Heinemann **ECONOMICS** A2 *for AQA*

Heinemann

ECONOMICS A2

for AQA

BY

Sue Grant *and* **Chris Vidler**

with **Charles Smith**

heinemann.co.uk
✓ Free online support
✓ Useful weblinks
✓ 24 hour online ordering

01865 888058

Heinemann

Inspiring generations

Heinemann Educational Publishers
Halley Court, Jordan Hill, Oxford OX2 8EJ
Part of Harcourt Education

Heinemann is the registered trademark of
Harcourt Education Limited

© Sue Grant, Charles Smith and Chris Vidler, 2003

First published 2003
Revised and updated, 2005

08 07 06 05
10 9 8 7 6 5 4 3 2

British Library Cataloguing in Publication Data is
available from the British Library on request.

10-digit ISBN 0 435330 81 0
13-digit ISBN 978 0 435330 81 1

Typeset by Hardlines Ltd, Charlbury, Oxford

Original illustrations © Harcourt Education Limited, 2003
Illustrated by Hardlines Ltd, Charlbury, Oxford

Cover design by Matt Buckley

Printed in the UK by Scotprint

Picture research by Sally Cole

Acknowledgements
The authors and the publishers would like to thank Dr
Charles Smith of Swansea Business School, AQA Principal
Examiner.

The publishers would like to thank the following for
permission to reproduce photographs: Alamy/Holt Studios,
p.214; Alamy/Image State, p.195; Alamy/Bern Mellmann,
p.25; Alamy/Sean Potter, p.86; Gareth Boden, p.17; Eye
Ubiquitous/Paul Thompson, p.44; Richard Jackson, p.101;
Milepost 92 half/Virgin, p.128; Rex/Action Press, p.234;
Rex Features/Ray Tang, p.155.

(Economics A2 for AQA)
This book has been reprinted with corrections to the
following pages: 30, 46, 66, 74, 77, 80, 82, 83, 88, 89, 91,
96, 173, 175, 179, 180, 183, 184, 187, 199, 202, 204, 220,
233, 242, 249, 250

Every effort has been made to contact copyright holders
of material reproduced in this book. Any omissions will
be rectified in subsequent printings if notice is given to
the publishers.

Tel: 01865 888058   www.heinemann.co.uk

Websites

There are links to relevant websites in this book. In
order to ensure that the links are up-to-date, that the
links work, and that the sites are not inadvertently
linked to sites that could be considered offensive, we
have made the links available on the Heinemann
website at www.heinemann.co.uk/hotlinks. When you
access the Heinemann website, enter the express code
0810P, and this will take you to the links you want.

Contents

Introduction

Welcome to *Heinemann Economics A2 for AQA*. This book has been specially written for students taking the AQA course. This means that it:

- follows the AQA specification closely
- has been written to ensure that all concepts are clearly explained in terms understandable by students taking this subject for the first time
- includes plenty of advice from examiners to help you get the best possible grade.

This introduction is divided into three parts. Firstly the links to your AS are made clear. This is followed by a more formal description of how the A2 part of your course is organised and finally you will be introduced to the special features of this book which have been designed to help you get the grade you deserve.

Your AS experience

How was it for you? We hope you got the grade you deserved. If you did not, think about a retake. Even if you scored well for AS, it can be worthwhile taking units again. It is easier to score marks for AS than it is for A2 and as the second year of your course involves more in-depth consideration of many of the topics you took in the first year you should get better and better at economics.

You should be:

- familiar with the special technical language associated with economics
- used to using graphical analysis to show that you can predict the outcomes of changes in economic and other variables
- developing skills of analysis and evaluation.

Your AS programme consisted of two sets of learning. You probably tacked micro economics first and followed this with macro. Finally, unit 3 involved applying what you had learned in the first two modules to case study material on housing, the environment or sport and leisure. This structure is reflected in the A2 course.

Module 5 is advanced micro economics and module 6 is advanced macro. Module 4 requires you to apply your skills to either an extended case study on Europe or coursework. At this stage you need to make a decision about the coursework and case study options, sort out any retakes and try to plan out your programme for study to spread pressure points over the whole year. Thus, if you are taking the coursework option try to make sure you have finished it by Christmas, take module 5 in January, and module 6 in June. This will give you the fall back of resubmitting coursework in the summer and having another go at module 5. Those electing to do the case study are advised to do module 5 in January and the case study and module 6 in June. There are fewer chances for retakes but there is quite a cross over in content between the advanced macro module and the European case study. There are, of course, other ways of dividing up your course and your school or college may not allow you to take exams in January. Whatever the constraints it pays to plan ahead especially to reduce pressure on yourself next May and June.

The main thing to know and never forget is that examiners can ask questions based on both the AS and A2 parts of your course. Don't throw away your notes from last year and don't forget to revise basic stuff like elasticity and aggregate demand and supply for your A2 examinations.

Moving up a gear

Most students find the second year of the course much more demanding than AS. You have got to know more, questions are less straightforward and usually require longer more detailed answers. This is because a higher proportion of marks is awarded for showing that you have the higher order skills of analysis and evaluation. The good thing about economics is that once you have mastered a particular topic it should stick in your brain.

As already indicated, module 5 – Business economics and the distribution of income and wealth – is advanced micro economics and consists of three linked elements:

- theory of the firm
- labour markets
- market failure and government intervention.

The theory of the firm involves a deeper understanding of revenue and costs faced by firms operating under different market conditions. This links directly into a consideration of why markets might be considered to fail and possible strategies for government intervention, which themselves might fail. Parallel to this is an element about how labour markets work and how this might explain differences in income and wealth, which also links into market failure/government intervention/government failure.

The advanced macro module – Government policy, the national and international economy – also consists of three linked elements:

- economic growth and inflation
- government policies
- international economics.

The first two of these involve a much more detailed consideration of what you did for module 2 for AS but the final part on the international economy is likely to be new to you. It involves looking at the costs and benefits of international trade, balance of payments and exchange rates.

Finally, choice time. Module 4 involves a choice between the case study and coursework options. Your teachers are bound to have a view as to which is the better option for you. Ask yourself the following questions.

- Do exams phase you? Yes/No
- Are you well organised? Yes/No
- Do you like to get into particular topics in depth? Yes/No
- Are you good at finding things out for yourself? Yes/No

Definitions

Units = examination papers.

Modules = what you have to learn.

■ Do you take pride in how your work looks? Yes/No

If there are more 'yes' answers than 'no' answers think about doing coursework. If the 'no' answers outweigh the 'yes' answers the case study might be better for you. Coursework will probably mean more work but you should end up with a more secure mark than you would from sitting the case study exam.

Finding your way

The text of *Heinemann Economics A2 for AQA* is set out in a similar fashion to that of the AS text. The major difference is that the individual sections are longer to give enough space to develop the more detailed treatments required for A2. At the end of each part there are sections devoted to exam preparation. This consists of advice from examiners who work for AQA on good practice when it comes to exams. They can give you a feel for what examiners actually look for when it comes to marking your work. Finally there are sample questions and answers and further examination style questions for you to develop the skills that will be tested at the end of your course.

Sample Section

The typical layout of each section is illustrated below.

Diagrams appear in the margin

Main text

Section title

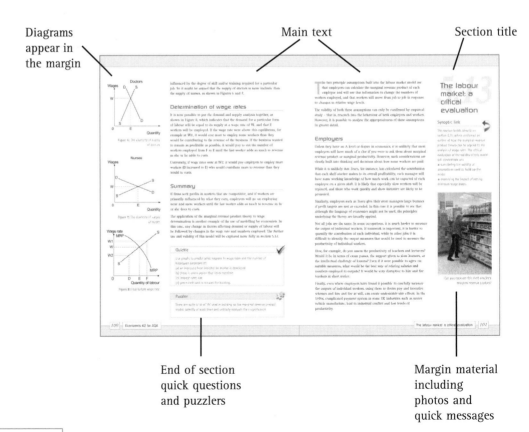

End of section quick questions and puzzlers

Margin material including photos and quick messages

The central body of text is designed to explain the key concept(s) featured in each section. This always ends with quick questions ('Quickies') to test your understanding. The margins of each section will contain a different selection of quick messages designed to help your learning. Where relevant, there are links to the work that you did for AS. Other hints relate to further research, weblinks, and controversial issues. Each is associated with a symbol and these are explained in more detail below.

 Synoptic links – Links to AS and other areas of study which are relevant to your understanding of the current section.

 Quickies – Quick questions designed to test your understanding of what you have just read.

 Key concepts – Ideas that are essential to understanding the section.

 Hot potatoes – Controversial issues you might want to argue about.

 Definitions – You must know these and get into the habit of defining the main terms you use in all your exam answers.

 Research tasks – Suggestions for more in-depth exploration

 Thinking like an economist – Questions and tasks that encourage you to apply economic analysis.

 Making connections – These enable you to use knowledge you have gained in earlier sections.

 Exam hints – Little ideas that might make all the difference when it comes to the exam.

 Puzzler –Tricky stuff to get your head round.

 Web links – Hopefully they are still there when you need them.

Good luck.

PART 4

Working as an economist

Working as an economist 4.1

The nature of the module

Module 4 is designed to enable you to develop your skills as an economist. It accounts for twenty per cent of the total A level marks, the highest weighting of any one module.

In this module you have a choice between being assessed by a case study or by coursework. If you decide on the coursework option you can undertake an investigation into any economic problem or issue. Your teacher may recommend that you undertake coursework on the same topic as the case study. This may be because your school is entering students for both the coursework and the case study and wants to provide you with the opportunity to switch to the case study, if necessary. The topic for the case study is the European Union.

The same skills are assessed in both coursework and the case study. In both cases you will be expected to analyse, interpret and evaluate data. In the case of coursework this will be in the form of a written report of 3500–4000 words. For the case study you will undertake a structured question based on a selection of given data.

The European Union

This topic is designed to provide a real world context in which you can apply the economic concepts you have learned during the course. For example, arguments for and against protectionism and the aims of competition may be explored in an EU context.

You will investigate a range of aspects of the nature, organisation and future of the European Union (EU). Part 4 seeks to explore the key aspects identified in the specification including the single market, the arguments for and against UK participation in the single currency, the likely impact of the entry of new members and the operation of the Common Agricultural Policy.

Maximising your grade

To achieve a high grade it is important, whether you have selected the coursework or the case study, to apply your knowledge and understanding of economic concepts and techniques to EU issues, to develop analytical and evaluative skills and to keep up to date on EU issues.

Particular emphasis is placed on evaluative skills, with 37.5 per cent of the marks being awarded for evaluation. Issues connected to the EU, especially whether the UK should join the single currency, can arouse strong feelings. Remember that as an economist you should assess arguments on the basis of relevant theory and evidence.

Developments are always taking place in terms of the performance of EU economies, the policies pursued by the EU and the degree of integration. You should keep in touch with these developments by reading relevant articles in newspapers and economics magazines and by visiting appropriate websites.

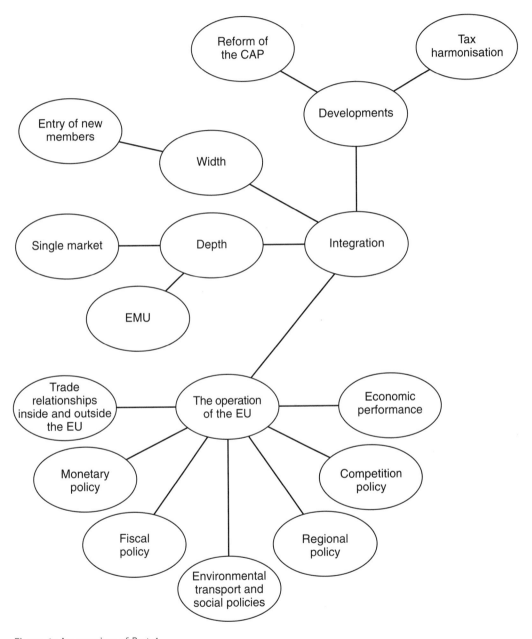

Figure 1: An overview of Part 4

The EU as a trading bloc

4.2

The European Union (EU) has changed its name a number of times as its member countries have become more integrated. In the 1950s, six European countries – Belgium, France, Italy, Luxembourg, the Netherlands and West Germany – started to work together in the European Coal and Steel Community and the European Atomic Energy Community. In 1958, the same six countries formed the European Economic Community (EEC). At the beginning, the area was a **customs union**. Now the EU has fifteen members, soon to be twenty-five, and is much more than a customs union.

Customs union

A customs union is a **trading bloc** that requires member countries to remove trade restrictions between each other. The member countries also follow the same foreign trade policy by imposing the same tariffs on non-member countries.

When the UK joined the European Community on 1 January 1973, it had to remove the taxes it imposed on imports coming from, for example, Germany, while it had to impose the European Community's common external tariff on imports from, for example, New Zealand.

This requirement to have a free trade approach with member countries while taxing products from outside the area has contributed to the change in the pattern of UK trade. Other EU countries are continuing to become more important as UK trading partners. In contrast, the importance of commonwealth countries continues to decline.

Common market

The EU moved from being a customs union towards being a **common market**, giving it not only free movement of products across national borders, but also the free movement of labour and capital. In a common market, it is not only tariffs on goods between member countries that are removed, but also non-tariff barriers (NTBs), including different product standards and restrictions on the movement of capital. One of the central aims of a common market is to increase actual and potential competition.

Economic and Monetary Union (EMU)

Economic and Monetary Union (EMU) involves the harmonisation of economic policies to promote greater economic integration. Economic union concentrates on the creation of a single market through the removal of artificial trade barriers and the development of common policies. Monetary Union involves the adoption of a common monetary policy, including a single currency and interest rate. The EU now operates the following, which augment member governments' national policies:

- a single currency (to which most members belong)
- a **Common Agricultural Policy (CAP)** and competition
- regional, social, transport and environmental policies.

Synoptic link

This section is linked to A2 sections 6.23 and 6.24 on protectionism.

Definitions

Customs union: a group of countries with free trade between them and a common external tariff on imports from outside the area.

Trading bloc: a group of countries with preferential trading arrangements.

Definitions

Common market: a group of countries with free movement of products, labour and capital.

Economic and Monetary Union (EMU): a group of countries that operate a single currency and co-ordinate economic policies.

Making connections

Explain what factors influence where the UK imports from.

Hot potato

Would the UK benefit from being a member of the United States of Europe?

To date, there has been limited harmonisation of fiscal policy. Greater harmonisation of policies would move the EU more towards a single economy – referred to by some as the United States of Europe.

Free trade area

A **free trade area** is a trade bloc where the member countries remove restrictions on the free movement of products between themselves. Apart from this there is no co-ordination of policies between member countries.

The EU was always more than a free trade area. Some of its member countries, however, were originally members of the European Free Trade Area (EFTA), and the EU has important trading links with both EFTA and NAFTA (the North American Free Trade Area, also known as the North American Free Trade Agreement). EFTA was formed in 1960. Over the years, six of its members – Austria, Denmark, Finland, Portugal, Sweden and the UK – left to join the EU. EFTA currently consists of just Iceland, Liechtenstein, Norway and Switzerland. NAFTA came into being in 1992 and consists of the USA, Canada and Mexico.

The EU's relationship with NAFTA

The EU and NAFTA are the world's two largest trading blocs. While a considerable amount of trade flows between the two blocs, the relationship is a somewhat fraught one. Both frequently accuse the other of unfair competition.

NAFTA complains about the EU's use of export subsidies on agricultural products. The EU is the world's main user of export subsidies. Subsidies make EU agricultural products artificially cheap in foreign markets. In turn, the EU claims that the USA distorts free trade by providing generous export credits to its farmers. These credits are short-term loans that, in theory, bridge the gap between the sale and payment of produce.

Trade disputes have broken out between the two trading blocs over a range of products including bananas, steel and beef. In 2004, the USA and the EU had been in dispute over genetically modified foods for more than five years. The USA was complaining about the EU's ban on GM food, imposed in 1999, which it claimed was costing US farmers more than US$300 million (£186 million) a year.

Definitions

Common Agricultural Policy (CAP): a series of policy measures regulating agriculture in the EU.

Free trade area: a group of countries with free trade between them.

Making connections

What are the benefits a country may gain from engaging in free trade?

Research task

Investigate how NAFTA compares to the EU in terms of economic size (real GDP – gross domestic product) and population size.

Thinking like an economist

Analyse the effect of a trade war on economic welfare.

Web link
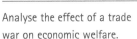

Find out more about the EU by going to the following website and entering express code 0810P: www.heinemann.co.uk/hotlinks.

Bananas at war

Quickies

1   What effect has the UK's entry into the EU had on its pattern of trade?
2   Distinguish between a customs union and a common market.
3   Explain what is meant by the harmonisation of economic policies.
4   Identify one similarity and one difference between EFTA and the EU as trading blocs.

4.3 The single market

Synoptic link

This section builds on AS section 1.18, and links to A2 sections 5.4, 6.22, 6.23 and 6.26.

In England, a firm based in, say, Southampton can sell goods and services to consumers in, for example, York without having a tariff imposed on them, without having to pass through border controls and without having to meet different quality standards. A dentist from Southampton can take up a job in York without obtaining a work permit and without having to possess different qualifications. A Southampton firm can also open a branch in York without any restriction on the amount of money it can move from Southampton to York. A consumer in Southampton can also easily compare the price of products produced by firms in Southampton and York, as both use the same currency. This is because England is a single market.

A single market in the EU would be similar. To achieve such a situation, the EU has been seeking to remove obstacles to free competition in the area. The process began with the formation of the EEC (see section 4.2) and is still ongoing. Along the way there have been a number of key measures that have sought to create a competitive market in product, labour and capital markets.

The Treaty of Rome

The Treaty of Rome (1957) set out the basic aims of what was to become the EU. These included:

- the elimination of tariffs and quotas on the import and export of goods between member countries
- the establishment of a common external tariff
- the abolition of obstacles to the free movement of people, services and capital between member states
- the establishment of common policies for agriculture and transport.

These were ambitious aims. The EU achieved the removal of tariff and quota barriers on the free movement of goods relatively quickly, as this is a condition of membership. However, in its first decades a significant number of obstacles to the free movement of people, services and capital between member states, and therefore competition on equal terms, remained.

Thinking like an economist

Explain how both the UK and other EU countries could benefit from the UK government permitting firms throughout the EU to tender for government contracts.

The Single European Act

The Single European Act (SEA) was passed in February 1986 and came into force in July 1987. Its main aim was to achieve the Treaty of Rome's objective of free trade within the EU by removing all remaining internal barriers and creating a fully integrated single market by the end of 1992. These barriers were not just on the movement of goods, but also on services, capital and labour.

The SEA outlined a series of measures designed to achieve competition on equal terms throughout the EU. These included:

- the ending of customs controls at the frontiers of member states
- the removal of non-tariff barriers – for example, **restrictive public procurement policies** by member governments

Definition

Restrictive public procurement policies: policies that favour domestic producers.

- reduction of subsidies by national member governments
- the mutual recognition of other member states' qualifications.

The SEA also committed the EU to work towards a common policy on a range of areas including the environment, research and development, and social and economic matters.

A series of directives came out of the SEA. For instance, one required major state contracts to be advertised at EU level with a reasonable time limit for bids to be received.

Progress on the SEA's measures turned out to be relatively slow. Much of the progress occurred on a case-by-case basis. This was, in part, because of the need to work out minimum quality standards on products and appropriate qualifications for different occupations.

The Maastricht Treaty

The Maastricht Treaty was signed in February 1992. It is also sometimes known as the Treaty on European Union.

This treaty sought to achieve some political objectives, most notably a common foreign and security policy. It also aimed to promote the single European market by encouraging the removal of remaining barriers to trade and increasing integration by replacing national currencies with a single European currency.

The treaty set out a timetable for EMU to be achieved in three stages.
- Stage 1 was already in progress, with the move towards a single market.
- The main features of stage 2 were to be increased co-ordination of national monetary policies and encouragement for governments to achieve greater similarity of economic performance (convergence).
- Stage 3 was to be the establishment of the European Central Bank (ECB) and the introduction of the single currency. The countries that belong to the single currency are collectively known as euroland, the eurozone or the euro area.

Making connections

Explain how the adoption of a single currency can promote free competition.

Progress towards a single European market

Some noticeable progress has been made towards the creation of a single European market. For example, **exchange controls** have been removed in all the member countries and this has increased the geographical mobility of capital. The geographical mobility of labour has been encouraged by the abolition of work permits and the mutual recognition of other member countries' qualifications. However, the single market programme still has some way to go. For instance, differences in tax rates and tax bases between countries and state aid are still distorting competition between member states.

Definition

Exchange control: restrictions on the purchase of foreign currency and on the export of capital.

Effects of a single market

The EU is seeking to achieve a single market, as it believes it will increase efficiency and economic welfare. The removal of barriers to competition should enable countries to take full advantage of comparative advantage. Greater specialisation and trade should raise output, lower costs and prices, and raise quality. Enabling efficient firms to sell freely to a large market should enable them to take greater advantage of economies of scale. The greater competition created should promote not only allocative and productive efficiency, but also dynamic efficiency.

The Cecchini Report of 1998 estimated that the completion of the single market programme may increase the real GDP of the EU by up to 6 per cent a year.

As well as the benefits, though, the movement towards the single market is bringing with it some threats to consumers, workers and firms. Overall, as already indicted, a single market should generate more income, but it may be more unevenly distributed. Some firms will thrive in the more competitive environment, but others will be driven out of business – requiring workers to develop new skills and possibly to move from one area to another. There is also a risk that one or a few firms could control such a market and abuse their market power.

Quickies

1 What were the aims of the Treaty of Rome?
2 On which barriers to free competition did the SEA concentrate?
3 How does a single currency promote competition?
4 Why does the move towards a single market increase the need for regional policy?

Puzzler

To enable UK traders to compete on equal terms with French traders, should the UK government cut excise duty on cigarettes and alcohol?

Throughout its history, several countries have joined the EU, thereby increasing its size. The largest single increase took place in 2004. To join the EU, countries have to meet a number of conditions. This was not an easy process for the accession countries since currently their economies exhibit significant differences from the current members.

The entry of the accession countries will have significant economic effects, not only for the countries themselves, but also for the original EU 15 member countries.

Extension of the EU

In 1957 six countries – Belgium, France, Italy, Luxembourg, the Netherlands and West Germany – signed the Treaty of Rome to form the European Economic Community (EEC), which came into existence on 1 January 1958. This was a customs union. The name changed to the European Community (EC) in 1967. Nine countries joined later:

- Denmark, Ireland and the UK in 1973
- Greece in 1981
- Spain and Portugal in 1986
- Austria, Finland and Sweden in 1995.

In addition, in 1990, East Germany merged with West Germany to form Germany. The area's name was changed again in 1992 to the European Union to reflect the greater degree of integration that was occurring.

The accession countries

At the Copenhagen summit in December 2002, the EU formally invited ten countries to join the EU. These ten accession countries joined on 1 May 2004. The countries are Cyprus, the Czech Republic, Estonia, Hungary, Latvia, Lithuania, Malta, Poland, Slovakia and Slovenia. All but two of these countries, Cyprus and Malta, are former command (planned) economies.

The accession countries' economies also differ from those of the original EU 15 in a number of ways. Perhaps the two most striking are the size of their agricultural sectors and their income levels. All the accession countries have larger agricultural sectors than the EU 15. On average, twenty per cent of their labour force is employed in agriculture, compared with an average of four per cent for the EU 15.

The accession countries, on average, also have smaller economies and lower income per head – some significantly lower. Table 1 compares the income per head of the EU 15 with that of the accession countries.

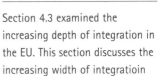

Widening of European integration

Synoptic link

Section 4.3 examined the increasing depth of integration in the EU. This section discusses the increasing width of integratioin in Europe.

EU 15	GDP per head	Accession countries	GDP per head
1 Luxembourg	28,534	1 Cyprus	8,298
2 Denmark	20,081	2 Slovenia	6,016
3 Ireland	17,044	3 Malta	5,908
4 Sweden	16,244	4 Czech Republic	3,504
5 UK	16,026	5 Hungary	3,354
6 Netherlands	15,416	6 Poland	2,895
7 France	15,059	7 Slovakia	2,430
8 Finland	15,015	8 Estonia	2,423
9 Austria	14,910	9 Lithuania	2,041
10 Germany	14,793	10 Latvia	2,000
11 Belgium	14,200		
12 Italy	12,201		
13 Spain	9,509		
14 Greece	7,022		
15 Portugal	6,807		

Table 1: A comparison of GDP per head in 2003 in €s

Conditions for entry

The conditions that the accession countries had to meet to join the EU were drawn up in 1993 and are known as the Copenhagen criteria. These include:

■ a functioning market economy
■ acceptance of EU legislation
■ a Western-style political system.

These conditions mean that, for instance, a new member country has to:

■ be willing to permit the free movement of products, capital and labour
■ accept the requirements of economic, social, energy and environmental policies
■ be able, eventually, to join the European single currency.

To reach the required standard, the accession countries had to make relatively rapid progress. For example, Poland had to take radical measures to reduce its levels of sulphur emissions and Hungary had to spend more than €15 million on improving its road and rail infrastructure.

The EU gave financial aid to the accession countries to help them meet the costs of complying to the EU's standards, rules and regulations. It agreed that there will be a transition period of integration, in part to meet the concerns of the EU 15.

Effects of membership on the accession countries

The accession countries joined the EU because they believe they will experience a net gain. Those countries that do join will experience a number of effects, potentially both advantageous and disadvantageous.

- Access to a very large and rich market. The accession countries will be able to sell to a market of more than 450 million people, many of whom enjoy high incomes.

- Increased competition. The single market has resulted in a greater degree of competition between member countries. The accession countries' firms will have to modernise and increase their performance in terms of productivity, quality and price – in other words, they will have to raise efficiency.

- A change in the pattern of trade. The absence of barriers with the EU and a common external tariff (CET) on products from outside the EU will encourage the new entrants to trade more with fellow EU members. Trade creation and trade diversion will occur. The first happens when membership of a trading bloc increases the amount of specialisation and trade due to the elimination of trade barriers between members. Trade diversion involves changing the pattern of trade with some trade being switched from non-members to members. The net effect on the accession countries' economies will depend on the cost of the products they bought prior to entry, the price of EU products without the CET on them, and the extent to which their output and exports rise.

- Increased investment from overseas. Firms from outside the EU – for example, Japan and the USA – are attracted to set up branches and production units in the EU because it is a such a large, rich market. In addition, countries from the EU 15 will be attracted to increase investment in the lower-cost accession countries.

- Access to EU funds. The countries will be entitled to receive financial support from the CAP and from the EU's structural funds.

- Reduction in sovereignty of macro economic policy. National governments will have to give up some of the control of their economies to EU institutions. Most noticeably, the accession countries will no longer be able to devalue their currencies or have their central banks alter their interest rates. There is a risk that the 'one size fits all' monetary policy may not be appropriate for countries at different stages of the economic cycle.

Effects on the EU 15

The entry of new countries is already having an impact on the EU 15 and will continue to do so for a number of years. The effects and possible effects include those listed below.

- Reform of the EU's policies and procedures. The entry of countries with large agricultural sectors and relatively low GDP per head is forcing the EU to adapt the Common Agricultural Policy and its expenditure

Thinking like an economist

Explain why entry into the EU may increase productive and allocative efficiency in a country.

Hot potato

Should a poor record in human rights debar a country from joining the EU?

programmes. A programme of EU budget reform was introduced under Agenda 2000, which restricted expenditure on enlargement and placed a limit on CAP expenditure.

■ The poorer EU 15 countries – Greece, Portugal and Spain – will receive less financial assistance from the EU.

■ There may be large-scale movements of labour. With higher rates of unemployment and lower wages in the accession countries, the EU 15 may experience significant levels of immigration. Of course, over time immigration may decline if the accession countries experience a rise in income and living standards.

The process of joining

In April 2004, all twenty-five of the current and future member states ratified (confirmed acceptance of) the Accession Treaty. Their integration into the EU will, to a degree, be a gradual process. Access to labour markets will be phased in. The countries received access to some aspects of the CAP straight away, including export refunds, but direct payments for farmers will be phased in over ten years.

Some aim to join the euro within four years, but for most it will be some time before their economies converge sufficiently to be able to consider membership of the single currency.

The larger EU

The 2004 enlargement is unprecedented in terms of both the number of countries joining and their levels of GDP per head. The twenty-five member EU:

■ will compose the largest trading bloc in the world

■ will have more bargaining power in its negotiations with, for example, NAFTA and the World Trade Organization (WTO)

■ should create greater political stability in Europe

■ will be more difficult to co-ordinate.

Whether the EU proves more effective in raising the economic performance and living standards of its members will depend on whether it is still moving towards its optimum size or whether it has past it.

Quickies

1   In which main ways do the accession countries differ from the EU 15?

2   Why is the existence of a functioning market economy necessary for membership of the EU?

3   Distinguish between trade diversion and trade creation.

4   Why has the entry of the accession countries stimulated reform of EU policies and procedures?

5   Should Turkey be allowed to join the EU?

onetary policy for countries in euroland (also known as the eurozone and euro area) is operated by the European Central Bank (ECB) and for the countries outside (currently Denmark, Sweden and the UK), by their governments.

The first few years of the operation of the single currency have allowed economists to assess how effectively the ECB is carrying out its role. It has also provided information for the continuing debate on whether the UK should join the single currency.

Synoptic link

This section links to A2 section 6.27, Economic and monetary union (EMU).

The objectives of monetary policy in euroland

The objectives of monetary policy for euroland were set out in the Maastricht Treaty. The key objective is to maintain price stability. Subject to that objective, the EU wants monetary policy to foster sustainable economic growth and high employment.

The role of the ECB

The ECB has a number of functions, including issuing banknotes, conducting foreign exchange operations and managing the official reserves of the member states. However, its most well-known function is to set interest rates. The ECB's Governing Council meets to consider a variety of economic indicators including, amongst others:

- exchange rate movements
- unemployment data
- wage changes
- retail sales
- business and consumer confidence surveys.

Initially, the inflation target set for the ECB was a year-on-year increase in the harmonised index of consumer prices (HICP) for euroland of below 2 per cent. This target came in for two main criticisms.

One was that it was too harsh. Measures of inflation, even the HICP, tend to overstate the rate of inflation. A target of less than 2 per cent is very low and concern was expressed that it risked pushing economies with an overvalued exchange rate into deflation.

The target, between 0 per cent and 2 per cent, was also essentially asymmetric. The assumption was that, in principle, the ECB wanted inflation to average 1.5 per cent. This meant that inflation could only go 0.5 per cent points above, but 1.5 per cent points below.

In May 2003, the ECB announced it was softening its inflation target and redefining its monetary policy strategy. It stated that it would attach less importance to an analysis of the money supply in making its interest rate decisions. Its inflation target was changed to 'close to, but below, 2 per cent'.

Euros changing hands in euroland

These changes make the target rather more symmetric but not fully symmetric and suggest that the ECB may set interest rates lower in the future.

Inflation targeting has a number of advantages. It allows the ECB's record to be assessed. Perhaps more importantly, if firms, workers and households believe that the target indicates the ECB is serious about controlling inflation, they will restrain their price rises, wage demands and spending and therefore not cause inflation to accelerate.

Record on interest rate changes

The ECB did not always achieve its initial inflation target. Between 2000 and 2003, inflation was above two per cent on a number of occasions – but not significantly so. As measures of inflation tend to overstate the rate of inflation, the new target may prove to be a more realistic one.

One of the main criticisms of European monetary policy has not been that inflation has been too high, but that the policy has tended to be too deflationary. It is thought that on several occasions the ECB has resisted cutting interest rates when there was no real risk of the inflation rate rising and when such a cut would have been beneficial for stimulating economic activity in a number of member states.

Another criticism is based on the so-called 'one size fits all' nature of European monetary policy. The interest rate decided by the ECB applies to all the countries in euroland. There is a risk that an interest rate that may be appropriate for the area as a whole may be inappropriate for some individual member countries.

Those member countries with overheating economies and high inflation will have low real rates of interest when they need high real interest rates. Meanwhile, economies with high levels of unemployment and low inflation will have high real interest rates.

If all the economies are operating at a similar point on the economic cycle, having the same interest rate would not be a problem. In practice, though, there are still significant differences in euroland economies. For instance, in 2003 unemployment in Spain was 11.8 per cent and only 3.7 per cent in the Netherlands. Inflation in Ireland was 3.3 per cent, but 0.9 per cent in Germany, as measured by the HICP.

The euro's record

The euro was launched on 1 January 1999 and became a physical currency, used by households and firms, three years later on 1 January 2002.

The value of the euro was initially rather weak, largely because of concern about the economic performance of euroland countries. In 2003, though, the value of the euro rose, mainly due to the weakness of the US dollar. This led

Making connections

Explain how a rise in interest rates could reduce inflation.

Thinking like an economist

Why does a low rate of inflation usually result in a high real rate of interest?

to some pressure being put on the ECB to cut interest rates to avoid the value of the euro rising too high.

One problem is that some countries joined the single currency at inappropriate exchange rates – for example, Germany went in at too high a rate and Ireland at too low a rate. This has put deflationary pressure on Germany and inflationary pressure on Ireland.

There is evidence, though, that the euro has promoted international trade, investment and competition. A single currency removes a key source of uncertainty. Euroland members no longer have to be worried about currency changes between them. This has made it easier for firms to plan ahead and to compare the costs of producing in different parts of euroland. These factors have encouraged them to undertake more investment.

Foreign direct investment (FDI) into euroland has also been attracted by both this greater certainty and by the ease of movement of capital. Trade within the area has grown, with the trade that France and Germany do with other euroland countries having increased significantly.

There is evidence that some suppliers took advantage of the changeover to the euro, at a time when some consumers were uncertain about its internal purchasing power, to raise prices. However, by making price differences more transparent, the single currency is now putting competitive pressure on euroland firms to keep their prices low.

Thinking like an economist

What determines the value of a currency?

The UK's position outside euroland

The UK economy has performed quite will outside euroland in the first few years of its existence. It has enjoyed low unemployment, low and stable inflation and an economic growth rate above that of the EU average. In contrast, unemployment in euroland has been relatively high and economic growth rates slow.

However, some economists and politicians argue that UK economic performance would be better if it joined the single currency. They point out that UK trade with other EU countries has grown more slowly than that of France and Germany. They also warn that while the UK remains the most popular destination for FDI in the EU, its share has fallen since 1999.

Will the UK join the single currency?

For the UK to join the single currency, it will have to meet the convergence criteria set down by the 2003 UK government (see Part 6, section 6.26). In October 1997, the Chancellor of the Exchequer, Gordon Brown, added that 'the key factor is whether economic benefits of joining for business are clear and unambiguous'.

Web link

Find out more about the ECB by going to the following website and entering express code 0810P: www.heinemann.co.uk/hotlinks.

Making connections

Explain how inward FDI affects long run aggregate supply.

For UK membership to stand any chance of reaping these benefits, it is important that the UK economy is converging with euroland. In early 2003, the National Institute of Economic and Social Research stated that the UK is now in a very similar position to the rest of Europe in terms of the symmetry of economic shocks. Gordon Brown is considering changing the UK's inflation target to that of the ECB. This would help to prepare the UK for membership. However, on 9 June 2003 he said that he did not think that his conditions had yet been met.

If the government thinks that the UK's economy is in line with euroland and all the necessary conditions have been met, it will put the decision on membership to the public in a national referendum.

Those in favour argue that in addition to increased trade, investment and competitive pressure due to using the same currency, membership may bring less volatility of interest rates. If so, this would make the UK housing market, and therefore the economy more stable, and would again promote investment.

Those opposed point out that euroland lacks sufficient labour market flexibility and a large enough central budget to offset economic shocks. They are also concerned about giving up autonomy over monetary policy, especially as the ECB has tended to operate a rather rigid monetary policy.

Quickies

1 In what circumstances is the ECB likely to raise the rate of interest?
2 In what ways was the ECB's inflation target changed in 2003?
3 In connection with European monetary policy, what is meant by 'one size fits all'?
4 In what circumstances would the UK join the euro?

Puzzler

Which presents the greater risk – a 'one-size-fits-all' interest rate or exchange rate fluctuations?

U nemployment is a significant issue for the EU, because it is high –
particularly in euroland. A major cause of this high unemployment
is thought to be a lack of labour market flexibility. Individual
member countries seek to reduce unemployment, although the measures that
members of euroland can take are constrained by the membership of the
single currency. The EU itself also seeks to reduce unemployment.

EU unemployment performance

	EU	euroland	UK	USA
2000	7.8	8.4	5.5	4.0
2001	7.4	8.0	5.1	4.8
2002	7.6	8.3	5.1	5.8
2003	7.9	8.7	5.2	5.7

Table 1: Unemployment rates %

Table 1 shows that unemployment is higher in the EU than the USA. It also
shows that unemployment in euroland exceeds both that of the USA and the
UK. The USA and the UK both have more flexible labour markets than those
in euroland.

Lack of wage flexibility

One cause of EU unemployment is claimed to be a lack of wage flexibility.
If wages do not adjust fully and quickly to changes in demand,
unemployment is likely to result. Figure 1 shows aggregate demand for
labour falling from **ADL** to **ADL1**.

If the wage rate does not fall, unemployment of **QX–Q** will result.

In recent years, there have been a number of occasions when the aggregate
demand for labour has fallen in the EU. One was the early to mid 1990s,
when the countries aspiring membership of the single currency introduced
deflationary fiscal and monetary policies in order to met the Maastricht
criteria. Another was the demand shock caused by the 11 September 2001
terrorist attack in the USA.

Wages in euroland are inflexible for a number of reasons – one being that
wages in the area are determined on the basis of national, collective
bargaining to a much greater extent than in the UK and the USA. This can
prevent wages reflecting different demand pressures in different areas. If
wages are the same in both depressed and prosperous areas, there will be
little incentive for workers to move to the prosperous regions and for capital
to move to the depressed regions.

Synoptic link

This section builds on AS sections
2.6 and 2.15, and links to A2 sections
6.6 and 6.8.

Research task

Using the *Economist* magazine
or website, find out the current
unemployment figures for the EU,
euroland, the UK and the USA. Assess
the relative performance of these
areas/countries.

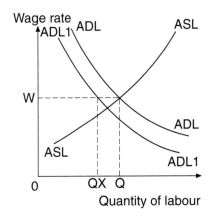

Figure 1: Aggregate demand for labour

Why might a fall in wage rates
result in higher rather than lower
unemployment?

It is thought that unions in a number of euroland countries have been pushing up wage rates above their equilibrium levels. Unions in Germany have been particularly militant in pursuit of wage rises. Additionally, while unions in France represent only a relatively small proportion of the labour force, they exert a considerable influence on the political determination of minimum wage and the length of the working week.

Rigidity of employment relationships

If employers believe that it would be difficult to dismiss workers should demand fall, they may be reluctant to take on many workers when demand is high.

Employment protection legislation in many EU countries makes dismissing workers a costly and lengthy process, with employers having to consult with unions and local and national authorities. In contrast in the USA, where there is less government intervention in labour markets, a fall in demand tends to result initially in a greater rise in unemployment, but later a larger rise in employment when demand increases.

Generous unemployment benefits and some state employment can reduce labour market flexibility. Unemployment benefits are higher in most EU countries than in the USA and UK and eligibility rules are more lax. It may be claimed that this reduces the incentive for the unemployed to search for work and to be prepared to accept offers of employment at the going wage rate.

The labour market can also be distorted by more generous pay and conditions in state employment than in private sector employment. In France, for instance, civil servants can claim a full pension after 37 years of employment compared to 40 years for their private sector colleagues.

Rigidity of employment relationships can also create unemployment by reducing the pressure on workers to accept change. If there is resistance to change what is sometimes called 'eurosclerosis', labour productivity will grow more slowly.

Government intervention and labour costs

Making connections

Explain two measures a
government could take to increase the
incentive to work.

Government intervention can cause unemployment by raising labour costs. In addition to the costs imposed by employment legislation, governments in the EU raise labour costs by imposing taxes on the employment of workers, such as National Insurance contributions and their equivalents, and imposing, for example, limits on working hours, health and safety standards, and maternity and paternity rights.

If government intervention pushes wage costs above their equilibrium levels, unemployment can occur. Of course, it is possible that government intervention will not have an adverse effect on employment if it is correcting market failure. For instance, if a labour market is a **monopsony**, the wage rate and employment may be lower if there is no government intervention.

Policy approaches

Euroland countries' choice of government policy measures is constrained by their membership of the single currency. Monetary policy is in the hands of the European Central Bank. Member states can use expansionary fiscal policy to stimulate aggregate demand and raise employment. However, government's use of fiscal policy is restricted by the Growth and Stability Pact.

When a government employs expansionary fiscal policy, its spending will rise relative to tax revenue. This may result in a budget deficit, but the Growth and Stability Pact requires national governments to keep their budget deficits below three per cent of GDP. An economy that is experiencing high unemployment is likely to have low tax revenue and high spending on unemployment and other benefits. If, though, its budget deficit is close to three per cent, its ability to raise its spending and cut tax rates would be very limited.

However, EU governments, both in and out of euroland, can use supply-side policies and, in the long run, supply-side policies are likely to be more effective in reducing structural and frictional unemployment. Germany and Austria have relatively efficient vocational training and this is thought to keep down youth unemployment in both countries. The Scandinavian members of the EU also make extensive use of training and help workers to search for jobs. The UK's New Deal is a supply-side approach (see Part 6, section 6.8).

Making connections

Explain how expansionary fiscal policy may reduce unemployment.

Costs of a more flexible market

A more flexible labour market should result in lower unemployment, but it is not without costs. Workers in a more flexible labour market will be likely to experience greater income inequality and greater fluctuations in pay. Any period of unemployment they experience should be shorter, but they will have a greater chance of being unemployed. Workers will also have to be prepared to be more adaptable and more mobile.

The Luxembourg Process

In November 1997, the Extraordinary European Council on Employment announced an unemployment initiative known as the Luxembourg Process. This initiative is based on four 'pillars':

- improving employability by providing on-the-job training
- encouraging the adaptability of firms and their workers through consultation between workers and employers' organisations (designed to increase both the adaptability and mobility of firms and workers)
- increasing equality of opportunity (possible measures here include improving child care facilities and encouraging firms to operate family-friendly employment policies; the main aims are to increase

female participation rates, to narrow the gap between male and female wage rates and to reduce female unemployment)

■ promoting entrepreneurship (measures here concentrate on making it easier for new firms to get started and include deregulation).

Within each of the pillars there are detailed policy guidelines. Each member country is asked to submit National Action Plans, which explain what policies the government is implementing in the context of the Luxembourg Process. The Council monitors the progress of these policies and can make recommendations to individual member states.

The Luxembourg Process is based on the belief that Europe's high unemployment arises largely from structural problems. It combines both direct intervention and market-based measures. It does not, however, explicitly seek to encourage greater flexibility of wages or employment conditions.

Making connections

Analyse the impact of the introduction of a national minimum wage on employment.

Quickies

1   Explain how a lack of wage flexibility can cause unemployment.
2   Identify three ways in which government intervention can raise labour costs.
3   How does membership of the single currency restrict a government's choice of policy measures?
4   What are the key features of the Luxembourg Process?

T he EU operates its own budget and influences member countries' budget positions and fiscal policies.

The EU's budget

The EU's budget, like a national government's budget, is a record of its spending and revenue. However, unlike a national government's budget, it must always balance. This is because the sole aim of the EU's budget is to raise the funds needed to finance the EU's spending programmes. It is not used to influence the level of aggregate demand in the EU. The EU's budget, as a percentage of GDP, is much smaller than a national government's budget. It was one per cent of EU GDP in 2002. This smaller percentage is accounted for by the narrower coverage of EU expenditure.

The main items of EU spending are the Common Agricultural Policy (CAP) and the structural funds used for regional development and social policy. Minor items of spending include development aid, spending on energy programmes and administration.

The EU receives its revenue from four key sources:
- customs duties
- agricultural levies
- VAT levy – set at one per cent of member countries' VAT revenue
- GNP (gross national product, or national income). Member countries contribute a proportion of their national income. A ceiling has been placed on this at 1.27 per cent of GNP for the period 2000–2006.

Some countries – for example, Ireland and Greece – are net beneficiaries of the EU budget. This means that they receive more from EU spending than they contribute to the EU budget. Other countries, including Austria and the UK, are net contributors. The UK was concerned about its initial relatively high net contribution and negotiated a significant rebate.

EU policy and member governments' budget positions

The EU influences member countries' budget positions in a number of ways. The fundamental way is that all member countries are expected to avoid 'excessive' budget deficits.

Those countries wanting to join the single currency have to meet specific convergence criteria. These contain two criteria that place a limit on fiscal deficits:
- a government must not have a budget deficit in excess of three per cent of GDP
- a government's national debt should not be above 60 per cent of GDP.

Synoptic link

This section builds on AS section 2.12 and links to A2 sections 6.16, 6.17 and 6.18.

Thinking like an economist

What effect is the move towards trade liberalisation likely to have on the sources of the EU's revenue?

Making connections

Explain why a government is likely to experience a budget deficit during a slowdown in economic activity.

Once in, the countries' governments have to submit convergence programmes to the European Commission and the ECOFIN (the Council of EU Finance Ministers) about how they are progressing towards the convergence criteria.

The Stability and Growth Pact

The Stability and Growth Pact states the medium-term objective for the budget positions of countries in the single currency should be close to balance or in surplus. Countries are allowed to react to normal cyclical fluctuations, but are required to keep to the budget deficit limit of three per cent of GDP, except in exceptional circumstances.

Euroland countries have to submit stability programmes and annual updates to the European Commission and ECOFIN. These have to explain how the government is moving towards the medium-term budgetary objective, what is expected to happen to national debt and how economic activity will influence its financial position.

The ECOFIN assesses these stability programmes. If it is concerned that a country will not achieve the fiscal targets of the pact, it will make recommendations on how the government can take the necessary adjustment measures. If a country exceeds the three per cent budget deficit limit, it will first receive a warning. If the deficit persists, it may be fined up to 0.5 per cent of its GDP.

Making connections

Explain how a government could reduce a budget deficit.

Web link

Find out more about the EU budget by visiting www.heinemann.co.uk/hotlinks and entering express code 0810P.

Assessment of the three per cent budget deficit limit

The EU argues that a limit has to be placed on the budget deficits that governments can operate in a single currency to ensure price stability and economic growth. If a government, or group of governments, operates large budget deficits, it will add to aggregate demand and possibly the money supply. This is likely to put downward pressure on the euro, which may generate inflationary pressure and result in a higher rate of interest for all member countries.

However, some argue that the Stability and Growth Pact is too harsh and needs reform. A budget deficit over three per cent may not be significant if it results from capital spending or if it stimulates higher employment and incomes.

Some argue that Gordon Brown's golden fiscal rule is more appropriate. This allows governments to borrow for capital spending but not, over the medium term, for current spending. However, Brown's public sector rule that national debt should not exceed 40 per cent of GDP is harsher than the EU's.

It is also claimed that fiscal flexibility is more important when governments cannot independently use monetary policy to influence the level of economic activity in their countries.

Tax harmonisation

As well as influencing member governments' budget and national debt positions, the EU is seeking to ensure that variations in the tax base and tax rates across member countries do not distort competition and so create inefficiency. Currently, there are considerable variations in the **tax burden** across the EU with, for instance, Sweden being relatively highly taxed and Greece relatively lightly taxed.

The Treaty of Rome stated as an objective the harmonisation of indirect taxes. A move towards this was made with the requirement for member countries to adopt VAT as their main indirect tax. The SEA also stated the objective of harmonising rates of VAT and excise duty. Agreement was achieved that countries' standard rates of VAT should not be below 15 per cent. Nevertheless, there are still considerable variations in the coverage and rates of VAT and the rates of excise duties across the EU.

There is also some evidence that this does distort competition, with countries with lower tax rates, but not necessarily lower costs of production, attracting more custom. Additionally, concern has been raised about how differences in corporation tax, taxes on savings and income tax are influencing direct and portfolio investment, and the ease that firms experience in recruiting key workers.

Definition

Tax burden: the total amount of tax paid as a percentage of GDP.

Quickies

1   How does the EU's budget differ from a national government's budget?
2   What limits does the Growth and Stability Pact impose on member governments?
3   How do the limits of the Growth and Stability Pact differ from Gordon Brown's fiscal rules?
4   Explain how variations in the tax base and tax rates can distort competition.

Puzzler

Why might a government be reluctant to reduce a budget deficit?

The Common Agricultural Policy

Synoptic link

This section develops the work on the CAP introduced in AS section 1.23.

Definition

Strategic industry: an industry regarded as important to the operation of the economy.

Making connections

Explain why agriculture might be regarded as a strategic industry.

The Common Agricultural Policy (CAP) consists of a series of measures to regulate agriculture in the EU. Throughout the world there is considerable government intervention in agricultural markets. This arises in part because of the instability of agricultural prices in free markets and because agriculture is often regarded to be a **strategic industry**. However, intervention can create problems and the CAP has come in for considerable criticism. This criticism is one of the factors behind the recent reforms of the CAP.

The objectives of the CAP

The objectives of the CAP were set out in Article 39 of the Treaty of Rome. They are:

- to increase agricultural productivity
- to ensure a fair standard of living for the agricultural community
- to stabilise agricultural markets
- to make the area self-sufficient in agricultural products
- to ensure affordable prices for consumers.

While the CAP has been relatively effective in terms of the first, third and fourth objectives, it has been criticised for its performance on the second and fifth objectives. Farmers' incomes have not risen in line with other incomes and consumers are paying relatively high prices.

Price support

One of the best known and most criticised features of the CAP is the policy of setting prices usually above the world equilibrium price. Figure 1 shows the effect of setting a minimum price of butter above the market price.

To maintain the price at this artificially high level, two main measures are used. The interventionist agency of the CAP buys up the surplus created and an import tax (tariff) is placed on produce from outside the EU. Some of the surplus is destroyed, some stored and some is exported at low, subsidised prices. The import tax is set so that the price of non-EU produce is above that of the minimum price.

This minimum price guarantee has a number of significant disadvantages that reduce welfare within and outside the EU. Consumer surplus is reduced as people have to pay higher prices, and tax revenue has to be used not only to buy up the surplus but also to store it. The import tariff and export subsidy distort comparative advantage and make it difficult for developing countries to sell agricultural products to the EU and at home.

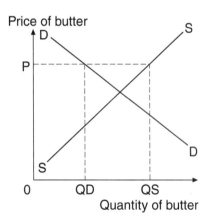

Figure 1: The effect of price support

Thinking like an economist

What effect would the setting of a minimum price above equilibrium have on producer surplus?

Other measures

As well as price support, the CAP includes a range of other measures designed to achieve its objectives. These include:

- production subsidies
- investment grants
- direct income payments unrelated to production
- conservation measures
- health regulations.

Arguments in favour of the CAP

Some arguments can be advanced in support of the CAP. It does seek to achieve a level playing field in agriculture by replacing different national policies with one EU-wide approach.

While it can be debated whether all farmers, particularly UK farmers, have benefited from the CAP in recent years, small farmers in Greece and Portugal, for instance, have enjoyed significant benefits. The help to some poor, rural areas has been important and in some cases – for example, by making hill farming viable – the CAP has protected the environment.

It can also be argued that the security the CAP has provided for farmers has encouraged investment, which has raised productivity and resulted in self-sufficiency (and above) in a number of agricultural products.

Criticisms of the CAP

The CAP has come in for severe criticism on a number of grounds, most of which emphasise the inefficiencies it causes.

- It is expensive to operate. It is the largest item of expenditure in the EU budget. In the mid-1970s, it accounted for 75 per cent of EU spending, although it had fallen to just below 50 per cent by the start of the 2000s. Many argue that much of this expenditure is not well spent – particularly expenditure on storing surpluses such as, for example, 'wine lakes' and 'butter mountains'.
- It reduces competitive pressure in the industry. Farmers have not faced the same pressures to keep their costs low and to be responsive to changes in consumer tastes as they would in a free market. The necessary restructuring that has been forced on other industries has been delayed. Farmers have not always acted in a commercial way – for instance, they didn't insure against foot and mouth.
- It enables small and inefficient farmers to survive. Significant advantage can be taken of economies of scale in farming. In a free market environment, many of the small farms in, for example, France would have to merge to form more efficient units.
- It discourages diversification. A significant number of farmers in the EU are over-reliant on one or two crops.
- It disadvantages consumers. As a result of the CAP measures, EU consumers pay higher prices and higher taxes.
- It creates unfair competition with developing countries. Tariffs imposed on developing countries' agricultural products make it difficult for them

Hot potato

Would UK farmers do better outside the EU?

Thinking like an economist

In what circumstances might a subsidy to producers increase economic efficiency?

to sell to the EU. The dumping of EU surpluses in their markets also makes it difficult for them to compete at home. The EU is the second largest exporter of agricultural products in the world, but it does not have a comparative advantage in the vast majority of these products.

- It causes a misallocation of resources both in the EU and worldwide. This reduces world output and world living standards.
- In some cases it causes environmental damage by, for example, encouraging land that is rich in wildlife but of poor agricultural value to be used for agriculture.

Pressure for reform

Internal criticism and consumer pressure are some of the driving forces behind the reform of the CAP. Other factors also contribute to the pressure on the EU to find ways to make the policy more efficient and cost effective.

One is concern that the cost might rise significantly with the entry of countries with large, low-productivity agricultural sectors. Another is pressure from the WTO, which wants the EU to open up its markets and compete on more equal terms with non-EU members. There is also environmental pressure, with concern being expressed about the harmful effects that intensive farming and the use of pesticides are having.

Reforms

The MacSharry reforms were proposed in 1992 by Ray MacSharry, the then Agriculture Commissioner, and finally approved in December 1995. These sought to bring CAP prices closer to world levels and to increase competitive pressures from outside by reducing the level of support prices on a range of products, including cereals. The emphasis on help for farmers was switched, in part, from price support to direct income payments. To qualify for these direct income payments, farmers (except small farmers) had to set aside at least 15 per cent of arable land. They were also given grants to turn land over to ecological, forestry or recreational use. These reforms did reduce surpluses and did improve the environment to a certain extent.

Thinking like an economist

What effect will a switch from price support to direct payments be likely to have on the distribution of income?

The next major reforms came in 1999. The Fischler reforms, named after Franz Fischler, the Agriculture Commissioner, introduced more cuts in minimum prices and further shifted help from price support to direct income payments.

Together the MacSharry and Fischler reforms have moved the cost of the CAP away from consumers towards taxpayers. This is because the effect of the changes made was to reduce agricultural prices but to increase direct income payments to farmers. They also lead to a more efficient allocation of resources within the EU and the world by lowering agricultural prices and making EU agriculture more subject to market forces. However, they did leave agriculture still relatively heavily subsidised.

A further set of reforms was introduced under the title 'Agenda 2000' and was motivated, in part, by the imminent enlargement of the EU. Yet again, support prices were lowered and there was a further switch from price support to direct subsidies. More emphasis was placed on environmental objectives. It also placed a limit on CAP expenditure.

Some believe the reforms should go further. These people point to the example of New Zealand, which ended agricultural subsidies in the mid-1980s. As a result, farmers became more efficient. They cut their costs and became more responsive to changes in consumer tastes, diversifying into new areas such as wine.

Comparison of some of the CAP measures

As mentioned earlier, the system of price support has been heavily criticised. Figure 2 shows that consumers lose out in a number of ways in comparison with a free market situation. They pay a higher price for the product (**P1** rather than **P**) and consume a smaller quantity (**QD** rather than **Q**). They also enjoy less consumer surplus (**P1AE** in comparison to **PAB**) and have to pay taxes, not only to fund the purchase of the surplus, but also to store it.

Consumers do better under a system of production subsidies. As Figure 3 shows, a subsidy causes the supply curve to shift to the right.

This results in consumers paying a lower price and enjoying higher consumer surplus (**P1AH**). Less tax has to be used because, while the subsidy has to be funded, tax revenue does not have to be used to purchase unsold stock – the market clears.

A subsidy might be justified on the grounds that farming can generate positive externalities. However, if the positive externalities are estimated incorrectly, there can still be overproduction.

Direct payments avoid the problem of overproduction, but they do have a number of disadvantages – most notably, high costs of administration and the possibility of fraud. The payments are conditional on farmers carrying out certain activities – for example, setting aside land for environmental purposes. This means that tax revenue is used not only to make the payments but also to check that farmers are meeting the requirements.

Quickies

1   Why do agricultural product prices tend to be unstable in free markets?
2   How do the operators of the CAP prevent the EU price of butter falling to the market level?
3   How does the CAP result in a misallocation of resources?
4   What is forcing the CAP to become more responsive to market forces?

Making connections

Explain how the CAP may result in allocative and productive inefficiency in agriculture?

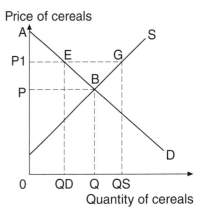

Figure 2: The effect of price support

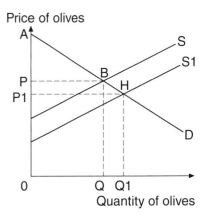

Figure 3: The effect of a production subsidy

Regional problems

EU regional policy seeks to work with national governments to reduce regional imbalances in the member countries and to help those regions lagging behind. The EU sees regional differences as a significant issue, as they can contribute to economic inefficiency and generate inequality and a lack of social cohesion. As a result, the EU spends a considerable amount on regional policy.

Regional problems

Regional disparities generate a number of problems. Poor (depressed) regions usually have low real GDP per head, high unemployment and net outward migration. They tend to be dominated by a few traditional industries, have poor transport infrastructure, low educational attainment, low productivity and difficulty attracting investment. Some of the poor regions are also heavily dependent on agriculture. These key features suggest that many poor regions are having difficulties adjusting their industrial structure to changing economic circumstances.

It is interesting to note that prosperous regions may also experience some problems. These include congestion, pressure on social capital and a shortage of workers.

The need for regional policy

Market theory would suggest that regional problems would soon be self-correcting. Unemployed workers would move from poor regions to prosperous regions, where more jobs and higher wages would be on offer. Capital would move from the prosperous regions to the poor regions, where factor prices would be cheaper and labour would be more available.

In practice, though, due to a variety of forms of market failure (including a lack of labour mobility), regional disparities are not self-correcting. Indeed, the disparities may increase. Poor regions tend to become poorer and rich regions richer.

Some of the best workers and some firms will move out of poor regions due to their relatively low incomes. This will further reduce demand in these poor regions and make them even less attractive sites for inward investment. In the rich regions, success often breeds success with firms moving to them. As a result, governments intervene in an attempt to reduce regional disparities.

With the limits imposed on national government fiscal policy measures and the 'one-size-fits-all' EU monetary policy, the role of EU regional policy is increasing. Before it joined the single currency, Greece, for instance, could have cut its interest rate and lowered the value of its exchange rate to stimulate demand across the country. There was also no limit on how much the government could spend on regional aid to its depressed regions.

Synoptic link

This section builds on the previous sections, 4.5, Monetary policy and the euro, and 4.6, European unemployment.

Thinking like an economist

Explain the link between low educational attainment, low productivity and difficulty attracting investment.

Making connections

Explain why the unemployed may find it difficult to move from poor to prosperous regions.

Aims of EU regional policy

EU regional policy seeks to remove regional differences in order to achieve greater equity, social cohesion and efficiency.

The EU is concerned with differences in economic prosperity – both between member countries and between regions within the countries. The EU currently contains some rich regions (including Ile de France and the south-east of England), but it also has poor regions (including most of Portugal, the south of Spain and all of Greece).

The accession countries are poorer than the current members and the EU provided them with pre-accession regional assistance. It will continue to give them help to bring their economies up to the EU average and to reduce regional imbalances for some time after their membership.

The EU also uses regional policy to increase economic efficiency. If there are unemployed resources in some regions, potential output is lost and productive efficiency is not achieved. The existence of unemployed resources in some regions (such as workers, factories, hospitals and schools) at the same time as there are shortages of resources in other areas will mean that allocative efficiency is also not achieved.

Having regions with different levels of economic activity makes it difficult to implement EU-wide policies. This is because policy measures will have a different impact on prosperous and poor regions. For instance, a decision by the ECB to raise its rate of interest may have little effect on a prosperous region but may raise unemployment still higher in a poor region.

EU regional policy objectives

Initially, the EU identified six objectives for regional policy. However, for the period 2000–2006 these objectives have been simplified under three headings:

- to help those regions lagging behind in their development (that is, having a real GDP per head of less than 75 per cent of the EU average, and helping the Finnish and Swedish sub-arctic regions, which would not be economically viable without assistance)
- to help regions in industrial decline (the EU seeks to help these regions and their firms and labour force to adapt to change)
- to support education, training and employment (such measures should increase the employability of workers through raising their skills and adaptability; it is thought these measures are particularly significant in the case of youth and long-term unemployment).

Regional policy spending

EU regional policy spending is intended to complement national government regional policy assistance. It comes through the European Regional Development Fund and through other programmes, including the

Making connections

Using a PPF (production possibility frontier) diagram, analyse the effect on the EU economy of a reduction in regional unemployment.

Thinking like an economist

Explain the links between the EU's three regional policy objectives.

Social Fund and the Cohesion Fund. Collectively, the EU funds used for regional assistance are referred to as the structural funds. This spending is largely in the form of non-repayable grants.

The EU devotes its funds to a range of projects and employment schemes. Objective 1 receives the greatest amount of funding, accounting for almost three-quarters of all EU structural fund-spending.

Structural funds account for approximately 35 per cent of the EU budget and are the second most important form of spending after the CAP.

Significance of EU regional policy

EU regional policy can claim a number of successes. For instance, the rise in educational attainment in Ireland can be partly attributed to EU regional aid. The improved quality of Irish education has raised productivity, encouraged more FDI and contributed to higher economic growth.

However, there are still considerable regional disparities and with the imminent entry of the accession countries, the disparities will widen. This suggests that EU regional policy will play an even more important role in the future.

Quickies

1   What are the characteristics of a poor region?
2   Why, in the absence of government intervention, are regional differences likely to continue?
3   What are the main disadvantages of regional differences?
4   Explain how educational and training projects can help poor regions.

The EU seeks to promote a common policy in a range of areas. These include the environment, transport and social policies. To date, some progress has been made, but a common approach has not been fully achieved in any of these areas. Differences exist in, for instance, the use of renewable energy resources, subsidies to public transport and the number of days holiday workers enjoy.

EU environmental policies

Over time, EU environmental policies have come to be based on three key principles:

- the 'polluter pays' principle
- the precautionary principle (that is, action should be taken to protect the environment where there are significant risks, even if scientific evidence is not conclusive)
- the need to achieve sustainable development.

The Single European Act sets out the EU's environmental aims as:

- to preserve, protect and improve the quality of the environment
- to contribute towards protecting human health
- to ensure a prudent and rational utilisation of natural resources.

The Maastricht Treaty emphasised the need to integrate environmental issues into all its policies and introduced the precautionary principle. In 1997, the Amsterdam Treaty made explicit reference to the need to achieve sustainable development.

EU environmental measures

Most of EU environmental policy makes use of regulations and taxes. For example, the EU sets targets for the recycling of waste, for carbon dioxide emissions and for the quality of sea-bathing water. It has promoted the use of some taxes, including the landfill tax (a tax on the amount of waste being buried in landfill sites) and the aggregates tax (a tax on extracted materials such as gravel and sand).

Fewer tradable permit systems are in use in the EU than in the USA, but this could be about to change with the development of the market in carbon trading. The EU now often makes use of its collective power and acts as a single negotiating body at international environmental conferences.

Transport

The Treaty of Rome set out the objective of the adoption of a common transport policy. Progress on this objective has been slow, in part because each member country has its own transport objectives.

Environmental, transport and social policies

Synoptic link

This section builds on AS sections 3.6–3.9 and links to A2 section 5.12.

Making connections

Explain two ways in which the 'polluter pays' principle could be enforced.

Research task

Investigate the EU's role at international environmental conferences.

One of the achievements of the EU in the transport market has been to ease frontier crossing restrictions

EU transport policy seeks to achieve an efficient allocation of resources within the transport sector. It also aims to meet individual transport market requirements at least resource cost and to achieve an equitable distribution of benefits and costs from transport activities.

The EU has had some achievements in the transport market, including:

- the easing of frontier crossing restrictions
- the removal of restrictions on road-haulage firms undertaking road-haulage business within other EU countries on their return journey.

It has also provided funding, through structural funds, for a number of infrastructure projects. However, the main impact on the transport market comes from the European Commission's (EC) competition policy. This has, for instance, liberalised EU air passenger transport.

Social policy

The EU's social policy seeks to establish common social standards across the area. The aim is to achieve social cohesion, equity and a level playing field. The Treaty of Rome set out the objectives of improving living standards, working conditions and occupational health and safety. It also sought to promote employment and the free movement of labour, plus equal pay for men and women doing the same work.

Initially, EU social policy tended to concentrate mainly on labour market policy and, in particular, measures to retrain unemployed workers. However, as it has developed it has focused not only on labour market policy but also on the reduction of poverty and social exclusion.

Much of EU social policy is operated by means of directives. These set out the objectives the EU wants member countries to achieve, but leaves it up to member countries how to achieve them. Many of the directives that have been issued are less restrictive than national regulations. For instance, The Working Time Directive, introduced by the EU in 1993 and adopted by the UK in 1998, sets out a maximum working week of 48 hours. For all the EU member countries, except the UK and Denmark which had no limit, this was less stringent than their existing legislation. The UK has negotiated an opt-out that allows employers to ignore the limit if staff agree.

The Social Chapter

The Social Charter was adopted at the Strasbourg Council in 1989. It emphasised that in the development of a single market, social aspects should be given the same importance as economic aspects and that job creation should be given top priority.

Some economists were concerned that the single market could lead to social dumping – the driving down of employment and social conditions to the lowest level. With greater mobility of capital comes the risk that firms may move from countries with strong employment rights and high taxes to countries with few restrictions on firms. This would be likely to reduce working conditions and pay, and make it more difficult for governments to fund social benefits.

The Social Charter formed the basis of the Social Chapter, which was included in the Maastricht Treaty. It seeks to harmonise social legislation and lists the 'fundamental rights' of EU workers, including:

- the right to belong or not belong to a trade union
- the right to strike
- the right to have safe working conditions.

In addition, it emphasises the need to promote vocational training, the protection of children, gender equality and consultation between firms and their workers.

The UK initially opted out of the Social Chapter. It was concerned that it would raise firms' costs and make the UK a less attractive destination for FDI. However, the new Labour government of 1997 did sign up to the Social Chapter. It has introduced a number of the Social Chapter's directives.

As well as the Working Time Directive, it implemented the Works Council Directive in 1998 and the Parental Leave Directive in 1999. The former directive means that all UK-based firms with a labour force of 1,000 or more and with 150 or more workers based in more than two EU countries, have to set up consultation committees that deal with transnational issues. The latter directive increased paid maternity leave from 14 to 18 weeks, and gave both men and women the right to have three months' unpaid leave after the birth of a child.

Quickies

1 How might a landfill tax improve the environment?
2 Why is it difficult to achieve a common EU transport policy?
3 What are the aims of EU social policy?
4 Why did EU social policy become more significant with the development of the single European market?

Puzzler

Will globalisation increase or reduce the risk of social dumping?

4.11 Competition policy

Synoptic link

This section links to A2 section 5.19 on competition policy.

The EU's competition policy is administered by the Competition Department of the European Commission (EC). Its authority comes from articles laid out in the Treaty of Rome and subsequent legislation.

The policy aims to achieve a more efficient allocation of resources by increasing competitive pressure on firms throughout the EU. In pursuit of this aim, the policy tackles what it perceives to be unfair competition in markets involving more than one member state. Such unfair competition includes the formation of cartels, price discrimination and government subsidies. EU competition policy acts alongside national competition policy.

The theory behind EU competition policy

EU competition policy is based on the belief that competitive pressure will raise economic efficiency. The advantages claimed for a competitive market include consumer choice, low prices, high quality and a quick response to changes in consumer demand.

A competitive market provides both a carrot and a stick to firms to be economically efficient. The incentive (carrot) is that if a firm can lower its costs and produce what consumers want, it will attract more consumers and so earn higher profits. However, the punishment (stick) is that if a firm does not keep its costs and prices low and does not respond to what consumers want, it will make a loss and may go out of business.

This competitive pressure may come from the existence of a large number of firms in the industry (actual competition) or concern that failure to achieve economic efficiency will result in the entry of new firms (potential competition).

EU competition policy focuses less on the number of firms in any particular industry and more on the behaviour of the firms. A firm or group of firms may have significant market power, but if it or they act in a way expected of a competitive market, the European Commission (EC) is unlikely to intervene.

Restrictive practices

Restrictive practices between firms within a member state are left to national governments to deal with. However, the EU bans agreements between firms that restrict competition and affect trade between member countries. The assumption behind the ban is that such restrictive practices are against the public interest. For example, the formation of a cartel is likely to result in higher prices and may also lead to less choice and lower quality.

In October 2002, the EC found Nintendo (the Japanese video games manufacturer), John Menzies (the sole UK distributor of Nintendo products) and distributors in six other European countries guilty of operating a price-fixing cartel that pushed up prices. Nintendo was fined £94 million and John Menzies £5.5 million.

Making connections

Distinguish between a perfectly competitive market and a perfectly contestable market (see page 96 for more about contestable markets).

Making connections

Explain why cartels are often short-lived.

Monopoly power

EU policy on firms with a dominant market position is based on the belief that the possession of such a position does not necessarily mean a firm will act in an anti-competitive way. The EU is not concerned with the mere existence of monopoly. What does concern it is abuse of monopoly power. The EC will take action if it finds that a firm is abusing its dominant position.

There are several ways in which a dominant firm can use its power to exploit consumers. The most obvious is to restrict output and so raise price, reduce consumer surplus, increase producer surplus and increase profits. The firm may also engage in price discrimination, charging different prices to different groups of consumers for the same product, again in order to increase profits. Additionally, it may seek to reduce potential and actual competition.

In the first case, it may use limit pricing (that is, setting a price below the maximum profit level in order to discourage the entry of new firms). In the second case, the firm may be more aggressive, setting a price low enough to drive out existing competitors.

If a firm is suspected of abusing its market power, the EC will investigate. If found guilty, the firm will be fined and ordered to stop the uncompetitive activity.

Mergers

Since 1990, the EC has had the authority to assess mergers and acquisitions over a given value and where less than two-thirds of the combined turnover comes from one member state. In such circumstances, the parties to the merger must notify the EC. The Commission then decides whether or not to carry out an investigation. If it does carry out an investigation, it may allow the merger with conditions or may decide to stop it.

In practice, the EC investigates very few mergers and prohibits even fewer. The EC has been criticised for what is seen as its too permissive approach. However, it is not an easy task. This is because while a merger may not always be in the public interest, in some cases it may increase economic efficiency. A larger, combined firm may be able to take greater advantage of economies of scale, may have more confidence and funds to innovate and be able to compete more effectively in world markets.

Government aid

The EC prohibits government aid if it distorts or threatens to distort competition and affects trade between member states. There are a number of ways a government may assist its firms – including subsidies, investment grants and preferential purchasing. Exceptions may be allowed if the assistance serves some EU purpose. What the EC is concerned about is that

Research task

Using newspapers, magazines or websites, find a recent case in which the EC has taken action against what it perceived to be an abuse of monopoly power. Decide whether you think the EC's action was justified.

Making connections

What conditions are necessary for price discrimination to occur?

Making connections

Explain the main motives behind mergers.

	Total state aid in € bn	Total aid as % of GDP
Finland	2.1	1.58
Denmark	2.4	1.36
Belgium	3.3	1.34
Luxembourg	0.3	1.30
Ireland	1.3	1.20
Germany	23.3	1.14
Greece	1.3	1.04
Portugal	1.2	1.04
France	15.8	1.10
Italy	12.0	1.01
Austria	2.1	0.99
Netherlands	4.0	0.98
Spain	4.7	0.74
Sweden	1.9	0.71
UK	10.6	0.66
EU	86.3	0.99

Table 1: State aid in EU member states in 2001

state aid can prevent a 'level playing field' being achieved, with domestic firms being able to charge lower prices and undercut rival countries' firms at home and abroad.

In recent years, the EC has begun to scrutinise state aid much more closely, as it is now seen as one of the main threats to competition in the EU. Between 1997 and 2001, state aid throughout the EU fell from €98 billion to €86 billion under pressure from the EC to reduce state assistance to unprofitable firms. As Table 1 shows, the UK spent less of its GDP on state aid to industry than any other EU country.

The EC is urging governments to redirect their state aid from propping up unprofitable firms towards environmental protection, the development of small- and medium-sized businesses, job creation programmes, and research and development.

The car market

In October 2002, the EC introduced measures to increase competition in the car market and reduce the wide differences in car prices in the EU. The measures will come into force in October 2005 and include the following.

- Dealers can advertise and open showrooms anywhere in the EU.
- Dealers can sell more than one brand of car in the same showroom.
- Dealers do not have to offer repair services but if they do not, they will have to sub-contract to a suitable repairer.
- Supermarkets can become dealers if they meet manufacturers' quality criteria.

Quickies

1 Explain how competition may benefit consumers.
2 Identify two possible disadvantages and two possible advantages of a monopoly.
3 In what circumstances will the EC prevent a merger going ahead?
4 Using a diagram, explain the effect of a government granting a subsidy to a firm.

Britain and the euro

In April 2003 the Begg Commission, set up by BiE (Britain in Europe), produced a report on the consequences of Britain's non-membership of the euro. The Begg Report represented an attempt to shift the nature of the debate away from discussions about the pros and cons of going in, towards a discussion of the consequences of staying out.

In the media, two issues overshadowed the Begg report:
- the debate about Britain's role in the war against Iraq
- the Treasury's assessment of the Chancellor of the Exchequer's 'five economic tests' for membership of the euro. These tests concerned convergence, flexibility, investment, financial services and employment.

Summary – the consequences of saying 'no'

1. Saying 'no' to the euro would harm Britain's trade, inward investment, financial markets and competitiveness.
   - **Trade:** by keeping the pound, Britain is missing out on trade that is being created within the euro-zone, which already accounts for half our trade. Studies suggest that the euro has already added up to 30 per cent to trade among the countries that share it – and that this process is likely to continue.
   - **Foreign investment:** staying out of the euro is likely to reduce inward investment in Britain because foreign firms that want to access the large euro-zone market face higher costs, notably currency volatility, if they are based outside it. Foreign investment in the UK has already fallen sharply. This cannot simply be explained by the weakening of the US and global economies because Britain's *share* of inward investment into Europe has also fallen.
   - **Financial markets:** the euro will make the euro-zone more competitive in financial services. Already, some of the City of London's business has relocated to the euro-zone. Although some of this will occur whether or not Britain joins the euro, our euro decision is likely to affect the locations of some activities. For example, the European Central Bank (ECB) wants the euro's clearing and payment systems to be located within the euro-zone.
   - **Competitiveness:** the euro has reduced transaction costs and exchange rate risks and increased price transparency. For expensive consumer durables, such as electrical goods, euro-zone price dispersion has fallen dramatically. Survey evidence suggests British-based firms are pursuing different pricing strategies from their counterparts in the euro-zone. Staying out of the euro could increase companies' incentive to invest in further segmenting Britain from the euro-zone. If so, the small UK market would suffer from lower competition, fewer scale economies and higher prices.

2. There are no guaranteed benefits in delaying our euro decision, because entry conditions may not become more favourable in future.

- **Convergence of business cycles and economic structures:** Britain's business cycle and economic structure have already significantly converged with the euro-zone's. Trading links are closer, economic policy is more similar and financial structures are much more alike. Although convergence is not fully complete, joining the euro would increase it.
- **Convergence of interest rates:** while British long-term interest rates have already converged with the euro-zone's, our short-term rates have been consistently higher. Waiting is unlikely to close this gap, because it is structural as well as cyclical. Based on the US's proven system, the report discusses how to encourage households to borrow at long-term interest rates in order to overcome structural differences between British and euro-zone housing markets. These reforms are desirable whether or not Britain joins the euro.
- **Reaching the right exchange rate:** in recent months, there has been a welcome depreciation of sterling against the euro. The pound is approaching a reasonable euro entry rate.

3. An important window for institutional reform within the EU is opening. If Britain stands aside now, it will have less influence over these reforms.
   - **Fiscal-policy framework:** the EU's fiscal rules – the Stability and Growth Pact (SGP) – are flawed. Their quantitative definition of fiscal discipline is limited and inflexible, and sanctions from the European Commission are bound to be so sensitive that political considerations may prevent their imposition. The British government's fiscal rules are not perfect. They depend on the Chancellor's credibility as an enforcement mechanism and are not binding on future governments. A reformed SGP could be superior to Britain's domestic rules.
   - **Monetary-policy framework:** the British government may be more comfortable with the euro if the ECB takes less account of monetary aggregates and moves to an inflation-targeting system that is more like the Bank of England's. The ECB is currently reviewing its monetary-policy strategy, ahead of the EU's enlargement in 2004 and the appointment of a new ECB president.
   - **Financial regulations:** the euro-zone is at a turning point in choosing its financial architecture. In 2003 many decisions on the Financial Services Action Plan will be made, making it a particularly bad time to declare that Britain will be outside for the long-term.

Source: Adapted from Britain in Europe, Non-technical summary of the Begg Report, April 2003.

Activities

1 Imagine you are a member of an organisation called 'No to the euro'. Write a report giving as many counter-arguments as you can come up with to points raised in the Begg Report.

Thinking like an economist

Choose any two points made in the Begg Report and select a suitable economic diagram to illustrate the point. Write a paragraph explaining how your diagram is related to the specific issue.

Research task

Type the following words into a web search engine: five economic tests +euro. use suitable web resources to help you summarise the five economic tests in your own words.

Case Study: the European Union – the regional dimension

Study the extracts and all parts of this question very carefully before writing your answer. The whole report will be marked out of 84, including 4 marks for quality of written communication.

Setting the scene

It is the year 2005 and, following a referendum, a directly elected Assembly for the North West (ANW) has been created. One of the main functions of the ANW is to promote economic development in the region, which includes Liverpool, Manchester and Merseyside.

You are an economist working for Ms. Jacqui Mason, the Minister for Economic Development in the ANW. She has asked you to prepare a report drawing on the previous experience of other regions and explaining the role of the EU in promoting development in the regions.

When writing your report you should make use of the information in the extracts, together with any other relevant knowledge you possess.

Requirements of the report

The report should be entitled 'What can the EU do for us in the regions?' and should:

- explain what is meant by 'the regional problem' and how it can be measured
- discuss how regional policy can be expected to affect the economy of a region
- evaluate the effectiveness of EU regional policy
- conclude by recommending whether EU structural funds should be expanded in the future, giving reasons to justify your answer.

You will be given credit for demonstrating your ability to analyse, comment critically on and make effective use of the data provided.

Extract A: The structural funds

Disparities or imbalances between Europe's regions have long been recognised by the European Commission. As early as 1958 it was reported that the regional GDP per head in Hamburg (Germany) was five times greater than in Calabria (Italy).

The purpose of European structural funding is to promote the development of the poorer parts of the European Union. The European Summit of March 1999 agreed to allocate €195 billion (approximately £122 billion) to structural funds across the whole of Europe for the programme period 2000–

2006, most of which will be spent through three identified objectives (replacing the six objectives of the previous programme).

The EU Commission's guiding principles are as follows.

- Concentration of the funds on the areas of greatest need as defined by 'objectives'.
- Programming: multi-annual programmes are the norm, to promote a strategic approach.
- Partnership: partnerships are established to oversee and administer the funds involving local and regional decision-makers for the first time. Experience suggests that 'political' regions are better able to form partnerships than 'administrative' regions.
- Additionality: the additionality requirement ensures that spending in the regions would not simply replace spending by national governments, but be additional to it. In general, European structural funds must be 'matched', so the funds can only be used to pay for a proportion of the cost of eligible projects. The rest of the cost has to come from non-EU sources – the regional government budget or the national state.

Extract B: Previous objective I performance in the UK

Region	1995	1997	1999
Merseyside	68	72	71
Highlands and Islands	77	77	75
Northern Ireland	79	82	78
All UK objective 1	74	77	75

Table 1: GDP per head as a percentage of the EU average

The three main objectives agreed in 1999 were:

- to promote the development and structural adjustment of regions whose development is lagging behind. Objective 1 brings the highest level of funding from the EU budget
- to provide assistance to areas undergoing economic change, to declining rural areas, crisis-hit fishing areas and urban areas in difficulty
- to combat social exclusion by promoting lifelong training and education, encouraging job creation, and by countering the adverse effects of economic and social change. It is designed to create a 'learning region'.

Extract C

Table 2: Selected data for regions with highest and lowest rates of employment, 1999–2000 EU 27 = EU 15 and 12 applicants

Source: *Eurostat*, www.europa.eu.int/com m/regional_policy, 1 July 2003

	Region	Population 000s	Employment rate %	Unemployment rate %	GDP per head EU 27 = 100
Highest employment	Centro (Portugal)	1725.4	84.7	1.8	66.2
	Berkshire, Buckinghamshire and Oxfordshire (UK)	2113.9	82.0	1.9	151.3
Lowest employment	Calabria (Italy)	2057.6	39.7	27.7	72.2
	Corse (France)	260.3	37.7	12.5	93.1

For module 4, AQA gives you a choice of two examination units: paper EC4C (coursework) or EC4W (written exam). If you choose the written paper, then you are examined using a case study. The case study is unseen (it is not pre-released), but the general topic is known. At present, the topic for the case study is the European Union, and earlier chapters in this book give you some hints on the different aspects of this topic that could appear.

The most successful candidates sitting this paper are those who do not regard the case study as an 'easy option' requiring less preparation than coursework. Instead, they treat the case study as a type of coursework, researching topics, preparing reports and, ideally, presenting reports to their teachers and classmates in discussion groups.

A common weakness among candidates is to thoroughly prepare for a specific aspect of the EU (for example, 'Should Britain join the euro?') and then become disappointed and disorientated when they find that this is not the specific topic for their case study paper. Some are tempted to write an answer for their pre-learned topic regardless and, needless to say, such an approach earns very few marks.

It could happen that you find yourself faced with an aspect of the EU that you have never considered before. Do not panic! Read the case study carefully and you will find that enough information has been provided to enable you to comment sensibly on the issues. Also, the examiners will have been careful to ensure that the case study gives you opportunities to apply economic concepts and principles with which you are familiar. Bear the following points in mind.

- Do not worry too much about 'report format'. Simply remember that a report is from someone, to someone, and about something.
- Get into the scenario: write in the role that is assigned to you.
- Engage with the data, quote from it and use it to support an argument.
- Carefully follow the bullet-pointed tasks set out in the requirements of the report. There will be four or five of these, and it is sensible to divide your report into four or five corresponding sections. You might decide to have further sub-sections, but this is not necessary.
- Ensure that you demonstrate all the skills that the examiner will be looking for.

Mark schemes

The marking criteria are the same as for coursework:
- knowledge (10 marks)
- application (20 marks)
- analysis (20 marks)
- evaluation (30 marks)
- quality of written communication (4 marks).

The total is 84. The grade boundaries change from examination to examination for complicated technical reasons, so it is rather dangerous to quote these as if they are set in stone. However, you will need a mark somewhere in the 30s for a grade 'E' on this module, and probably somewhere in the 50s for an 'A'.

Experience suggests that the following two points would enable many candidates to improve their marks very efficiently.

- Pay more attention to 'application'. Try to insert some relevant economic theory and apply it to the data. Diagrams often help, for example, a production possibility curve, demand and supply diagram, or aggregate demand and aggregate supply diagram. Also use concepts that may or may not require a diagram, for example, opportunity costs, elasticity, the multiplier.
- Be critical. Do not accept judgements at face value. Challenge the data, and this should improve your marks for evaluation, enabling you to reach the higher mark bands.

As well as the general marking criteria that are used for all case studies, examiners are given some specific guidance for each particular case study. Here is the type of guidance that might be given for examiners marking the Exam practice case study in section 4.13.

Guidance

Examiners should approach the candidate's work with an open mind and credit should always be given where candidates respond in an unanticipated, but economically valid way.

Knowledge and understanding

Evidence of knowledge and understanding may be shown by the candidate who considers the general features of the regional problem (for example, by considering core-periphery disparities) and the main purpose of EU regional policy (economic and social cohesion). Candidates can show knowledge of the different indicators of regional development used in the data (for example, GDP per head, employment, unemployment). Understanding would be demonstrated by evidence of the candidate's ability to comment on possible linkages between these indicators.

Application

Economic principles that could be used to interpret the data include the multiplier and supply-side theory, particularly those aspects that focus on investment in human capital (education and training). An example of appropriate application would be an AS/AD diagram with AS shifting to the right as a result of successful regional policy. Candidates could make predictions about the future of European regional policy when the EU is expanded to twenty-five members, and when the current 'below average' regions such as the North West are likely to be much nearer EU averages.

Analysis and evaluation

For analysis candidates might, for example, comment on the fact that in the previous objective 1 programme (which affected Merseyside, part of the scenario's North West region) some regions either improved their position only slightly or even worsened their position.

For evaluation, candidates could challenge assumptions. For instance, the stated aim of reducing disparities in GDP per head does not appear to necessarily correlate with employment/unemployment levels. It might also be noted that the new structural funding programmes stress employability rather than employment, their supply-side benefits take time to be built up, and can be neutralised very quickly by a demand-side shock, such as a sudden large business closure. Specific evidence is most likely to be present when candidates start to make their recommendations and support their conclusions. However, if evaluative skills are demonstrated elsewhere in the report the candidate should be rewarded.

General

Weaker candidates will simply copy chunks out of the data. This approach would suggest lower level performance. However, if the data is appropriately selected and re-ordered to be relevant to an aspect highlighted in the scenario, this should tend to put a candidate's work in the middle levels. To move higher, the candidate should go beyond the selection and re-ordering of material from the case study.

Generally, stronger candidates should be writing closely to the scenario and giving specific analysis of the consequences of a proactive regional policy for the North West, which is 'bottom up', assessing local needs, rather than 'top-down'.

Further reading

4.15

4.2
B. Hill. *The European Union*, 4th edition. Heinemann, 2001. Chapter 1.

4.4
B. Hill. *The European Union*, 4th edition. Heinemann, 2001. Chapter 9.

4.5
B. Hill. *The European Union*, 4th edition. Heinemann, 2001. Chapter 6.
M. Russell & D. Heathfield. *Inflation and UK Monetary Policy*, 3rd edition. Heinemann 1999. Chapter 10.
D. Smith. *UK Current Economic Policy*, 3rd edition. Heinemann, 2003. Chapter 9.

4.6
G. Hale. *Labour Markets*. Heinemann, 2001. Chapter 5.

4.7
B. Hill. *The European Union*, 4th edition. Heinemann, 2001. Chapters 1 & 10.

4.8
B. Hill. *The European Union*, 4th edition. Heinemann, 2001. Chapter 4.

4.9
B. Hill. *The European Union*, 4th edition. Heinemann, 2001. Chapter 5.
D. Smith. *UK Current Economic Policy*, 3rd edition. Heinemann, 2003. Chapter 8.

4.10
B. Hill. *The European Union*, 4th edition. Heinemann, 2001. Chapters 3 & 10.

4.11
B. Hill. *The European Union*, 4th edition. Heinemann, 2001. Chapter 3

PART 5

BUSINESS ECONOMICS AND DISTRIBUTION OF INCOME

Business economics and distribution of income: an introduction

5.1

Welcome to Part 5 of A2 Economics. This introduction includes:

- an overview of what you can expect to study
- links with the AS part of this course
- an explanation of the difference between AS and A2
- general advice on how to maximise your grade.

Overview of module

Although the specification does not follow this pattern, it might be helpful to see Part 5 as consisting of five different but overlapping areas (illustrated in Figure 1 on page 60:

- theory of the firm (sections 5.1–5.6)
- market structures (sections 5.7–5.11)
- the labour market (sections 5.12–5.15)
- distribution of income and wealth (sections 5.16–5.17)
- government intervention (sections 5.18–5.23).

Theory of the firm

This includes detailed treatment of costs and revenue which you need to know to be able to predict how firms are likely to behave in relation to three key variables: price, output and profits. This will involve you using graphical analysis to aid your understanding of how firms behave.

Market structures

This builds on theory of the firm and consists of three different models: perfect competition, monopoly and oligopoly.

The labour market

Here, you are required to develop a more detailed understanding of how factor markets works concentrating on markets for labour. As with the other areas of Part 5, you have to learn a series of graphs and how they might be used to explain differences in wages and incomes between different groups. Examining labour markets provides a good exemplification of the possible limits to the usefulness of economics in understanding complex human institutions.

Distribution of income and wealth

This is another separate but related topic designed to help you understand how income and wealth are very unequally distributed in UK society, leading to problems of poverty for a significant minority of the population.

Government intervention

Finally, sections 5.18–5.23 explain how and why the government intervenes in all the different markets identified above. This involves a mixture of graphical and written analysis that you need to develop to show you have reached the A2 standard.

Links with AS

You should quickly appreciate that much of the content of Part 5 is similar to that which you learned in Part 1 'Markets and market failure'. For example, in Part 1, you will have dealt with competitive and concentrated markets. For A2, a deeper theoretical understanding is required. Another way of seeing the differences is that for AS most of your treatment of markets was descriptive, whereas at A2 you are required to use graphs and be more precise in your analysis.

At AS you would have touched on factor markets, but not in the depth required for A2. Thus, the term 'marginal revenue product' (MRP) will be new to you, as will consideration of inequalities in income and wealth.

Finally, government intervention in these markets builds and develops on the work that you did for AS in sections 1.22–1.24 of your text.

AS and A2

Students may find that units 5 and 6 are the hardest to do well on. There are a number of reasons for this.

For the AS exam, 60 per cent of your marks are for what some people think are lower order or easier skills of knowledge, understanding and application. The remaining 40 per cent are for analysis and evaluation. The split for Units 5 and 6 is 50/50, which means you have to give more longer answers and fewer short ones in your exam.

These longer answers will require you to have a better overall understanding of topics such that you can evaluate the usefulness of particular micro economic models. This means that you have to be able to step back from your work and see both the value and the limitations of these models in helping us to understand how businesses and labour markets work in the real world. You must show that you can see synoptic links between the different topics that you do for economics.

Maximising your grade

Obviously, knowing your stuff is the essential prerequisite for you doing well. However, there are issues that you and your teachers need to consider, and these mainly relate to the sequencing or scheduling of your learning.

Some schools and colleges don't follow the specification as laid out by AQA or in this book. Tackling the labour market and the distribution of income can be fitted in some places after AS at the end of the summer term. This means that the bulk of the autumn term of year 2 can be devoted to module 5, and the exam can be taken in January. This approach means that you get a second chance to improve your mark in the following June. This strategy will not work for everyone, as it will depend on staff and whether or not your school or college budgets allow January exam entries.

However, the point is that it pays to devote as long a period as possible to this module. There is a lot to learn and the exam is challenging. But stick to it and you will win through.

Figure 1: An overview of Part 5

Section 5.2 is devoted to increasing your knowledge of how the objectives of firms are likely to affect the ways in which firms behave. This is a key element in helping you to develop your understanding of what is called the Theory of the firm. Most firms probably pursue a variety of objectives. These include:

- survival
- profit maximisation
- sales maximisation
- social and community objectives
- building shareholder value
- growth and expansion.

Synoptic link

Before you go any further make sure that you know about:
- monopolies (AS section 1.18)
- economies of scale (AS section 1.18)
- supply-side policies (AS section 2.14).

Survival

The survival rate of newly established businesses is not very high and many struggle to stay afloat. Competition is often intense and new businesses are often under-capitalised, which means they often have insufficient financial backing to survive unforeseen events.

Getting through the first year of trading is a difficult objective, and one that is likely to dominate the actions of owners of small businesses. However, it is not just small and new businesses that have to fight to survive. Established UK companies like Marconi and Cable and Wireless are currently struggling to survive and, like their smaller counterparts, are doing everything possible to stay in businesses.

If companies such as these don't try to ensure that they minimise any losses and don't strive to make as big a profit as possible, they probably won't survive.

Profit maximisation

Ensuring that a firm earns as much profit as possible is a similar objective to survival. It means that a business is as prepared to cut production as it is to expand, and it means that chasing profits is more important than any other objective. As will be shown on pages 76–8, a firm that wishes to maximise profits will go on expanding production and sales until the last unit sold adds as much to its revenue as it does to its costs. In this way a profit-maximising firm will always ensure that its profits are as large as possible.

If not making a profit - cut production

Sales maximisation

This is a similar concept and applies to those firms that sell as much as they can while still covering their costs. A sales maximising firm will go on producing and selling until the price that it receives for the last unit sold is the same as its cost of production. There is a subtle difference between this and profit maximisation, as will be explained in more detail in section 5.6.

Research task

Speak to the owner of a small business and try to find out how they prioritise business objectives.

Research task

Find out how far a local
voluntary organisation is run as a
business.

Social and community objectives

Profit and sales are not always the most important objectives for
organisations. Schools may set out to get the best examination results, but
they are rarely run to make as big a profit as possible or to attract increasing
numbers of students.

Local councils will probably say that they strive to meet the needs of the
local community, and many voluntary organisations will have similar social
directed objectives. Many companies in the private sector also claim to have
wider objectives than merely the pursuit of sales or profit. Ethical traders like
Fairtrade are becoming more and more significant.

Building shareholder value

This and similar sounding terms are often used in the UK by public limited
companies (plcs) whose shares are publicly traded on the stock exchange.
The value refers to the return that shareholders receive from owing shares.
This can be boosted by larger dividends and, most importantly, by higher
share prices. The determination of share prices is a complex and, some
would argue, irrational process and large companies use a range of
strategies to push up the price of their shares. In the USA, in recent years
this has included the use of dubious and illegal accounting practices.

Growth and expansion

This is almost the opposite of survival, and many medium-size and large firms
strive to grow and dominate the industry in which they operate. This is often
described as gaining market share – that is, the proportion of sales in a given
market going to one particular firm – and can be achieved in two ways.

Firms can out-compete their competitors and build sales by selling at lower
prices or by beating rivals in terms of quality. The same objectives can be
achieved by merger and takeover of rivals or related businesses. Currently
Vodafone is the third largest UK company by its relentless acquisition of rivals.

Research task

Get hold of three different
annual reports from plcs. What do
they tell you about how large
businesses prioritise objectives?

Reconciling competing objectives

Few, if any, firms are simple one-dimension organisations. Most follow a
clutch of different, potentially conflicting, objectives. Sorting out which is
most important is often difficult. Firms themselves are not always very clear
about how they prioritise their objectives. Economists are often forced to
make generalisations. At a very basic level, no organisation can survive if it
fails to ensure that revenue equals or exceeds costs.

As will be shown in section 5.7, small businesses probably need to go for
profit at the expense of other objectives, and it is possible to argue that larger
organisations are most likely to grow and build shareholder value. Some

businesses set minimum levels of profit or market share, which allows them to pursue other objectives. This is called 'satisficing'.

Historical trends

Economists have undertaken extensive research into trying to establish what motivators or drivers are most important in determining how firms actually behave. There is a lot of evidence to suggest that business behaviour is heavily influenced by the culture of different societies. Thus, traditionally, Japanese firms have put much more value on ensuring that a wide range of workers' needs are met – for example, health care, sport and recreation, child support and the like. US companies are often stereotyped as having a 'get up and go' attitude in which growth and expansion are highly socially valued.

In his recent book *The State We Are In*, Will Hutton argued that British businesses are too short-termist, and that quick returns and profits rather than long-term investment are the expectation. Economists have to be careful to avoid making sweeping generalisations, but it is clear that more and more business is being concentrated in the hands of fewer companies or corporations. These large transnational firms are often more powerful than all but the wealthiest countries, but understanding how major companies such as Ford, Sony, Exxon and Unilever work is a neglected area of research.

Ownership and control

The Canadian born economist J.K. Galbraith argued that the growth of corporations in the US has led to a breakdown in the traditional relationship between ownership and control of firms. When businesses are small, their owners usually run them. Clearly this is the case with sole proprietors and partnerships, and it is logical to argue that if people have put money into a business, they will run that business to ensure that they make reasonable profits. They are likely to be profit maximisers.

The growth of firms requires additional funds. In countries such as the UK, the stock market is an important source of finance. Shares are sold to raise capital. Shareholders own plcs. Thus, Marks and Spencer is owned by thousands of individual shareholders. Galbraith argued that these shareholders did not actively participate in decision making. As long as they received what they considered to be a reasonable share of profits – their dividend – he argued that their role would be passive. Decisions regarding company objectives would be left to paid employees: senior managers.

Galbraith argued that this group of people were strongly motivated by status, and that status was earned in the US by being associated with a company that was growing and expanding. He suggested that such key managers would be more interested in boosting sales and achieving greater market share than they would be in chasing the highest possible profit. They would

Web link

All major plcs have websites that are of varying degrees of use for economics students. To see two examples, go to the following website and enter express code 0810P : www.heinemann.co.uk/hotlinks.

Thinking like an economist

Section 5.2 highlights the different ways in which the same terms are used.

- What is generally meant by the terms 'capital' and 'investment'.
- How do economists define these terms?

be foolish to totally ignore shareholders, but as long as they were happy with their returns, managers would be left to get on with running the company.

Evaluating Galbraith's arguments

Galbraith's arguments about the divorce between ownership and control of large corporations have had a significant impact on how economists deal with large companies. Clearly it is dangerous to automatically assume that all business are profit maximisers, but at the same time companies that ignore the pursuit of profit are likely to find it difficult to survive in the long term.

It is possible to argue that widespread share ownership means that individual shareholders exert little power. However, shares are not evenly distributed. They are not all owned by little old ladies living in Eastbourne. In the UK, it is very common for directors of plcs to also be major shareholders. Such people are likely to regard themselves as both owners and those in control.

The only way in which Galbraith's arguments and those who disagree can be properly evaluated is by undertaking empirical research of individual companies.

Quickie

Business objectives and their prioritisation will affect how firms behave, especially in terms of setting levels of output and/or price. Which of the following is likely to set the lowest prices?
1 A profit maximiser.
2 A sales maximiser.

Exam hint

Never forget the following mantra: a firm seeking to maximise profits must ensure that marginal cost equals marginal revenue.

Puzzler

Economists have to make simplifying assumptions. How valid is the assumption which says profit maximisation is more important than any other objective?

All firms, regardless of their mission statements, objectives, ownership and what they might say about themselves, have to make decisions about two key factors: costs and revenue. If firms are going to survive, they need to ensure that, one way or another, their revenues are at the very least the same as their costs. Most businesses strive to ensure that revenue exceeds costs. This positive difference is described by economists as profit. Should costs exceed revenue, a loss is made. The economic analysis contained in this section and in section 5.4 is based on this very simple reasoning.

Thus, examination of data about costs and revenue is important in helping you to develop a better understanding of the behaviour of firms. This applies just as much to organisations that are not primarily motivated to make profits – for example, government agencies and voluntary groups. This section is devoted to developing an understanding of how economists look at average costs of production in the short run. Section 5.4 is devoted to long run costs. This is followed by consideration of those factors that affect the revenue firms can earn.

Short run costs of production

All payments made by a firm in the production of a good or provision of a service are called costs. Economists use the convention followed by many businesses of distinguishing between overheads and running costs.

Overheads

Overheads are costs of production that businesses have to pay regardless of their level of output. Thus, a bookstore is likely to be faced with bills for rent, business rates and repayment of loans, which will remain the same regardless of how many books are sold. These expenditures are classified as fixed costs and the convention is that these do not change in the short run, which is defined as that period of time in which it is not possible to change the quantity of an input of a particular factor of production (usually called factor input).

Running costs

Running costs, such as payment of wages, stock purchases and the like, which will change as sales change in the short run, are classified as variable costs.

Classifying fixed and variable costs

In practice, it is not always easy to decide whether a particular cost should be classified as fixed or variable. For example, contracts and salaries might be agreed to cover a particular length of time, making them fixed, whereas maintenance costs might change considerably as output changes making them variable.

Costs of production: 1

Synoptic link

This section builds on the work that you did for AS on supply curves (see AS section 1.8). This may not be immediately obvious. But remember, you have already learned that supply curves almost always slope upwards from left to right. The detailed analysis on costs will provide you with an improved rationale as to why this is the case.

Key concept

Overheads are the same as fixed costs.

Total costs

The addition of fixed to variable costs gives total costs, which include all the costs faced by a firm in the production of a good or a provision of a service.

Key concept

$$\text{Average costs} = \frac{\text{total costs}}{\text{output}}.$$

Average costs

The total cost divided by the output of the business gives the short run average total cost, which is usually abbreviated to short run average cost, or even just average cost. This is probably the most useful of these measures, as it indicates the cost of producing each item or providing a service. The average cost is sometimes referred to as the unit cost.

Definition

Marginal cost: the change in cost brought about by changing production by one unit.

Marginal costs

Finally, economists and business people make use of the concept of **marginal cost**, which is the additional cost of producing an extra unit of output of a particular good or service. Thus, if a clothing manufacturing company were to produce an extra suit, it would be faced with the costs of additional materials and labour, but would not have to pay out any more for design or machine-setting costs.

Short run costs

Economic analysis of the behaviour of firms focuses on either the short or the long run. In the short run, as has already been indicated, a firm will have at least one fixed factor of production. In the long run, a firm can change all its inputs. This section is concerned with the analysis of changes in the short run, and a series of logical deductions can be made on the basis of this classification. The data contained in Table 1 is based on the actual costs of running a bookshop and illustrates how short run costs are likely to behave.

Table 1 shows it is easy to work out the monthly total costs (total variable cost plus total fixed cost) of running the bookshop (column 2 plus column 4). From this, it is possible to derive the average cost of selling convenient bundles of books. In this example, 2,500 books were sold in March. If this figure is divided into the total costs of £8,850, the average cost of selling each book is £3.54

Fixed costs	£	Variable costs	£
Rent	2,000	Purchase of new stock	2,000
Uniform business rate	1,000	Postage	300
Bank loan repayment	750	Telephone	200
Depreciation of computer and other equipment	50	Overtime	500
Insurance	50		
Wages	2,000		
Total fixed cost	5,850	Total variable cost	3,000
		Total cost £8,850	

Table 1: Average monthly costs of Forest Bookshop (March 2002)

Graphing average costs

By collecting cost data relating to different levels of output or sales, it is possible to construct graphs illustrating the relationship between costs and different levels of sales. To take an agricultural example, farmers are likely to have a fair idea of the best number of livestock to keep given the acreage and quality of their farmland. In Table 2, average costs of producing each lamb on a 250-acre farm are related to different 'outputs' of lambs.

Table 2 shows what a good farmer would know without having to make such calculations – that is, the most appropriate number of ewes to keep given the size of farm and cost of different factor inputs. In this example, if no lambs were sold, the farmer would still be faced with certain fixed costs which will probably be dominated by fencing, rent and repayment of loans.

A small flock of around 30 ewes might be expected to produce 50 lambs. Variable costs for feed, veterinary and the abattoir would be incurred. However, given the relatively high level of fixed costs, it would cost £120 to rear and slaughter each lamb. Production of 200 lambs would be more 'economic', as better use would be made of the available land. However, each lamb would still cost £45 to produce.

Increasing the flock to 300 ewes could produce 500 lambs and even better use would be made of the farm, giving an average cost of £38 per lamb. Continued expansion of the flock would, however, push up average costs to £65 a lamb when 1,000 are produced and £73 if 1,500 were raised. Breeding more lambs would put pressure on the available grass, lead to the purchase of more hay and concentrates, and probably a greater incidence of disease.

In short, if this farmer wanted to be most efficient and keep short run costs to a minimum, he or she should produce around 500 lambs a year.

The average cost data contained in the table is illustrated in Figure 1. Output is measured on the horizontal axis and average costs of production on the vertical. This (short run) average cost curve is 'U' shaped. As output expands, efficiency increases and short run average costs fall. They reach a minimum, or 'optimum', point beyond which short run costs rise indicating declining efficiency. This will apply to the short run costs of any firm and is known by economists as the **law of diminishing marginal returns**, which will always occur if the use of a variable factor is increased while another factor input remains fixed. In Figure 1, more and more fodder and concentrates were purchased to feed an expanding flock of sheep, but the size of the farm remained the same.

Similarly, if a factory manager wanted to increase production in the short run he or she would not be able to rapidly expand the size of the factory,

Annual sales of lambs	Fixed costs £	Variable costs £	Total costs £	Average costs £
0	5,000	0	5,000	
50	5,000	1,000	6,000	120
200	5,000	4,000	9,000	45
500	5,000	14,000	19,000	38
1,000	5,000	60,000	65,000	65
1,500	5,000	105,000	110,000	73

Table 2: Sales of lambs

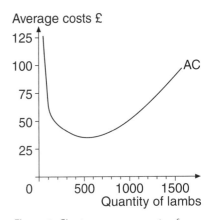

Figure 1: Short run average costs of sheep farmer

Definition

Law of diminishing marginal returns: this applies to short run costs faced by a firm. It 'states' that if a firm seeks to increase production in the short run, its average costs of production will first fall, then bottom out, then rise. This is means that the short run average cost curve is always drawn as being 'U' shaped.

nor buy new machines. Employees could be asked to work overtime and more workers could be taken on. If this process were to continue, a point would be reached when overcrowding and the sheer mass of workers would contribute to rising short run average costs.

Graphing marginal costs

As indicated on page 67, any change in costs brought about by changing production by an additional unit is described as a marginal cost. These costs can be calculated by looking at how total costs change according to changes in output. Table 3 relates to total costs incurred on a daily basis by a garage specialising in undertaking MoTs

The garage owner is faced with fixed costs of £150 a day – rent, business rates, wages, loan repayment and so forth. As more MoTs are carried out,

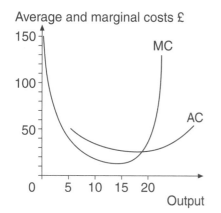

Average and marginal costs £

Figure 2: Marginal and average costs

Daily number of MoT tests	Total daily costs £	Average costs £	Marginal costs £
0	150		
1	150	150	150
2	180	90	30
3	196	65.3	16
4	211	52.75	15
5	224	44.8	13
6	236	39.3	12
7	247	35.3	11
8	257	32.1	10
9	266	29.5	9
10	274	27.4	8
11	280	25.4	6
12	285	23.75	5
13	292	22.5	7
14	301	21.5	9
15	311	20.7	10
16	331	20.7	20
17	355	20.9	24
18	385	21.4	30
19	423	22.3	38
20	471	23.6	48

Table 3: Total daily costs incurred by garage specialising in MoTs

resources are used more efficiently – reflected in both falling average and marginal costs.

As with the sheep farmer, the garage owner will find that costs will bottom out and then begin to increase. In this example, undertaking 16 rather than 15 MoTs causes a big rise in costs – perhaps extra labour is required. As work increases, the garage becomes more crowded and congested, and both average and marginal costs rise. This is illustrated in Figure 2. Marginal costs are plotted against the midpoint of each unit change in output, and the marginal cost curve will cut the lowest point of the average cost curve.

In the short run, average and marginal cost curves will always have the same relationship to each other. The application of the law of diminishing marginal returns means that any attempt to increase output by changing the use of one factor while the use of others remains fixed will initially lead to falling average and marginal costs. An optimum will then be reached, where average costs are at a minimum and, thereafter, growing inefficiency will lead to rising average costs. This observation that short run average cost curves are 'U' shaped is one with which all students of economics should become familiar.

Quickie

Assume the Forest Bookshop is able to sell twice as many books in April 2002 than it did March. Construct your own table of data reflecting these higher sales. What will be the effect on the following?

1 Fixed costs.   3 Average costs.
2 Variable costs.   4 potential profits.

Thinking like an economist

John Maynard Keynes argued that we should focus on the short run because in the long run we are all dead. Do you agree?

Exam hint

Get used to drawing average and marginal cost curves. Draw the 'U' shaped average cost curve first, then the marginal cost curve – a bit like the Nike swoosh. The upward final bit passes through the lowest point on the average cost curve. Finally, don't *ever* forget to label your axis – costs on the vertical and output on the horizontal.

Costs of production: 2

5.4

Having focused on short run costs in sections 5.2 and 5.3, this section looks at long run costs. The long run is defined as that period of time in which it is possible for a firm to alter any or all of its factor inputs. Traditionally, economists have considered that the distinction between the long and the short term is very important in analysing costs and the behaviour of firms. There is now more debate about this approach, and at the end of this section there is an outline of alternative approaches. You need to understand both traditional and newer approaches to the analysis of costs.

Traditional theory

This builds on the analysis in section 5.3. Thus, the long run is about the sheep farmer purchasing more land, the bookseller expanding its premises and the garage installing new car-testing machinery. The effect of expanding production on long run average costs is likely to depend on a number of factors. The following three scenarios apply to the sheep farmer doubling the size of his or her farm.

Constant returns to scale

Suppose the cost of a loan to purchase additional land is the same as was already being paid for the original 250 acres. Assume that there will be proportionately similar increases in costs for labour, winter feed, fencing and veterinary fees. In this situation, the average short run cost of producing each lamb would not be very different from the short run cost on the smaller farm.

This means that at the optimum level of output, each lamb would cost about £38 to produce. However, the farmer can now produce 1,000 lambs a year whereas on the smaller farm, diminishing returns occurred if more than 500 lambs were produced.

This is illustrated by Figure 1, which shows unchanged average costs of production and a possible long run average cost curve.

Diseconomies of scale

In this case, the cost of borrowing additional money might be greater and the newly acquired land might be less productive. Here, long run costs would be rising, as shown in Figure 2. At the farmer's optimum level of output, the short run average costs of producing each lamb would be greater than was the case with the optimum level on the smaller farm, giving a rising long run average cost curve.

Economies of scale

In contrast to the previous scenario, the newly acquired land might be cheaper and more productive. It may pay the farmer to transport his or her own livestock, and suppliers of winter feed might be prepared to supply larger orders at a discount. In this case, optimum short run costs of production would

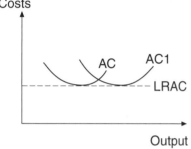

Figure 1: Constant returns

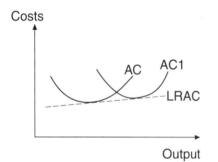

Figure 1: Diseconomies of scale

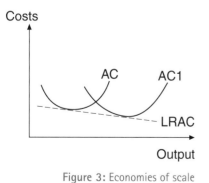

Figure 3: Economies of scale

fall. This means that not only would the farmer be able to produce more lambs, but also he or she would be able to produce each one more cheaply. In this case, Figure 3 clearly indicates that long run costs are falling.

Returns to scale

These three scenarios illustrate the concept of returns to scale, which is used to judge the impact on costs in the long run of changing any or all factor inputs. Scenario 1, where average costs of production remain the same, is described as an example of constant returns to scale. Scenario 2 involves rising long run costs, which can also be described as diseconomies of scale. Scenario 3 is about economies of scale which are falling long run costs.

Factors affecting returns to scale

Unlike short run costs, there is no law or certainty governing the shape of the long run average cost curves. A number of factors will determine whether or not they are likely to rise or fall. These can be sub-divided into internal and external returns to scale.

Internal economies of scale

Internal economies of scale relate to a growth in the size of the individual firm and include technical factors, organisational factors and market power.

Technical factors

As firms grow, producing and selling larger outputs can make it 'economic' to automate or mechanise particular stages of production in order to drive down costs. Henry Ford used production line techniques to mass produce cars that were much cheaper than those produced more traditionally. Similarly, wide-bodied planes such as the Airbus 300 series have lower running costs per passenger mile compared to a smaller aircraft such as the Boeing 707. Larger planes tend to be more fuel-efficient.

In the same way, as manufacturing firms grow and produce larger saleable outputs they are more likely to be able to afford more expensive but more efficient computer applications and automated production methods.

Organisational factors

The growth of firms and production of larger outputs enables firms to apply the division of labour and principles of specialisation. Those who work for small firms may have to undertake a range of jobs, and will find it hard to develop cost-saving skills and expertise in particular fields. As firms grow, they can afford to employ specialists in finance and marketing and so on, and this can result in cost savings, leading to falling long run average costs.

Thinking like an economist

Why can division of labour and specialisation drive down long run costs?

Growth and higher revenues can allow firms to invest more heavily in research and development. This is especially important in those industries in which the rate of change is rapid – for example, electronics and pharmaceuticals. These sectors of the global economy tend to be dominated by giant firms such as Sony and GlaxoSmithKline. Their growth leads to greater research efforts, which lead to the development of new products and the establishment of new sources of competitive advantage.

Market power

Firms that grow larger can exercise more power in the various marketplaces in which they operate. Expanding output can allow companies to negotiate larger discounts from suppliers. In the UK, the major supermarkets are said to be able to compel prospective suppliers of foodstuffs to accept ever-lower prices while maintaining ever-higher standards.

Larger, wealthier companies can afford to devote larger amounts of their resources to advertising, which is particularly important in branding and the development of global markets. Transnational companies have the power to influence governments and are in a stronger position than smaller companies to use bribery or take advantage of corrupt business practices.

Larger companies are also likely to have larger market shares and such monopoly power enables them to use different pricing strategies to limit competition. They are more likely to be able to cut prices to drive out smaller competitors.

Making connections

Can you see the link between external economies and diseconomies of scales and externalities?

External economies of scale

These can be very beneficial to some firms, as they can bring the benefit of long run cost reductions without additional expenditure by individual firms. External economies of scale relate to changes in long run costs that are associated with the expansion of a particular industry rather than an individual firm.

External economies of scale are often associated with the growth and concentration of particular industries in defined geographical areas. This can attract related businesses, reducing transport costs and making collaboration more possible. Local schools and colleges are more likely to provide relevant vocational training, which will also benefit local businesses, helping them to reduce long run average costs. These factors help to explain why biotech businesses are attracted to the Cambridge area and software manufacturers to Silicone Valley in California.

Diseconomies of scale

However, there are factors that can lead to the increasing size of firms being associated with rising long-term costs. Such diseconomies of scale can also be both internal and external to the firm in question.

Internal diseconomies of scale

These can be classified in the same way as economies of scale. Technical diseconomies of scale often relate to technological constraints. For example, ships that are built beyond a certain size require different methods of construction, which can result in increasing average costs. Their size might be such that ports and particular routes are no longer usable.

Organisational diseconomies are probably relatively more significant as the growth in size of businesses is often associated with increases in red tape and bureaucracy. Companies employing tens of thousands of workers are more difficult to manage, communications can be slower and less effective, and both workers and managers might be less motivated. All these factors might contribute to rising long run costs.

Growing size does not automatically bring greater market power. Large, dominant companies might be slower in responding to market trends. They are likely to be more distant and less responsive to the demands of their customers. There are many examples of companies that have expanded and lost touch with their customers. Xerox was once the world leader in the photocopier market but it is now struggling to survive. In the UK, businesses such as Marconi and ICI have been forced to demerge and downsize in order to try to survive.

External diseconomies of scale

In the same way that particular geographical areas can be associated with the complementary growth and development of related businesses, the decline of particular firms and industries can drag down the fortunes of others. Some of the worst social and economic problems in the UK are associated with the failings of particular industries – shipbuilding on the Mersey and Clyde and coalmining in South Wales, Yorkshire and Nottinghamshire are two obvious examples where many small businesses have not survived because of external changes.

Summary

In traditional economic theory, there is no automatic formula that can be applied to the average costs of firms as they grow in size in the long term. In some industries – for example, motorcar manufacture – potential economies of scale that benefit firms able to produce in large scale for a global market are enormous. In others, especially where more traditional methods of production are used, diseconomies of scale may be more significant.

Hot potato

Is small beautiful?

Research task

Choose a business that you are confident you can find out more about. Identify its main fixed costs, variable costs, the length of time it takes to vary inputs of land, labour and capital, and the existence of significant economies or diseconomies of scale.

5.5 Modern approaches to costs

Some economists have questioned the wisdom of making a rigid distinction between short and long run costs, while others have studied the actual nature of costs faced by firms in different industries. This research has had two broad outcomes.

Outcome 1

In many modern businesses, flexible working and modern technological developments mean that the distinction between the short and the long run can become blurred. Thus, modern technologies can link factories in one country to others across the world. If more machine parts are needed, it is not necessary to construct a new factory or plant; new orders can very easily be sub-contracted to other suppliers in some other part of the world. Similarly, improvements in the transportation of materials mean that individual components can be shipped around the world quickly and relatively cheaply. These developments are related to the globalisation of production and businesses.

Outcome 2

Many firms find that initial growth in output and sales is accompanied by dramatic cost savings – that is, economies of scale are significant. Thereafter, unit or average costs remain similar, regardless of output, until a point is reached at which average costs rise dramatically.

If these two sets of research findings are applied to traditional approaches of classifying costs, they have a significant effect on how the behaviour of firms is analysed. This is shown in Figure 1. There is no short run average cost or long run average cost, just an average cost 'curve' that might be 'trench' shaped.

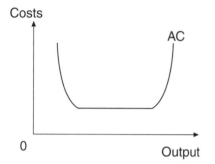

Figure 4: Modern approaches to average cost curves

Cost-plus theories

The use of the trench-shaped diagram and its accompanied rationale has led some economists to develop an alternative approach to analysing decision making within large businesses. It is suggested that firms may calculate their long run average costs and then add a profit margin in order to determine their long run supply curve. This is illustrated in Figure 2. It is important to note that any change in demand between output Q and Q1 will not lead to a change in price. The firm in question will prefer to alter production to ensure that demand and supply are kept in equilibrium.

Implications

If modern approaches to long run costs are adopted, the application of this model to predicting the likely behaviour of firms will lead to very different outcomes compared to the use of more traditional models. The use of these two models to predict the response of a firm to an increase in demand is shown in Figures 3 and 4.

Thinking like an economist

Remember cost plus pricing theories when you tackle oligopoly and price stickiness.

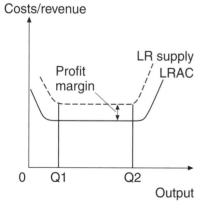

Figure 2: Cost-plus pricing

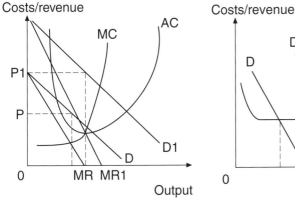

Figure 3: Traditional theory of the firm

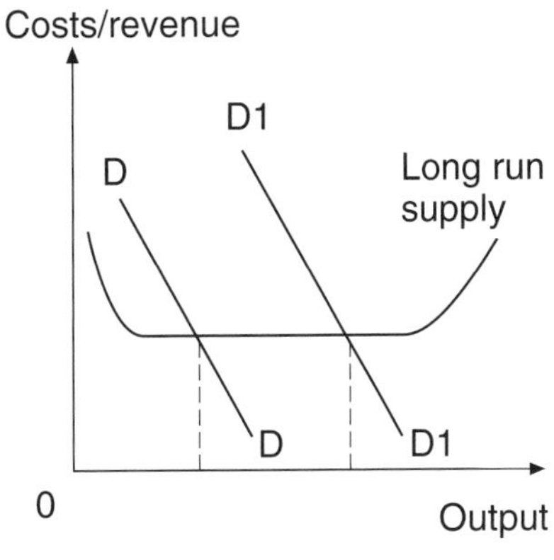

Costs/revenue

D1

D

Long run supply

D

D1

0   Output

Figure 4: Alternative theory of the firm

Figure 3 shows that any change in demand will result in a change in output and price, whereas in Figure 4 shows that an increase in demand from D to D1 leads to a change in output but not in price.

Summary

The last two sections have presented two different ways of treating costs faced by firms. Traditional economic analysis is based on a rigid distinction between the short and the long term. This provides a rationale for the existence of the U-shaped average cost curve and the concept of returns to scale. Alternative treatments regard the distinction between short and long run as artificial, and consider that firms can be much more flexible and responsive in their reactions to changing market conditions.

Quickie

Draw a long run average cost curve diagram that shows gradual economies of scale followed by both internal and external diseconomies of scale.

Exam hint

■ Sorting out the balance between economies and diseconomies of scale is a good lead-in to an assess/discuss/evaluate question, and using technical and organisation factors provides a way of structuring your answer to such high scoring questions.

Research task

Using other texts and journal articles, research different approaches to modelling average costs. Is the modern approach outlined in this section more helpful to you in making sense of the behaviour of firms? Go to www.heinemann.co.uk/hotlinks and enter express code 0810P to use a website that might be helpful in locating suitable articles.

Total, average and marginal revenue

5.6

Synoptic link

You should remember from your AS that if the price elasticity of demand for a product is relatively inelastic any cut in price is likely to decrease total revenue, whereas if demand is relatively elastic a cut in price will raise total revenue.

This section will help you to develop an understanding of different measures of revenue and how this appears in graphs. This is added to earlier work on costs and business objectives to provide an introduction to the Theory of the firm.

Revenue

'Revenue' is the term used by economists to describe those flows of money that are received by a firm. This is distinct from 'costs', which refers to those payments made by firms.

Different firms earn revenue in different ways. For example, private sector business revenues will be largely determined by the value of sales of goods and/or services. Charities largely depend on donations made by the public. Schools and colleges rely on funding provided by government agencies according to formulas based on student numbers. In short, all firms need revenue from somewhere.

The analysis in this section is based on an example of a firm operating in the private sector, but it can also be applied to public and voluntary sector organisations.

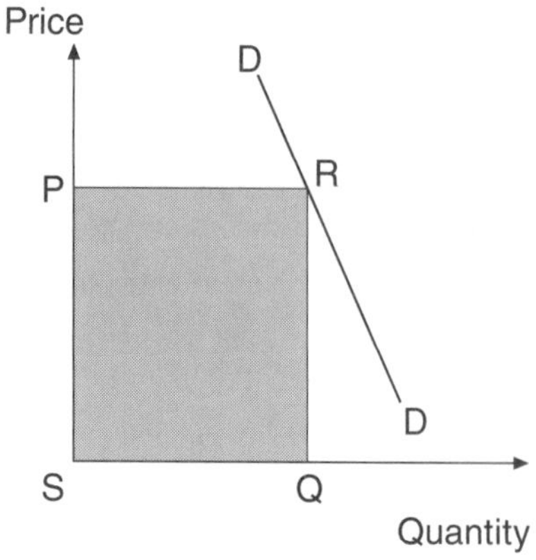

Calculating average revenue and total revenue

Calculating average revenue (AR) and total revenue (TR) is straightforward for those businesses that rely on the sales of a good or service. The demand curve shows the relationship between sales and different prices. In Figure 1, P is the price that will be paid if Q is sold. In other words, P is the average revenue. Total revenue is simply price multiplied by the number of items sold: $P \times Q$. Therefore, the shaded area PRQS represents the total sales revenue earned.

Figure 1: Total revenue

Definition

Marginal revenue: the change in revenue brought about by changing production by one unit.

Marginal revenue

Marginal revenue (MR) is defined as the change to revenue that occurs if sales are changed by one unit. In Figure 2, if sales are increased from 10 units to 11 units, revenue will rise by £28. (Ten units sold for £50 each, giving a total revenue of £500, but to sell 11 units the firm has to accept a lower price of £48 per unit, giving a new total revenue of £48 × 11 = £528.)

If sales are further increased, the marginal revenue will continue to decline. In other words if the demand curve is sloping downward to the right, more goods can only be sold at a lower price, which means that MR will always be less than AR. Thus, if the demand curve for a product or service is represented by a straight line, the marginal revenue curve will bisect the angle formed by the average revenue (or demand) curve and the vertical axis as shown in Figure 2. Note that the marginal revenue is plotted against the mid points of sales represented on the horizontal axis.

Putting costs and revenue together

The graph covered in section 5.3 showing short run costs (remember the U-shaped AC and the MC Nike swoosh) can be superimposed on top of the average and marginal revenue figure developed in Figure 2. This is done in Figure 3. It should be clear that this illustrates a business that would not be likely to survive. At any point on the diagram, average costs are above average revenue or price. This firm is clearly making a loss in the short run.

On the other hand, Figure 4 shows a range of outputs at which average cost is both above and below average reserve. Between Q and Q2 the business would be making some level of profit.

Profits

At this stage in the analysis of a firm's behaviour it is important to clarify how economists define the term 'profit'. They use the term 'normal profit' to define the amount of additional return, once all costs have been met, that is just sufficient to keep a business working at its current level of production. Anything above this is called 'supernormal' or 'abnormal' profit. If a firm is making less than normal profits, it is making a loss.

Business objectives

The work that you did in AS section 1.8 on business objectives needs to be brought into the analysis, because understanding these is helpful in determining the level of output chosen by an individual firm. Three scenarios will be considered:

- survival
- sales maximisation
- profit maximisation.

To survive, a business must choose an output between **Q** and **Q2** (see Figure 4). If a business wanted to maximise on sales, it would produce Q2. It is slightly more complicated using graphical analysis to identify the profit maximising output. Profit maximisation quite simply means producing the largest profit possible. This output is found by applying what is known as the profit-maximising rule. This means choosing the output **Q1** at which **marginal costs** (MC) and marginal (MR) revenue are equal. At this output, the gap between average revenue and average costs is maximised. If a firm chooses this output, total profits equal to the shaded area *abcd* would be earned. As AR is greater than AC (average cost), these would be called supernormal or abnormal profits.

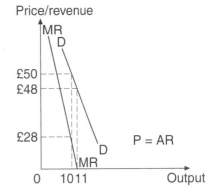

Figure 2: Derivation of marginal revenue

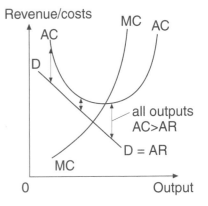

Figure 3: Loss maker

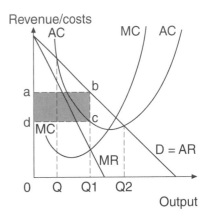

Figure 4: Profit maker

Definitions

Marginal cost: the change in cost brought about by selling one more unit.

If the firm decided on an output to the right of Q1, marginal costs would exceed marginal revenue – in other words, expanding production beyond Q1 would raise costs by a larger amount than any increase in revenue, reducing total profits. On the other hand, any point to the left of Q1 would mean that marginal costs were less than marginal revenue, meaning that if output were expanded, revenue would grow by more than costs. Only at the point at which MR equals MC will profits be maximised.

Summary

The revenue earned by a firm will be determined by the interaction of price and the demand for its good or service. Data on revenue and costs can be put onto the same graph, and this can be used to predict the levels of output chosen by different types of firms, according to their business objectives.

Quickie

Suppose a business is known to want to maximise profits. How will it change production if the following things happen?
(a) Demand increases.
(b) Variable costs increase.
(c) Fixed costs increase.

P erfect competition is the name given to a theoretical construct useful in understanding the behaviour of small firms operating in highly competitive markets. Economists have developed this model on the basis of a series of simplifying assumptions. They consider that a perfectly competitive market consists of a large number of small firms, with each doing the following:

- producing an identical or homogenous product
- contributing only a tiny proportion of the final output of the industry
- selling to customers who also have a perfect knowledge of the behaviour of all the firms operating in the industry
- having perfect knowledge of the behaviour of other firms in the industry
- having absolute freedom to enter or leave the industry.

The combined effect of the first three assumptions is very important. It means that an individual firm operating in a perfectly competitive market will have no ability to set or influence the price of the product or service it produces. Such a firm is obliged to accept the price that is set by the market as a whole.

Should an individual firm try to set a price above that set by the market, customers would purchase cheaper substitutes being offered by all the other firms in the industry. Conversely there is no advantage to be gained from selling below the market price; this would merely reduce profits or create losses.

Finally, because each firm produces so little, each can sell its entire output as long as it accepts the market price. This leads to a demand curve facing the individual perfectly competitive firm that will be perfectly elastic – as shown in Figure 1, where the market set price is P. This perfectly elastic demand curve means that any extra output will be sold for P. In other words, the marginal revenue curve will be identical to the demand or average revenue curve.

Short run equilibrium of the perfectly competitive firm

The short run average cost (U shaped) and the marginal cost curve (remember the Nike swoosh?) can be superimposed on top of the D=MR=AR facing the individual firm. Here, three different scenarios are possible:
- loss
- supernormal, or abnormal, profit
- normal profit.

Loss

In Figure 2, average costs at greater than price, regardless of the output chosen by the perfectly competitive firm, will result in a loss. The loss will be minimised if the firm chooses output Q, where marginal cost is equal to marginal revenue.

Competitive markets
5.7

Synoptic link

Remember dealing with competitive markets (AS sections 1.16–1.17)? You should be able to describe the characteristic of a competitive market. In this section, and sections 5.8 and 5.9, this initial understanding is developed further largely through diagrammatic treatments of what is known as the model of perfect competition.

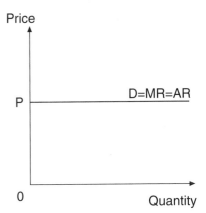

Figure 1: Short run market price and individual demand curve for a perfectly competitive firm

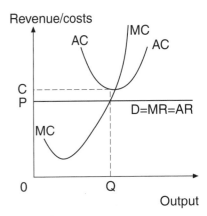

Figure 2: A loss-making perfectly competitive firm

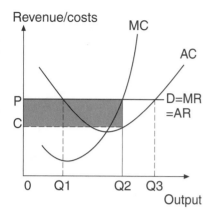

Figure 3: A supernormal profits graph

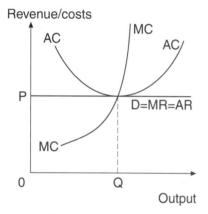

Figure 4: A normal profits graph

Supernormal, or abnormal, profits

In Figure 3, the demand for the product is such that between outputs Q1 and Q3 average revenue exceeds average costs – in other words, supernormal profits can be earned. If the firm wishes to maximise profits, it should follow the rule of equating marginal cost with marginal revenue, which would lead to output Q2. The shaded area shows the level of supernormal profits.

Normal profits

The third scenario is one in which the average cost curve is at a tangent to the demand curve. In other words, average costs are equal to price. In this situation, a perfectly competitive firm will be earning normal profits. Choosing an output other than at which marginal cost equals marginal revenue would result in making a loss – see Figure 4.

Long run equilibrium of the perfectly competitive firm

Figure 4 also illustrates what will happen in the long run. The reasoning for this is simple and follows on from the assumptions outlined at the beginning of this section.

If firms are earning supernormal profits, other businesses will find out and be attracted by the prospect of making greater profits. They will produce more of the product in question, and this extra production will result in a long-term increase in supply.

If this occurs, the price will be forced down. The subsequent effect will be to eliminate the supernormal profits. The relationship between changes in the whole market and their impact on an individual firm are illustrated in Figure 5, where the increase in supply forces down the price from P to P1.

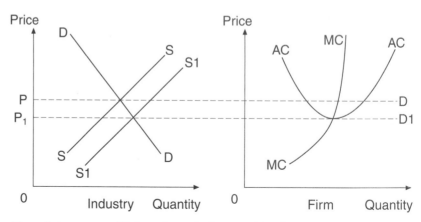

Figure 5: Long run equilibrium of a perfectly competitive firm

The converse of this is also true. If prices are below average costs, losses will be made. Some individual businesses will not be able to sustain losses over a period of time and they will go out of business or switch to the production of more profitable alternatives. If this happens on an industry-wide basis, some firms will leave the industry and total output will fall. This reduction in supply will lead to a rise in price and a return to normal profits. The relationship between the firm and the industry is illustrated Figure 6.

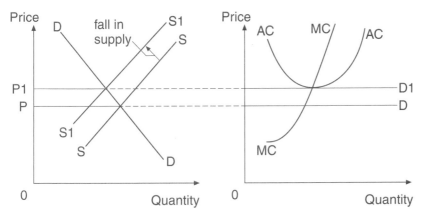

Figure 6: Elimination of losses

Summary

The neat analysis above is very important and is used to justify government intervention to promote competition. The application of this model produces a set of important predictions.

- Efficiency in terms of minimising the average costs of production would occur.
- Excessive profits could only be earned in the short run.
- Firms would have to attempt to maximise profits.
- Firms would have to respond to changes in demand.
- The desire to survive should ensure that firms are continually innovating in order to try to gain competitive advantage over other firms.
- Inefficient firms will be driven out of business.

In short, perfect competition would ensure the survival of the fittest. However, these predictions apply only if the assumptions required to build up the perfectly competitive model are met in the real world.

Quickie

Which of the following come closest to conforming to the assumptions of a perfectly competitive market?
(a) Retail groceries.
(b) Pork production.
(c) The stock market.

Hot potato

'The perfectly competitive market is so unrealistic that its use as a tool of economic analysis is extremely limited.' Do you agree?

Thinking like an economist

Remember the information from AS about model building (section 1.5)? This is what economists love to do. Sometimes, their models work and are useful in predicting and explaining what goes on in the real world. Sometimes they are useful in helping to develop logical arguments. Sometimes they do not work, either because they oversimplify or because they are too unrealistic. What do you think of the model of perfect competition?

Exam hint

Make sure you can reproduce the diagrams in this section. Don't forget all the labels and be careful when it comes to identifying supernormal profits or losses.

5.8 Perfect competition and the allocation of resources

Synoptic link

To develop further your understanding of how, given certain assumptions, perfect competition can lead to an optimum allocation of resource, re-read your AS text on productive and allocative efficiency. The argument is that if we lived in a perfectly competitive economy, goods and services would be produced at the lowest possible cost (productive efficiency) and in accordance with the demands of consumers (allocative efficiency). This section uses diagrams to demonstrate these two hypothetical possibilities, then helps you to assess this proposition critically.

Productive efficiency

The starting point for this analysis is to consider the equilibrium of the perfectly competitive firm and industry. This is illustrated in Figure 1, and it is important to note that, given the assumptions of perfect competition, the individual firm will be obliged to produce the output at which average costs are minimised. The profit-maximising rule of equating MC with MR has to be applied if the firm is to avoid making a loss, and that coincides with the lowest, or optimum, point on the average cost curve.

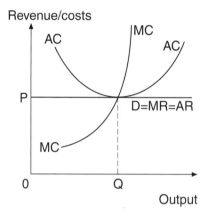

Figure 1: Perfectly competitive equilibrium

Figure 2: Perfectly competitive supernormal profit

Just suppose that the owner of one firm operating in this industry has a 'eureka' moment and discovers a new, quicker, cheaper way of making the product. If the new production technique is quicker and cheaper, the average cost curve will shift downwards to the right, dragging the marginal cost curve with it. The profit maximising firm will expand production to Q1, and will now be making supernormal profits shown by the shaded area in Figure 2.

This situation will only persist in the short run, as all competitors have perfect knowledge of what is going on within the industry. They will find out how the innovating firm has been able to cut production costs and copy the more efficient means of production. New firms might enter the industry.

This long run change will involve an increase in the industry-wide supply of the product. This rise in supply will force prices down and the firm that began the process with its 'eureka' moment will be back to earning normal profits.

An added twist to this argument is that if particular firms are slow in copying the more efficient means of production, they will find themselves making losses as output in the industry increases. Loss-making firms will be forced out of the industry. This is illustrated in Figure 3.

The logic of this analysis is that if the assumptions underpinning the perfectly competitive model were to be met, competition between large numbers of firms producing identical goods would ensure that there would be a continuous incentive to develop cheaper, more efficient ways of producing goods and providing services.

Figure 3: How a loss-making firm could be forced out of the industry

Perfect knowledge

The reward for this would be short-term supernormal profits. The sanction for not keeping up with competitors would be losses and business failure. The real beneficiaries would be the public, who would be assured of a constant stream to newer, better, more cost-effective products and services.

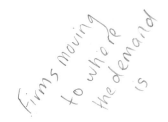

Allocative efficiency

This refers to consumer sovereignty. Allocative efficiency is achieved when firms produce where P = MC. In a perfectly competitive market, it is consumers who ultimately determine which of the world's resources are used to produce what products and services. This can be analysed diagrammatically by considering what happens if consumers' tastes change for some reason.

Suppose there is an increase in demand for DVD players at the expense of VCRs. Two changes will take place: there will be a shift to the right in the demand curve for DVDs; there will be a shift to the left in the demand for VCRs. This will lead to a rise in price to P1 for DVDs and a fall in price to P1 for VCRs – as shown in Figure 4.

When translated into changes in demand facing the perfectly competitive producers of DVDs and VCRs, the latter will be faced with potential losses and the former supernormal profits. This is shown in Figures 5 and 6.

The long run response to this situation is that losses will force some firms to drop out of the VCR market, while new firms will be attracted into the DVD markets. New long-term equilibriums will be reached in which both sets of firms earn normal profits but the industry output of DVDs will have increased, while the production of VCRs will have been reduced.

The essence of the analysis is that, if the assumptions are true, perfect competition will force businesses to change production in line with customer demands. If they fail to respond, they are likely to go out of business.

However, the analysis does not stop here. More successful companies will make larger short run profits. They will be able to pay more to attract scarce

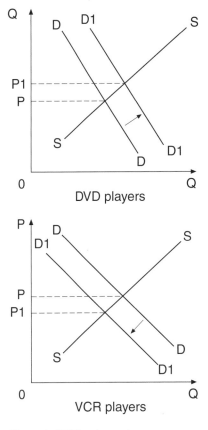

Figure 4: Shifting demand curves

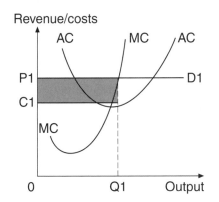

Figure 5: DVD producers

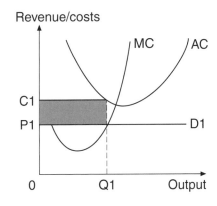

Figure 6: VCR producers

factors of production. Owners of these factors will sell their capital, land, labour or enterprise to the highest bidder and resources will be diverted to the production of goods that are most in demand. Therefore, if all industries were perfectly competitive, there would be an optimum allocation of resources. Consumers would determine what is produced, and these goods and services would be produced at the lowest possible cost.

Critically assessing the perfectly competitive model

This can be done by asking two sets of related questions.

- Are the assumptions valid?
- What is the effect on the model if any of the assumptions are relaxed?

The assumptions used to develop this model are:

- homogenous outputs
- several firms
- perfect consumer knowledge
- perfect producer knowledge
- freedom of entry and exit.

Homogenous outputs

One way of testing this assumption is to ask whether a particular product or service can be identified with an individual producer. Clearly, branding is designed to ensure that we differentiate most consumer products from each other.

Companies use branding to build up brand loyalty, which ultimately means that customers are prepared to pay more for one brand than another. Take away the packaging or label, and goods become much more homogenous – one computer is much like another. Moreover, the closer we get to raw materials, the harder it is to distinguish between the output of one producer as distinct from another.

You need to ask: 'If the assumption of absolute homogeneity is relaxed, and the other assumptions are held in place, will the perfectly competitive model result in productive and allocative efficiency?'

Several firms

It is not hard to think of industries that are made up of many individual producers who are forced to accept the price set by the market. Most producers of agricultural products and those that can be simply produced using little capital or expertise probably fall into this category.

However, as shown in later sections of this module, production in some industries is increasingly controlled by fewer producers. The crucial question you must try to answer is: 'If the assumption of many firms is relaxed, and the other assumptions are held in place, will the perfectly competitive model result in productive and allocative efficiency?'

Perfect consumer knowledge

This is not a very realistic assumption. It is argued that the average consumer knows only the likely price of fewer than twenty different items in a supermarket stocking 15,000 different products. Individually, we may be expert about some products and services. But collectively, the evidence is that we might be nearer to perfect consumer ignorance than we are to perfect knowledge.

Perfect producer knowledge

This is harder to assess. Successful businesses need to have a good knowledge of developments within their industry. By the same token, it is in the interest of firms to keep things secret. Sometimes this is protected by law, as with patents. Although there are exceptions – such as the formula for making Coca-Cola – it is reasonably safe to assume that over a long period of time producers have relatively good knowledge of their industry.

Freedom of entry and exit

Some economists argue that this is the crucial assumption and there is no clear 'yes' or 'no' answer as to its validity. Three factors are likely to be important:

- what are the costs of entry or exit?
- what are the objectives of businesses within a given industry?
- the legislative framework – are there legal barriers to entry and exit?

The cost of entering many modern industries such as telecommunications, electronics or vehicle production are likely to provide an enormous barrier to entry, and existing businesses will tend to be hostile to incomers. On the other hand, barriers will be fewer in industries where smaller-scale production is the norm.

Hot potato

Has the development of the Internet encouraged greater competition? Give reasons for your answer.

Thinking like an economist

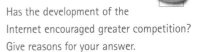

Just because the assumptions underpinning perfect competition are very rarely met, it does not mean that the analysis in this section can be ignored.

Quickie

Use diagrams to predict what will happen to short run supernormal profits of an individual firm if:

(a) new entrants are attracted to the industry

(b) demand for the product increases

(c) customer ignorance is reduced.

Concentrated markets

Synoptic link

This section develops the descriptive treatment of monopoly and competition developed from your AS.

Key concept

The largest businesses are increasingly dominating world trade. Transnational corporations are now responsible for producing ten per cent of world GDP and one-third of world exports.

Lloyds Bank's takeover of Cheltenham and Gloucester Building Society is an example of a conglomerate merger

'Concentrated markets' is the term used to describe those industries in which production is in the hands of one or a relatively small number of firms. Monopoly refers to an industry in which there is one firm. Oligopoly is much more common and applies to industries dominated by a small number of businesses. First, it is useful to note why firms grow to become monopolists or oligopolists, and how this might be measured.

The growth of firms

Firms can get bigger in two different ways. They can grow by:
- internal expansion
- external growth (mergers and takeovers).

Internal expansion

Firms grow in size by increasing total sales or turnover. This can be achieved by:
- either out-competing rivals and gaining greater market share
- or being part of an expanding market.

Both approaches require development of greater productive capacity. To some degree these growth strategies can become self-financing, because retained profits can be used to provide the finance for expansion. Internal growth can lead to economies of scale and lower long-term costs of production, which can provide greater competitive advantage and therefore help further growth.

Firms that successfully pursue such policies will also usually find it easier to raise additional funds, either from banks or from the stock market. Most oligopolistic firms are plcs, but this also makes expanding companies liable to takeover – especially if they are competing in the same market as larger, better-resourced firms.

External growth (mergers and takeovers)

Firms can also grow in size and economic power by merger when two businesses agree to collaborate to form one. More commonly, one business takes over another, either by outright purchase or by the accumulation of a controlling interest of shares. Both external forms of growth are usually referred to as mergers. These take three forms:
- vertical – by which one firm merges with another involved in different stages of the production chain (for example, electricity supply companies buying into electricity generation)
- horizontal – when mergers take place between companies at the same stage of the production chain (for example, Wal-Mart and Asda)
- conglomerate merger – where firms from different industries merge (for example, a tobacco company taking over an estate agency chain).

Merger activity provides a rapid means of building up market share. It helps to protect firms from competition and to ensure greater control over the productive process. However, as will be outlined in section 5.9, it can also reduce customer choice and increase monopoly power.

Merger activity tends to be greatest towards the peak of the economic cycle. Successful companies generate profits, which can then be used to part-finance further acquisitions.

Demergers

Over the last decade, there has been an increase in demergers. Increasing competition and globalisation can leave large conglomerates at a disadvantage compared to firms more clearly focused on a particular economic activity. Improvements in technology (especially ICT), the further development of subcontracting, multi-skilling of workers and the development of flatter, more customer-focused organisations are combining to reduce the cost advantages enjoyed by conglomerates.

The fashion in business is increasingly to 'concentrate' on core activities. Selling off non-core activities is another way of financing further focused growth and development. An example is the restructuring of GEC. Its defence-related business was sold off to British Aerospace, and the company has been renamed Marconi to concentrate on growth in the ICT sector.

Measuring concentrated markets

Economists use a simple device to illustrate whether or not production in a given market is in the hands of a few or many firms. These are called concentration ratios and involve the calculation of the share of output of the leading firms in a given market.

Industrial sector	Five-firm concentration ratio
Tobacco	99.5%
Iron and steel	95.3%
Motor vehicles	82.9%
Cement	77.7%
Water supply	49.7%
Footwear	48.2%
Bread and biscuits	47%
Carpets	21.8%
Clothing	20.7%
Plastics processing	8.8%

Table 1

Hot potato

The monopoly model is as much help as the perfectly competitive one in helping us to understand how businesses operate in the 'real' world. Do you agree?

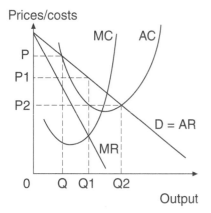

Figure 1: Demand and cost conditions facing a monopolistic firm

Thus, a three-firm concentration ratio would involve adding together the market shares of the three largest firms. The Labour government elected in 1997 uses a five-firm ratio to produce a measure of competitiveness in key economic sectors, which gives the information outlined in Table 1.

Examination of these ratios reveals the possible existence of two inter-related influences determining levels of competitiveness:

- differing levels of economies of scale – for example, steel and cement
- differing extent of barriers of entry – for example, clothing and water supply.

Monopoly

In order to understand the behaviour of both monopolists and oligopolists, it is useful to understand how economists have built up a theoretical model of monopoly in a similar way to that of perfect competition. This model is based on two related simplifying assumptions:

- production of a whole industry is in the hands of one firm
- complete barriers prevent the entry and exits of firms.

These assumptions mean that the demand curve for the individual firm will be the same as that for the industry as a whole. Moreover, there is no distinction – as there is with perfect competition – between the short and the long run. If a monopoly is total, barriers to entry are absolute and this prevents other firms competing away excess profits. The monopolist will be able to set the price or quantity sold, and therefore has considerable freedom to pursue particular economic and social objectives.

Possible price, sales and output levels can be analysed graphically – as shown in Figure 1, where demand and average revenue are above average costs at outputs between Q and Q2. This means that a monopolistic firm could set a price anywhere between P and P2, and make more than normal profits.

In this case, a profit-maximising monopolist would produce at Q1 and a sales maximiser at Q2. Barriers to entry would ensure that this short run situation was also the long run position.

If monopolies existed that conformed to this model:

- average costs of production would not necessarily be minimised
- excessive profits could be earned in the long run
- firms would not have to attempt to maximise profits
- firms would not necessarily have to respond to changes in demand
- there would be little incentive to innovate
- customer choice could be restricted.

Comparisons with perfect competition

Figure 2 demonstrates that, in the short run, prices under monopoly will be higher than those with perfect competition and output would be lower. Under perfect competition, firms are forced by competitive pressures to produce where MC equals price. If this applied to a whole industry, perfectly competitive output would be at Q and price at P, whereas a profit-maximising monopolist would charge P1 for a smaller output of Q1.

This conclusion depends on one implicit assumption – that both monopolist and perfectly competitive firms would be faced with the same average and marginal cost conditions.

One argument used to justify the existence of monopolies is that they are able to enjoy the benefits of economies of scale that may arise in increasing size, which then leads to falling long run average costs. The effects of this possibility are illustrated in Figure 3, where AC1 and MC1 represent lower long run costs that might be generated by economies of scale enjoyed by the monopolist. In this case, the profit-maximising monopolist will charge P1 for output Q1, compared to P and Q for the perfectly competitive industry.

Summary

Graphical analysis has been used to compare output, prices and profits under the two extremes of perfect competition and monopoly. The use of this analysis indicates that prices might be lower and outputs higher under conditions of perfect competition than under monopoly. However, this simple comparison ignores the existence of economies of scale and the greater freedom that a monopolistic firm has to pursue differing objectives.

Quickie

Which of the following are closest to being monopolies as defined in this unit?
(a) Microsoft®.
(b) Network rail.
(c) Littledean Village Store.

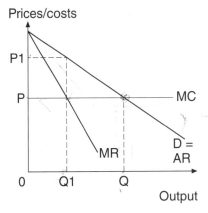

Figure 2: Monopoly and perfect competition compared

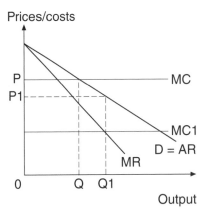

Figure 3: Monopolist benefiting from economies of scale

Thinking like an economist

Don't jump to conclusions based on the analysis in this section. In the real world it is hard to fine pure monopoly or perfect competition. However, you will find that firms behave in some of the ways that have been described in this section.

5.10 Oligopoly

Definition

Oligopoly: a market dominated by a few large firms.

Oligopoly literally means competition among the few. There are two principle assumptions that underpin this model. The first is the existence of barriers of entry to and from the industry. These will vary from industry to industry, but their existence makes the analysis of oligopoly more similar to that of monopoly. The second principle is the interdependence of decision-making. The assumption is unique to this model and means that individual firms make decisions about prices, marketing, product design and so on with reference to how they perceive their competitors will respond. Each firm is affected by the actions of others.

Barriers to entry

Oligopolists are protected by barriers to entry and are likely constantly to erect new barriers in order to maintain long-term market share and profits. Barriers to entry and exit are likely to include the following.

- Capital costs – especially in capital and technology intensive industries such as Sony Music.
- High levels of sunk costs – that is, those fixed costs attributable to capital equipment that cannot be transferred to other uses (for example, the Channel Tunnel needed specialised capital equipment to build).
- National and global branding. Nike, Adidas and other leisurewear firms have spent billions of pounds on promoting a global image that would be both costly and difficult for a newcomer to match.
- Patent and copyright – especially important in pharmaceuticals (for example, GlaxoSmithKline).
- Technological expertise – especially when backed up by large research and development expenditures (for example, Nokia).
- Takeover. Dominant firms often respond to the threat of new entrants by taking them over (for example, Microsoft®).

Interdependence

The second assumption is very significant because it makes it much more difficult for economists to model the behaviour of an oligopolistic firm.

The behaviour of one firm will depend on its perceptions of how other firms will react to changes. The responses of other firms will depend on their perceptions of the responses of others. It is harder, therefore, to predict how oligopolistic firms are likely to behave.

Economists have developed further limiting assumptions about the objectives of oligopolists to make their work easier. They include the following.

- Competition. Oligopolistic firms will wish to compete with their rivals to gain greater market share.
- Collusion. This refers to firms coming together to avoid the risks associated with competition. Colluding firms may seek to set common prices or levels of output for each.

Competitive oligopolists

Predicting the outcomes of decision making by oligopolists is difficult. To take a current example, Volkswagen needs to decide on the recommended selling price for its new Polo. It is currently selling a basic version of the Polo for £8,999. However, some competitors, such as the Nissan Micra, are available more cheaply while others, such as the Vauxhall Corsa, are more expensive.

There are fears in the automobile industry that car prices are likely to fall. So what should Volkswagen do? If it cuts its price and competitors follow suit, it will end up with the same market share. If it cuts its prices and competitors fail to respond, its market share may increase. What if Vauxhall or Nissan make larger price cuts?

One approach used by economists to try to make sense of such competitive behaviour is by use of game theory, first developed by psychologists when trying to predict human responses in a similarly unpredictable situation. At a simple level, this can be restricted to looking at the behaviour of one firm and the possible responses of another. This is illustrated in Figure 1.

- To begin with, assume that the market for small cars is shared equally between Volkswagen and Nissan. They charge the same price of £8,999 for cars with similar specifications, and they both receive profit of £200 million. This is depicted in box A of the matrix.
- The outcomes of Volkswagen cutting £1,000 from its recommended price will depend upon the responses of Nissan. If it keeps its original price, Volkswagen will gain a bigger market share and a larger proportion of the industry profit. This is illustrated in box **B.**
- Alternatively, Nissan could copy Volkswagen, leaving both with an equal market share but reduced profits because of the price cut. This is shown in box D.
- A fourth option is that Volkswagen maintains its price at £8,999, but Nissan cuts its to, say, £7,999. In this case, both Volkswagen's market share and profits will be cut as shown in box C.

		Nissan £8999	Nissan £7999
Volkswagen	£8999	A Each shares market, earning £200m profit	C Nissan takes larger market share + £350m profit
Volkswagen	£7999	B VW captures larger market share + £350m profit	D Equal market shares, each with profit of £100m

Figure 1: Game theory matrix

This approach to the analysis of the behaviour of oligopolists yields an important prediction. For Volkswagen, option B would give the best possible return, but it is also the most risky. It depends on Nissan ignoring an aggressive price cut. Option C is the worst outcome, while options D and A are the least risky. Logic dictates that Volkswagen ought to collude with Nissan.

The essence of game theory is that there is a range of possible outcomes in response to market changes or changes in the behaviour of firms. Game theory focuses on alternative strategies that firms may pursue. Cautious firms will elect a strategy that is least risky. This is called a maximin strategy, whereas an approach that involves taking greater risks to gain higher levels of profit is called a maximax strategy. If both approaches lead to the same outcome, firms are said to be playing a dominant strategy game.

Kinked demand curves

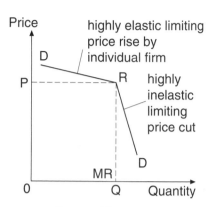

Figure 2: Kinked demand curve

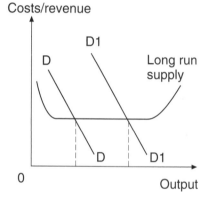

Figure 3: Theory of firm

An alternative theoretical treatment of the behaviour of oligopolists is that associated with the American economist Paul Sweezy. Sweezy observed that even if oligopolists were in competition with each other, prices in such markets tended to be stable. He used a simplified form of game theory, reasoning that as pricing decisions by oligopolists were interdependent, an individual firm would be very reluctant to raise its prices because it would fear that none of its competitors would follow suit.

On the other hand, he argued that an individual firm would be reluctant to cut its prices because this decision would be copied by competitors. In other words, the oligopolist would be faced with an elastic demand curve in terms of price rises and an inelastic curve for price cuts. This is illustrated graphically in Figure 2. This theory has been attacked by a number of economists as lacking in any empirical evidence. Figure 3 illustrates a different explanation of price stability under oligopoly.

Collusive oligopolists

Game theory can be used to demonstrate that it is in the interests of oligopolistic firms to collude – that is, form agreements to reduce the risks attached to competition (especially price competition). Collusion can take three forms.

- Open, in which firms make a formal collective agreement. This is called a cartel and will usually bind its signatories to agreed price levels and/or production quotas. With some exceptions, cartels are illegal in the UK and in most other Western countries.
- Informal, in which firms find ways of evading legal restrictions in order to maintain common prices. It is thought that informal agreements are common in the UK, especially in the markets for electrical goods, cars and perfume. However, as this form of activity might be the target of government investigation and intervention, it is hard to find evidence of secret agreements.
- Tacit behaviour, in which individual oligopolists arrive at common policies without formal or informal agreements. Some industries are dominated by a particular firm and others will follow its pricing decisions. In the UK, ESSO is seen as a leader in terms of petrol prices, Kellogg for breakfast cereals and Nike for trainers. Common prices and other apparent collusion can arise when firms in industries follow common pricing formulas and pay similar amounts for factor inputs. Most pubs mark up the price of beers and lager by 100 per cent; local stores add 40 per cent to the cost price of confectionery and similar products; and restaurants add 500 per cent to the cost of ingredients to price their menus. This can lead to competitive firms charging similar prices for the same meals.

Collusion, though attractive to oligopolists as a means of reducing risks and safeguarding profits, has particular dangers.

Non-collusive behaviour

Although there must be a strong temptation for oligopolists to avoid unnecessary risks by colluding with each other, some businesses are likely to be more aggressive and confrontational. Stable relationships between oligopolist firms can be upset by the following.

• *New technologies.* The ways in which goods and services are produced is constantly changing. As this process is likely to occur unevenly across the firms making up an industry, some firms are likely to find themselves producing goods more cheaply than their competitors. For example, digital technologies are revolutionising the printing and media industries. Those businesses in the forefront of this change are likely to try to use their lower production costs to drive competitors out of the industry.

• *Changes in ownership.* As with technology, the ownership of plcs in the UK is not always static. Changes at the top can lead to changes in business strategy, especially if the goal is to drive up shareholder value. The hostile acquisition of rivals and aggressive behaviour in building up market share are non-collusive strategies. In particular, some firms may start price wars by deliberately selling close to, or below, costs of production with a view to driving out competitors.

Summary

Analysing the behaviour of oligopolists is far more complex than for firms operating in other market structures. Graphical analysis is less helpful, as outcomes in terms of pricing, output and profits are less predictable.

Particular industries may be characterised by high levels of competition, while in others tacit agreements result in high levels of price stability and little or no competition.

Thinking like an economist

What evidence would you search for to try to establish the validity of the following models to analyse the behaviour of large firms?
- Maximin gaming strategy.
- Maximax gaming strategy.
- Kinked demand curves.

Quickie

Which of the following industries comes closest to satisfying the assumptions of oligopolistic competition?
(a) Brewing.
(b) Airlines.
(c) Electricity generation.

Puzzler

Construct a matrix to predict possible outcomes of interdependent decision-making in an industry of your choice.

5.11 Market power

conomic theory demonstrates that firms that are monopolies or oligopolies have considerable market power to set prices, determine customer choice, limit competition and prevent new market entrants. These firms are also often very large, commanding turnovers greater than most countries in the world, and able to use this economic power to influence the behaviour of governments. Economists differ in their assessments of the impact of such large firms, but have developed further theories and techniques to help measure market power and advise governments of possible intervention strategies. This section is devoted to:

- price discrimination
- consumer and producer surplus
- contestable markets.

Research task

Identify three firms that use price discrimination. How do they do it?

Price discrimination

One method of assessing the degree of power that any firm has in the marketplace is to establish the degree to which it is able to charge different customers different prices for the same product or service. This is called price discrimination and is an aspect of market power used by firms to boost revenue and profits.

Most of us are used to being charged a range of different prices for particular goods or services. Airfares are a good example. Customers flying from London to New York can pay anywhere between £200 and £1,000 for the same seat in the same aircraft. In order to benefit from price discrimination, airlines need to ensure that the following conditions must be fulfilled:

- the firm must have some degree of market power and be a price maker
- demand for the good or service will be spread between different customers, each with differing price elasticities of demand for the product or service
- these different market segments have to be separated from each other
- the proportion of fixed to total costs is likely to be high.

Market power

Only those firms that are facing a downward sloping overall demand curve for their products or services will be able to charge different prices to different customers. The more monopoly power a firm enjoys, the more it can price discriminate. On the other hand, those firms that are closer to being perfectly competitive will have only a limited opportunity to charge different prices to different customers. Clearly, there is a limited number of airlines flying between London and New York. Those that offer the most flights will be able to set prices rather than having to accept the 'market' price.

Differing price elasticities of demand

A discriminating monopolist will wish to charge higher prices to some of its customers and will be prepared to sell the same product or service to others at a lower price as long as this boosts overall revenue.

Airlines exploit this by charging much higher fares to those who have to fly at particular times or whose airfare is likely to be part of an expense account. Other market segments, such as young people travelling around the world, are likely to be much more price sensitive and will only be attracted by lower fares. Another important segment for some airlines is the holiday market. Holiday companies may make block bookings of seats but will expect significant discounts. Finally, seats that are hard to sell can be sold through 'bucket shops' (travel agencies specialising in cheap tickets) and those travel agencies dealing in last-minute bookings.

Separation of markets

Elaborate strategies such as those outlined above will only work if it is impossible for one set of airline customers to sell on its cheaper tickets to passengers who would otherwise be prepared to pay higher fares. This is relatively easy for the airlines, because tickets can only be used by a named person. Other price discriminators use time to separate markets. Train tickets bought at different times of the day cost different amounts and can be used only on specified trains.

Relatively high fixed costs

The bulk of the costs of flying from London to New York are fuel, maintenance and debt repayment. Once committed to the flight, the airline has low levels of variable costs. Put another way, marginal costs of carrying additional passengers are low. It costs little more to carry 350 passengers than it does to carry 349. Hence, the airline will add to its profits once it has covered the costs of extra meals, ticketing and costs associated with the 350th passenger.

If variable costs are relatively more significant, marginal costs will be higher and a profit-seeking company would be more limited concerning discounts.

Consumer and producer surpluses

Another way in which economists attempt to assess the impact of non-competitive behaviour by firms is by the use of two concepts:

- consumer surplus
- producer surplus.

Consumer surplus

This concept uses graphical analysis to illustrate the benefits that customers gain from consuming a particular product or service. Figure 1 illustrates consumer surplus and P represents an equilibrium price with the level of sales at Q.

The last customer is prepared to pay the market price for the product, but all earlier customers would have been prepared to pay more. For instance, Q1 customers would have been prepared to pay more than P, and Q2 customers

Exam hint

Remember that successful price discrimination requires different price elasticities of demand.

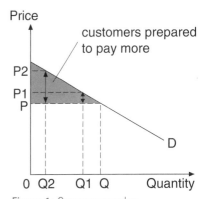

Figure 1: Consumer surplus

would have been prepared to pay still more. The vertical distances indicate how much more some customers would have been prepared to pay. Taken together, the shaded area represents an additional benefit enjoyed by consumers of this product. This is referred to as consumer surplus.

Producer Surplus

A similar analytical approach can be made to gains made by producers of a good or service. In Figure 2, Q producers receive P for their total output, but some producers would have been prepared to supply the good or service for less. Q1 producers were prepared to supply for P1, whereas Q2 producers were prepared to accept even less at P2. The shaded area, therefore, represents producers' surplus.

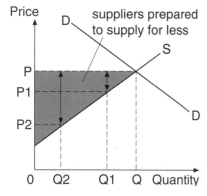

Figure 2: Producer surplus

This concept is applied to understanding the impact of monopoly power. Figure 3 shows that a profit-maximising oligopolist or monopolist will produce at Q and charge P for its output, whereas a perfectly competitive industry facing the same cost structure will produce at Q1 and charge P1 for its output.

Consumer surplus under monopolistic conditions will be the equivalent of area *a*, but under perfect competition it would be larger and equal to *a + b + c*.

Producer surplus, on the other hand, is bigger under monopoly consisting of *d + b* compared with a perfectly competitive producer surplus of *d + e*. In other words, this graphical analysis shows that producers gain while consumers lose.

Overall, *c + e* represents losses under monopoly of both producer and consumer surpluses. This area is known as deadweight welfare loss of monopoly.

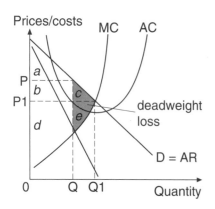

Figure 3: Deadweight welfare loss of monopoly

Contestable markets

This is an alternative approach based more on the adaptation of traditional theory to assess the degree of competition that may occur within an industry. The theory of contestable markets is based on the premise that firms will operate competitively if they fear competition in some way. There are a number of variants of this theory, and it is argued that a monopolist will behave like a competitive firm if:

- there is a fear of takeover
- barriers to entry and exit are minimised.

Fear of takeover

No plc is free from the fear of takeover, and senior managers of such firms have to compete with other businesses on the stock market. Rising share prices are associated with business success and will be fed by stock market perceptions of potential profits, levels of customer service, responsiveness to changes in demand and so on.

Monopolistic and oligopolistic firms that fail to pursue those and other objectives associated with competitive behaviour will, the theorists argue, be punished by the stock market and share prices will fall, making such firms more liable to takeover. It could be argued that this describes the position of Marks and Spencer in 2000/2001.

Minimization of barriers to entry and exit

A market is said to be perfectly contestable if barriers to entry and exist are zero. If this were the case, other firms would be attracted to those industries in which supernormal profits are being made.

In order to prevent increased competition, firms operating in a contestable market will keep prices down, and ensure that profits are kept to normal levels. Exit barriers need also to be minimised. If sunk costs are significant, firms already in an industry will be deterred from leaving, as they cannot transfer such resources to other uses. Moreover, new entrants will be deterred if they were unable to transfer capital elsewhere.

Summary

This section has been devoted to an explanation of some of the techniques economists use to measure the extent and possible effects of the exercise of monopoly power. The ability of firms to charge different prices to different sections of their markets was also considered. Graphical analysis has been used to indicate the possible harmful affects of monopoly power. Finally, there was an introduction to contestable market theory.

Quickie

Which of the following operates the most comprehensive policies of price discrimination?
(a) Mobile phone providers.
(b) Package holiday suppliers.
(c) The railway operating companies.

Puzzler

How might consumer and producer surplus be affected by the following?
(a) Reduction of barriers of entry in an industry.
(b) The establishment of a cartel in an industry.

Exam hint

There is lots of scope in this section for questions that test your higher order skills. Be prepared to assess, evaluate or discuss the degree of competition in a given market. Remember to develop a number of arguments and make a clear conclusion.

The labour market

The labour market model can be used to predict what would happen if the demand or supply of labour changes and the significance of the elasticity of demand or supply. This section takes the earlier analysis forward by considering:

- **marginal revenue productivity theory**
- the supply of labour
- the determination of wage rates in competitive markets.

Synoptic link

The tools of economic analysis developed in the AS part of your course can be developed to analyse how labour markets might work. For AS it is reasonable to assume that the demand for labour is likely to slope down from left to right, and that the supply of labour is likely to slope upwards to the right, giving a possible equilibrium wage rate. This is shown in the figures in this section, in which the wage rate is given at W and the numbers employed at E.

Definition

Marginal revenue productivity theory: the significance of the additional value created by employing additional workers. This is derived from multiplying additional output by the price for which it can be sold.

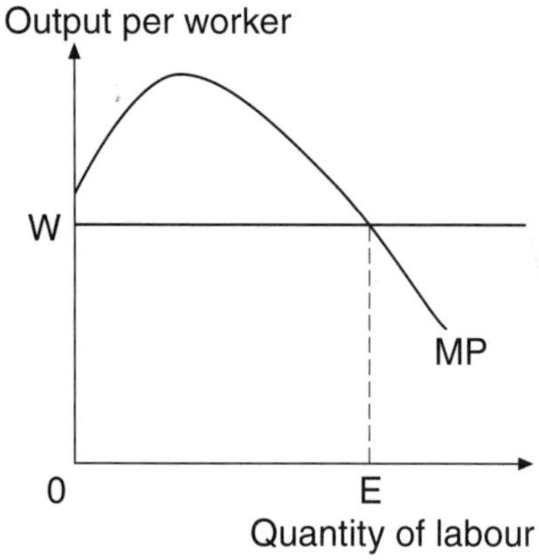

Marginal revenue productivity theory

The demand for any factor of production is a derived demand. Factors are not demanded in their own right; they are demanded because they can be combined to produce goods and services that, under competitive conditions, can be sold for a profit.

It follows that entrepreneurs will be primarily interested in the contribution that the use of a factor is likely to make to profitability. This will, in turn, be dependent on the interaction between the amount each factor contributes to overall production and the price that can be gained from selling the product or service.

In section 5.3, the law of diminishing marginal returns was outlined. To recap, in the short run output can only be increased by using more of a variable factor. Average costs of production will drop as output is expanded, an optimum where average costs are minimised will be reached and, thereafter, average costs of production will rise showing increasing inefficiency. This provides a rationale for the U-shaped average cost curve.

If this is applied to labour productivity, output per workers will rise, reach a peak and then fall. The application of the law of diminishing marginal returns can also be interpreted as meaning that the output per worker will increase until an optimum is reached. After this, growing inefficiency in the short run will result in lower output per worker. This produces a hump-shaped marginal productivity curve, as shown in Figure 1.

As has always been noted, the bottom line for any producer is likely to be not just what every worker can produce in physical terms but the value of that output.

The demand for labour is a derived demand, and it follows that the value of any worker's output will be influenced by the price that can be gained for what has been produced.

Thus, multiplying the additional output produced by each worker by the price that can be gained from selling that output gives the marginal revenue product of that worker. The additional revenue gained will be determined by the demand for that output.

The shape of this demand curve will depend on the degree of competition in that particular market. If the market is perfectly competitive, any additional output will be sold for the same price as the proceeding unit. This means

Figure 1: Marginal productivity curve

that the marginal revenue product curve will have the same shape as the marginal product curve.

However, if the market is less than perfectly competitive, additional output will only be sold at a lower price. This will have the effect of increasing the gradient of the marginal revenue product curve. These two possibilities are illustrated in Figures 2 and 3.

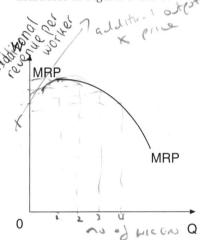

Figure 2: Marginal revenue product curve in a competitive market

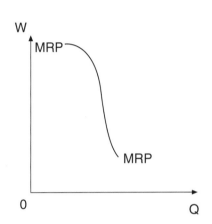

Figure 3: Marginal revenue product curve in a less-competitive market

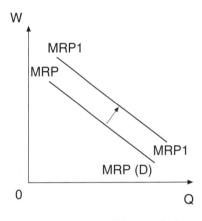

Figure 4: Upwards shifting marginal revenue product curve

Thus, if a kitchen fitter employs an additional joiner who can assemble two kitchens per week, and each kitchen earns the company an additional £1,000 net of other expenses, the weekly marginal revenue product of this worker would be £2,000.

It follows that any change in either the demand for the product or the productivity of any individual worker will have an effect on the MRP curve. This increasing demand for the final product will increase the revenue received for each unit shifting the marginal revenue product curve upwards to the right as shown in Figure 4.

Falling labour productivity would have the opposite effect, leading to a downward and leftward shift of the marginal revenue product curve, as shown in Figure 5.

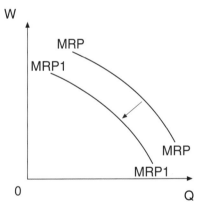

Figure 5: Downwards shifting marginal revenue product curve

The supply of labour

This is more straightforward than the demand for labour. What you learned for AS should be enough to give you a sufficient understanding of the main influences on the supply of any given type of labour.

Economists acknowledge that a range of non-monetary factors affect the willingness of workers to undertake particular jobs, but assume that higher wage rates will lead to an increase in supply of labour and vice versa. The elasticity of supply of a particular kind of labour will be primarily

Exam hint

Read through this again and check your understanding by drawing marginal revenue product curves for both a perfectly competitive and concentrated market for the final product.

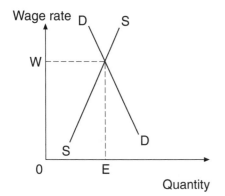

Figure 6: The elasticity of supply of doctors

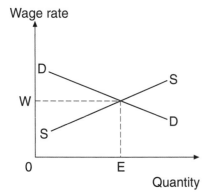

Figure 7: The elasticity of supply of nurses

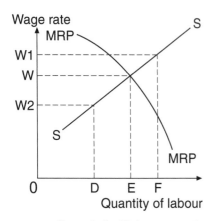

Figure 8: Equilibrium wage rate

influenced by the degree of skill and/or training required for a particular job. So it might be argued that the supply of doctors is more inelastic than the supply of nurses, as shown in Figures 6 and 7.

Determination of wage rates

It is now possible to put the demand and supply analysis together, as shown in Figure 8, which indicates that the demand for a particular form of labour will be equal to its supply at a wage rate of W, and that E workers will be employed. If the wage rate were above this equilibrium, for example at W1, it would cost more to employ some workers than they would be contributing to the revenue of the business. If the business wanted to remain as profitable as possible, it would pay to cut the number of workers employed from F to E until the last worker adds as much to revenue as she or he adds to costs.

Conversely, if wage rates were at W2, it would pay employers to employ more workers (D increased to E) who would contribute more to revenue than they would to costs.

Summary

If firms seek profits in markets that are competitive, and if workers are primarily influenced by what they earn, employers will go on employing more and more workers until the last worker adds as much to revenue as he or she does to costs.

The application of the marginal revenue product theory to wage determination is another example of the use of modelling by economists. In this case, any change in factors affecting demand or supply of labour will be followed by changes in the wage rate and numbers employed. The further use and validity of this model will be explored more fully in section 5.12.

Quickie	

Use graphs to predict what happens to wage rates and the number of bricklayers employed if:
(a) an improved frost inhibitor for mortar is developed
(b) there is union action that limits overtime
(c) interest rates rise
(d) green-belt land is released for building.

Puzzler	

There are quite a lot of 'ifs' used in building up the marginal revenue product model. Identify at least three and critically evaluate their significance.

The two principle assumptions built into the labour market model are that employers can calculate the marginal revenue product of each employee and will use this information to change the numbers of workers employed, and that workers will move from job to job in response to changes in relative wage levels.

The validity of both these assumptions can only be confirmed by empirical study – that is, research into the behaviour of both employers and workers. However, it is possible to analyse the appropriateness of these assumptions in greater detail.

Employers

Unless they have an A level or degree in economics, it is unlikely that most employers will have much of a clue if you were to ask them about marginal revenue product or marginal productivity. However, such considerations are clearly built into thinking and decisions about how some workers are paid.

While it is unlikely that Tesco, for instance, has calculated the contribution that each shelf-stacker makes to its overall profitability, each manager will have some working knowledge of how much work can be expected of each employee on a given shift. It is likely that especially slow workers will be replaced, and those who work quickly and show initiative are likely to be promoted.

Similarly, employers such as Tesco give their store managers large bonuses if profit targets are met or exceeded. In this case it is possible to see that although the language of economics might not be used, the principles underlying the theory are broadly applied.

Not all jobs are the same. In some occupations, it is much harder to measure the output of individual workers. If teamwork is important, it is harder to quantify the contribution of each individual, while in other jobs it is difficult to identify the output measures that would be used to measure the productivity of individual workers.

How, for example, do you assess the productivity of teachers and lecturers? Would it be in terms of exam passes, the support given to slow learners, or the intellectual challenge of lessons? Even if it were possible to agree on suitable measures, what would be the best way of relating salaries and numbers employed to outputs? It would be very disruptive to hire and fire teachers at short notice.

Finally, even where employers have found it possible to carefully measure the outputs of individual workers, using these to devise pay and incentive schemes and hire and fire at will, can create undesirable side effects. In the 1970s, complicated payment systems in some UK industries such as motor vehicle manufacture, lead to industrial conflict and low levels of productivity.

5.13 The labour market: a critical evaluation

Synoptic link

This section builds directly on section 5.11, which contained an outline of how the marginal revenue product theory can be applied to the analysis of wage rates. The critical evaluation of the validity of this model will concentrate on:

■ considering the validity of assumptions used to build up the model

■ examining the impact of setting minimum wage levels.

Can you measure this shelf-stacker's marginal revenue product?

One of a number of causes of this industrial conflict was the existence of very complicated piece-rate payment systems, which were meant to link productivity and pay but had the effect of creating hundreds of different pay scales and thereby creating more problems for managers than the schemes were worth.

This analysis needs testing against the actual behaviour of employers, but it is probably reasonable to conclude that:

- employers who pay workers with no regard to their productivity and contribution to profitability are unlikely to be successful
- the development of rigid and complicated payment systems and constant hiring and firing of workers can cause lasting damage to worker/employee relationships and thereby damage profitability.

For these reasons it might be helpful to consider a different kind of demand curve for labour – one that is broader and less well defined at the edges, as Figure 1 shows.

This acknowledges that it is hard to measure the output of each worker. Not only that, it is disruptive to constantly change pay or levels of numbers of workers employed. It also shows that at any given wage rate, W employers would be prepared to employ between E and E1 workers, only changing the numbers employed if marginal revenue product were to change significantly.

Figure 1: A labour demand band

Workers

As far as workers are concerned, the response to the simple question 'Does money matter?' is likely to be 'Of course it does, but...'. Most of you reading this book would be better off financially if you were doing something else – for example, stacking shelves at Tesco. You might make the perfectly reasonable economic argument that studying economics is a means to boosting your long-term earnings because it will help you (we hope) to get a better-paid job in the future. But any job? Are you prepared to:

- do something boring for the rest of your life
- move away from family and friends
- work unsocial hours
- do a job that you regarded as unethical
- be treated badly by an employer
- work in dangerous conditions?

Clearly, these considerations will have different effects on different individuals. But it will obviously have some effect, and for this reason it is perhaps a mistake to represent the supply of labour as a single upward sloping demand curve from left to right showing a very precise relationship between pay levels and the willingness of particular workers to do a given job.

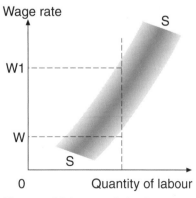

Figure 2: A labour supply band

Habit, social obligation and inertia are all factors that will have the effect of limiting the mobility of labour between different occupations. However, as with employers and the profit motive, it would be foolish of economists to ignore the significance of pay rates and their influence on the supply of labour. You will know by now that economists like symmetrical arguments.

It will therefore come as little surprise that it might be more helpful to represent the supply of labour as a band rather than a curve.

This is illustrated in Figure 2, which shows that a given number of workers will be prepared to work at a particular job for between W and W1. Some of these workers will seek work elsewhere if the wage rate falls below W. The supply of workers will only increase at wage rates above W1. This revised application of the demand and supply model may be more realistic.

The imposition of minimum wage rates

Governments of different countries intervene in labour markets to try to ensure that workers receive what might considered a socially acceptable level of pay. Currently in the UK, workers aged 22 and over should receive at least £4.85 per hour.

Legal minimum wage rates were introduced by the Labour government in 1998. At the time it was argued that the effect of these might be to create unemployment in those industries in which prevailing levels of pay were set below the legal minimum. This argument is demonstrated in Figure 3.

This figure shows that if the wage rate is set at W1, demand for labour will be E1, whereas the supply would be E2. In other words, fewer workers would be employed than would be the case if the wage rate were at the equilibrium of W. What appears to have happened as a result of the introduction of a minimum wage is that the unemployment levels fell. This could be explained in one of two ways:

- either the introduction of the minimum wage coincided with an increase in demand for workers
- or the increase was not sufficiently large to change the behaviour of employers and workers.

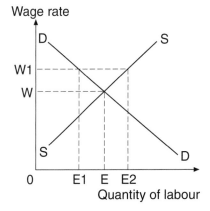

Figure 3: Minimum wage and its impact on labour

Summary

Traditional theory of wage determination is based on the assumption that both workers and employers are primarily influenced by wage rates in deciding both the demand and supply of labour. This may be an over-simplification of behaviour and may limit the usefulness of this part of economic theory. On the other hand, wage rates clearly influence both the demand and supply of labour. Representing these as two bands might be a more useful model to apply to the complexities of labour markets.

Research task

Try to develop a sound methodology that you could use to investigate the extent to which the assumptions underpinning economic explanations of differences in wages actually apply to the behaviour of employers and workers in your local area.

Quickie

How might wage rates for catering workers in the UK be affected by the following?
(a) Increased barriers to asylum seekers coming to the UK.
(b) A cut in interest rates.
(c) An increase in the value of the pound.

5.14 Investigating less competitive labour markets

Definition

Monopsony: this refers to a factor market in which there is theoretically only one employer of a given factor of production.

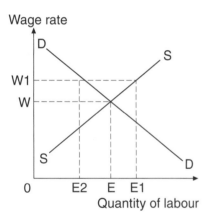

Figure 1: The effect of a trade union on the labour market

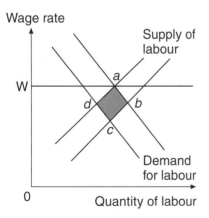

Figure 2: An alternative labour market model

Many factors affect how labour markets actually work in practice. Two important considerations are the effect of trade unions, and the impact of **monopsonistic** employers.

Trade unions

Trade unions can have a direct impact on labour markets. This should come as little surprise, as they were set up to improve the pay and conditions of workers. Although their functions have become more diverse, it is argued that they exist to serve the best interests of their members, and protecting and improving on pay and conditions of those at work will always be important.

Trade unions and employers may engage in collective bargaining to agree pay and conditions. This can happen at national level, where employers and unions will come together to determine nationally agreed pay and conditions – the fire brigade's union and local authority organisations representing their employers. The same process may take place at plant level. But in other cases, in which employers do not recognise trade unions, little may be achieved collectively.

Trade unions in the UK developed in the nineteenth century at a time when workers were often exploited. Pay rates were often low, workers' safety was ignored and employment was commonly very insecure. In these cases, the power relationship between individual workers and their employers was very one-sided. If an individual worker objected to some aspect of employment, he or she could be fired or sacked at will. Although not all workers were members, trade unions were able to counter this imbalance in power. The threat of strike or other industrial action posed a direct threat to the profitability of the business in question.

Economists have used the models of the labour market to try to assess the impact of trade unions. New classical (right wing) economists have tended to argue that anything that disturbs the free working of labour markets will have a negative effect on employment. Figure 1 can be used to indicate that any union efforts to push up wage rates from W to, say, W1 will result in unemployment of E to E2.

In some ways, there is little empirical support for this argument. This is because in the UK, increasing union activity has been associated with increasing rather than decreasing employment levels. On the other hand, it is possible to find examples where trade union militancy has resulted in the unemployment of workers – for example, the print unions in the 1980s.

The argument that trade union activity pushes up unemployment is, therefore, rather crude, which is where the revised labour market model introduced in section 5.12 may be useful.

In this case the lozenge shaped area **abcd** shown in Figure 2 contains a range of different combinations of wage and employment levels, which would all be acceptable to both workers and employers. Should trade unions attempt to push wages up above W, then it is likely that conflict between unions and employers would occur that could result in unemployment. This might provide a more convincing explanation of the possible impact of trade unions on competitive labour markets.

Monopsonistic employers

The preceding analysis is based on the assumption that there is competition between employers for particular types of workers. This might not always be the case. Many workers in Cornwall, for example, are dependent on a small number of large employers who are able to use their market power to pay lower wages than would be found in other parts of the country. In extreme circumstances, there may be only one employer of a particular type of labour – a monopsonist. Thus, the local police force is the only employer of policemen and women in a particular area.

In theory, a monopsonistic employer can force down wage rates below the level that would be set in a more competitive market. This possibility is represented in Figure 3, in which ACL represents the supply of labour showing the average wage rate that is paid to each worker.

If a monopsonist wanted to attract another worker, it would have to pay more than the average cost of the labour it currently employs. Moreover, it would probably have to pay this higher rate to all those workers it already employs.

Conversely, employing fewer workers will cut the firm's wage bill. Thus, the marginal labour cost to a monopsonist will be higher than the average cost. If this firm wishes to maximise its profits, it will go on employing workers until the last person taken on adds as much to the firm's revenue he or she does to costs. This level of employment is represented by employment level E, but the monopsonist will only have to pay out W in wages. However, if this market were competitive, competition between rival employers would drive the wage rate up to W1 and lead to the employment of E1 workers.

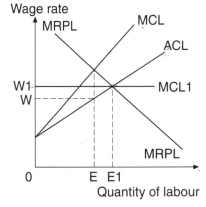

Figure 3: A monopsony labour market

Bilateral monopoly

What if a monopsonist is faced with a workforce that is 100 per cent unionised? Both those demanding labour and those regulating its supply will be in monopoly situations.

Unfortunately, the graphical analysis used to model what happens in labour markets is of limited use. Wages and levels of employment will be influenced by demand and supply conditions, but they will be determined by the relative bargaining strengths of the two sides.

If the trade union is relatively strong, it will be able to push up wage levels and maintain levels of employment until that point at which the survival of the business is threatened.

On the other hand, a relatively powerful employer will be able to push wages down to the level that it would pay if workers did not have a trade union to defend pay and conditions. In this case, wages will be forced down to subsistence levels – as is the case in the UK with some outworkers and in developing countries like Cambodia and the Philippines, where trade unions are not recognised by companies such as Nike and Gap.

Quickies

Use graphical analysis to suggest how a monopsonist might respond to:

(a) an increase in demand for the product produced

(b) the threat of a strike from a trade union representing the majority of the workforce

(c) adverse publicity because of exploitation of workers in developing countries.

T his section takes account of a current trend in economics to focus on institutions as much as theory in order to develop a more effective understanding of how economic institutions work. In some cases, it is hard to use traditional economic analysis to explain why particular groups of workers get paid different amounts to other groups of workers. There is evidence of different forms of **discrimination** in the job market relating to:

- gender
- ethnicity
- social class.

Discrimination in the labour market

Synoptic link

This section follows directly from the previous two A2 sections on the labour market (5.12 and 5.13).

Definitions

Discrimination: when a group of workers and potential workers is treated differently than other workers in the same job in terms of pay, employment, promotion, training opportunities and work conditions.

Gender

Although women in the UK are protected by legislation that makes it unlawful to pay them less than men if they do the same or similar work, there are persistent differences in the pay received by men compared to that received by women. This is illustrated in Table 1.

Average earnings (£) of full-time employees, GB, 2002			
	Hourly	Weekly	Annual
Women	10.22	383.4	19,811
Men	12.59	513.8	27,437
Pay gap (%)	81.2	74.6	72.2

Source: New Earnings Survey (NES) 2002, Table A1.

Table 1: Differences in incomes between men and women, 1998

The Labour government in power in 2003 uses the concept of the gender pay gap to measure progress made in narrowing the gap between the earnings of men and women. This indicates that the gap between the hourly earnings of men and women is narrowing. In 1974, women earned 30 per cent less per hour than men. In the last 27 years, this gap has dropped to 19 per cent. But, as with the other data, these statistics probably underestimate the gender gap, as men tend to work long hours.

The Labour government in power in 2003 has identified five key factors to explain the gender pay gap:

- human capital differences
- part-time working
- travel patterns
- occupational segregation
- workplace segregation.

Human capital differences

These are the differences in educational levels and work experience. Historical differences in the levels of qualifications held by men and women

Average hourly earnings of full-time employees in highest/lowest paid occupations, GB, 1998		
	Pay (£)	Female % of employees
General managers - government, large organisations	20.21	34
Legal professionals	19.45	41
Health professionals	18.94	45
Specialist managers	18.88	32
Business and financial associate professionals	18.18	34
Other occupations in agriculture etc.	5.15	22
Sales assistants & check-out operators	5.01	75
Catering occupations	4.94	63
Hairdressers, beauticians & relaxed occupations	4.84	89
Other occupations in sales & services	4.72	74

Note: Data are shown at minor occupation group level. There may be some high/low paid occupations for which data are not available.

Source: NES 1998, Table A12; LFS, Spring 1998.

Table 2: Average hourly earnings of full-time employees in highest/lowest paid occupations, 1998

have contributed to the pay gap. However, women are still more likely than men to have breaks from paid work to care for children and other dependants. These breaks have an effect on women's level of work experience, which, in turn is argued to affect pay rates.

Part-time working

The pay gap between women working part time and men working full time is particularly large and, as a large proportion of women work part time, this is a major contributor to the gender pay gap. Some of this gap is due to part-time workers having lower levels of qualifications and less work experience. However, it is also due to part-time work being concentrated in less well-paid occupations.

Travel patterns

On average, women spend less time commuting than men. This may be because of time constraints due to balancing work and caring responsibilities. This can have an affect on women's pay in two ways. They will have a smaller pool of jobs to choose from. It may also result in lots of women wanting work in the same location (that is, near to where they live), which will result in lower wages for those jobs.

Occupational segregation

As identified earlier, women's employment is highly concentrated in certain occupations (60 per cent of working women work in just ten occupations), and these are often the lowest paid occupations, see Tables 2 and 3. In addition, women are still under-represented in the higher paid jobs within occupations – the 'glass ceiling' effect, which is used to describe the difficulties women have in gaining promotion to higher pay jobs within organisations.

Average weekly earnings by occupational group, GB,1998

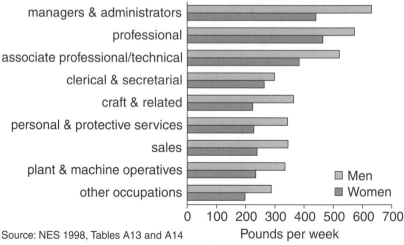

Source: NES 1998, Tables A13 and A14

Table 3: Average weekly earnings by occupational group, 1998

Workplace segregation

At the level of individual workplaces, high concentrations of female employees are associated with relatively low rates of pay. And higher levels of part-time working are associated with lower rates of pay, even after other factors have been taken into account.

Other factors that affect the gender pay gap include:

■ job grading practices
■ appraisal systems
■ reward systems and retention measures
■ wage-setting practices
■ discrimination.

In short, gender discrimination is deeply rooted within out society and is as much the result of social influences as it is economic.

Ethnic discrimination

Although it is unlawful in the UK, workers from ethnic minority groups tend to be paid less than those who are white. This is illustrated in Table 4. It appears that the factors resulting in discrimination against females in the workplace also apply to those from minority ethnic groups.

Average hourly earnings(£) of full-time employees, GB, 1998/99		
	Women	Men
White	7.50	9.29
Black	7.78	8.32
Indian	6.84	9.34
Pakistani/Bangladeshi	6.33	6.87
Mixed/other origins	8.71	9.38
All ethnic groups	7.51	9.27
Note: Ethnic minority data are based on small samples, so should be interpreted with caution.		
Source: Labour Force Survey (LFS), Spring 1998 to Winter 1998/99.		

Table 4: Comparison of the pay of workers from ethnic minorities

Racism can actually contribute to greater inequalities. If an employer believes that workers from minority ethnic backgrounds are somehow less productive than their white colleagues, the employer will perceive that their marginal revenue productivity is lower than it actually is. Economic analysis predicts that the wage rate paid to workers from minority ethnic backgrounds will be below the allocatively efficient level, as Figure 1 shows.

This discrimination is likely to have a knock-on effect throughout the labour market. Those who cannot gain employment with the discriminating employer will seek employment with those employers who do not discriminate. This will increase the supply of labour to the non-discriminating employers and lower the wage rate, as shown in Figure 2.

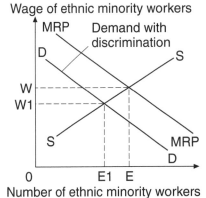

Figure 1: A discriminating employer labour market

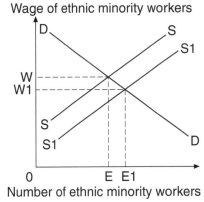

Figure 2: The effect on a non-discriminating employer labour market

Web links

Find out more about discrimination in the labour market by visiting the following website and entering express code 0810P: www.heinemann.co.uk/hotlinks.

Social class

It is, perhaps, less likely that employers actively discriminate according to the class that workers are perceived to have come from. However, the persistence of occupational immobility indicates that there are still strong social pressures limiting the access of children from working-class backgrounds to study at university and work in some professions. Lack of appropriate qualifications can provide a significant barrier to occupational mobility.

The costs of negative discrimination

Negative discrimination can impose costs on a number of groups.

- The group discriminated against clearly suffers. People within it are likely to be paid less than other workers doing the same job. They are also likely to find it harder to get jobs that fully utilise their abilities, or indeed any job. They may also be overlooked for promotion and may not be selected to go on training courses. The existence of discrimination may discourage members from the discriminated group from applying for well-paid jobs and working for higher qualifications.
- Producers who discriminate have a smaller pool of labour to select from. They may also not make the best use of any ethnic minority or female workers they employ. This will raise their costs of production and make them less competitive against rival firms at home and abroad.
- Consumers will experience higher prices if producers discriminate.
- The government may have to pay out more welfare benefits to groups that are discriminated against, and may have to spend time and money on legislation to end discrimination and tackle social tension.
- The economy will lose out as a result of the misallocation of resources. Output will be below the potential output, which could be achieved if the group were not discriminated against in terms of employment, pay, promotion and training.

Theories of negative discrimination

Various theories have been put forward to explain negative discrimination, including:

- Becker's theory
- statistical discrimination.

Becker's theory

Gary Becker, Professor of Economics at Chicago University (USA), argues that some people may be prepared to experience higher costs rather than come into contact with members of a particular group. In effect, the individuals pay in the form of lower profits to avoid employing, for example, women workers and in the form of higher prices to avoid buying from firms employing female workers.

Statistical discrimination

This arises because of imperfect information. Some economists argue that employers discriminate as a result of seeking to reduce their costs. They do not know in advance the productivity of job applicants and may find it difficult to measure the productivity of existing workers. So when deciding who to employ, how much to pay and who to promote and train, they make decisions on generalisations about groups of workers.

For example, an employer may assume that workers aged 50 years and over are less productive and will have a shorter time with the firm than younger workers. As a result, the employer may use age as a screening device when deciding on job applicants, may not promote older workers or send them on training courses, and make them redundant first.

Positive discrimination

Positive discrimination occurs when a group of workers and potential workers are treated more favourably than other workers. Employers may overestimate the marginal revenue productivity of a particular group – for example, workers who have degrees from particular universities or who attended particular schools. This will result in them paying a higher wage and employing a greater number of the particular category than the allocatively efficient levels.

Recently, there has been considerable attention paid to the pay levels received by directors of large companies. This is illustrated by the story on BBCi: 'Shareholders of advertising agency WPP have approved chief executive Sir Martin Sorrell's hefty pay package.' (30 June 2003)

Summary

When left to market forces, labour markets do not usually achieve an allocatively efficient allocation of resources. This is due to a number of reasons. There are frequently dominant buyers and sellers, workers are not perfectly mobile, there is not perfect knowledge on either the part of workers or employers, and there can be attachment between the two. In addition, the employment, promotion and training opportunities and wages offered to different workers are not always based on their marginal revenue productivity. This is because employers' offers can be influenced not only by imperfect information, but also by discrimination. Negative discrimination imposes a range of costs. Two significant ones are higher costs and lower output.

Hot potato

Why does the 2003 Labour government's Skills Task Force argue that the UK is suffering a 'significant competitive disadvantage' because 30 per cent of workers do not have GCSE qualifications or the vocational equivalent?

Research task

Investigating gender and ethnic differences in pay is a popular and good coursework choice. There is lots of data available. Investigate whether there is a glass ceiling in your school, college or place of work?

Quickie

In the UK in 2002, solicitors earned, on average, £900 a week, while secondary school teachers earned £610. As a group, draw up a list of reasons why, in the light of this wage differential, most teachers did not become solicitors.

Distribution of wealth and income

Throughout most of the twentieth century, income and wealth became more evenly distributed. However, the last two decades of the twentieth century saw a reversal of this trend and, now, at the start of the twenty-first century, a quarter of the UK population live in households with incomes below half the national average.

Synoptic link

This is essentially an A2 topic, although inequalities and the working of the price mechanism were mentioned in sections 1.20 and 1.22 of your AS course. This section seeks to examine how differences in income from employment and other sources arise and why these differences occur.

Wealth

Wealth is a stock of assets that have a financial value. The distribution of wealth can be considered in terms of how it is distributed between the population (size distribution), the forms in which it is held and according to the characteristics of those holding wealth. Wealth is very unequally distributed among the UK population. Table 1 shows the size distribution of marketable wealth between 1976 and 2000.

United Kingdom				Percentages	
Marketable wealth					
Percentage of wealth owned by:					
	1976	1986	1996	1999	2000
Most weatlhy 1%	21	18	20	23	22
Most weatlhy 5%	38	36	40	43	42
Most weatlhy 10%	50	50	52	55	54
Most weatlhy 25%	71	73	74	75	74
Most weatlhy 50%	92	90	93	94	94
Total marketable wealth (£ billion)	280	955	2,092	2,861	2,968
Marketable wealth less value of dwellings					
Percentage of wealth owned by:					
Most weatlhy 1%	29	25	26	34	32
Most weatlhy 5%	47	46	49	59	57
Most weatlhy 10%	57	58	63	72	72
Most weatlhy 25%	73	75	81	87	88
Most weatlhy 50%	88	89	94	97	99

Source : Inland Revenue personal wealth

Table 1: Marketable wealth between 1976 and 2000

This table shows that, although there was a dip in 1986, the distribution of wealth in the UK has become more unequal. If the value of dwellings is excluded, half the population shares one per cent of the nation's wealth while almost a third of wealth is owned by the most wealthy one per cent of the population.

Wealth distribution between different groups

As would be expected, wealth is unevenly distributed between age categories. For example, people in their 40s and 50s have had more time to accumulate savings than people in their 20s and 30s, and do indeed have greater wealth.

However, the amount of wealth held also varies between ethnic groups and genders. White adults have more wealth than adults from ethnic minorities. The group that currently has the lowest holding of wealth per head is people with a Bangladeshi background. Men also have more wealth than women.

Causes of the inequality of wealth

The causes of the inequality of wealth are obviously linked to the sources of wealth and include the following.

- The pattern of inheritance. In the UK, significant holdings of wealth have traditionally been passed on to the next generation on the basis of primogeniture (the right of the eldest son to inherit to the exclusion of others). Indeed, major estates and connected titles are still passed on to the eldest son. But in countries where property and other assets are distributed among the children on the death of their parents, wealth becomes more evenly distributed over time.
- Marriage patterns of the wealthy. The wealthy tend to marry other wealthy people. This further concentrates wealth in the hands of the few.
- Inequality of income. As already noted, people with high incomes are more able to save and earn interest.
- Different tendencies to save. Those who save a higher proportion of their income will accumulate more wealth than those who save a smaller proportion.
- Luck. This plays a part in terms of the success of businesses that people start and in terms of who wins money.

Distribution of income

Income is less unequally distributed than wealth. Within a country the distribution of income can be considered in terms of how income is shared out between the factors of production (functional distribution of income), between households (size distribution) and between geographical areas (geographical distribution of income).

The functional distribution of income

Income is a flow of money over a period of time. Income can be earned by labour in the form of wages, by capital in the form of interest, by land in the form of rent and by entrepreneurs in the form of profits. In the UK, wages still account for the largest percentage. However, this percentage is

Hot potato

Why has inequality in wealth increased over the last twenty-five years?

Web link

For more research into inequality go to the following website and enter express code 0810P: www.heinemann.co.uk/hotlinks.

falling. In 1987, 61 per cent of household income came from wages, but by 1997 it was down to 56 per cent. By contrast, income from dividends, interest and rent (collectively known as investment income) has been rising.

| | Percentage of households in each weekly income group | | | | | | | | Average gross weekly income[1] (£) | |
	Under £100	£100 but under £150	£150 but under £250	£250 but under £350	£350 but under £450	£450 but under £600	£600 but under £750	£750 or over	Per house-hold	Per person
United Kingdom	10	10	16	12	11	14	10	18	480	205
North East	18	10	19	12	10	13	8	11	380	165
North West	11	11	17	13	11	14	9	14	430	183
Yorkshire and the Humber	9	10	17	14	13	14	10	13	432	182
East Midlands	9	10	15	13	13	15	10	16	449	191
West Midlands	10	9	16	11	12	15	10	17	462	189
East	8	7	16	12	10	16	11	20	510	218
London	10	8	13	10	10	11	10	28	615	264
South East	8	9	12	11	10	14	10	26	586	258
South West	8	10	17	13	12	17	9	15	449	194
England	10	9	15	12	11	14	10	19	496	212
Wales	11	12	19	14	13	14	9	10	376	158
Scotland	12	10	17	12	11	13	9	14	419	183
Northern Ireland	12	13	21	13	11	12	8	10	370	142

1 Excluding Housing Benefit and Council Tax Benefit (rates rebate in Northern Ireland).

Source: Family Expenditure Survey, Office for National Statistics; Northern Ireland Statistics and Research Agency

Table 2: Distribution of household income, 1998–2001

In addition to earned income and investment income, households can receive income in the form of social security benefit. The relative shares of earned income, investment income and transfer payments depend on a variety of factors, but principally on the level of employment and the relative power of labour and capital.

Measuring the size distribution of income

A common method of measuring the degree of inequality of income and wealth distribution between households is the Lorenz curve. This is named after the US statistician Max Otto Lorenz.

As well as measuring the extent of industrial concentration, Lorenz curves can be used to compare the distribution of income and wealth over time and between countries.

The horizontal axis measures the percentage of the population, starting with the poorest. In the case of income distribution, the vertical axis measures the percentage of income earned. A 45 degree line is included. This is called the line of income equality, because it shows a situation in which, for example, 40 per cent of the population earned 40 per cent of the income and 80 per cent of the population earned 80 per cent of the income. The actual cumulative percentage income shares are then included on the diagram.

In practice, this will form a curve that starts at the origin and ends with 100 per cent of the population earning 100 per cent of income, but which lies below the 45 degree line. The greater the degree of inequality, the greater the extent to which the curve will be below the 45 degree line. Figure 1 shows that income is more unevenly distributed in Country A than in Country B.

The Gini coefficient measures precisely the degree of inequality shown on a Lorenz curve. It is the ratio of the area between the Lorenz curve and the line of inequality and the line of income inequality to the total area below the line. In Figure 1, this is the ratio of **a/a + b**. Complete equality would give a ratio of 0 and complete inequality 1. So, in practice, the ratio will lie between 0 and 1, and the nearer it is to 1, the more unequal the distribution of income.

Size distribution of income in the UK

In recent years the distribution of income in the UK has become more unequal. The widening of the gap between those with high incomes and those with low incomes was particularly noticeable between 1980 and 1990.

There were a number of reasons for this rise in income equality. One was the cut in the top tax rates, which benefited the rich most. Another was the rise in top executive pay, which was sparked initially by privatisation. At the other end of the income range, there was a decrease in the real value of benefits – particularly Jobseeker's Allowance – and a rise in the number of lone parents.

The percentage of families with dependent children that are headed by lone parents more than doubled between 1971 and 1996. The lack of support in bringing up the children means lone parents are often not in work or only in part-time jobs.

Causes of income inequality between households

These include the following.

- Unequal holdings of wealth. As wealth generates income in the form of profit, interest and dividends, differentials in wealth cause differences in income.
- Differences in the composition of households. Some households may have, say, three adults working, whereas other households may have no one in employment. Indeed, low income is closely associated with a dependency on benefits.
- Differences in skills and qualifications. Those with high skills and qualifications are likely to be in high demand and hence likely to be able to earn high incomes.
- Differences in educational opportunities. Those who have the opportunity to stay in education for longer are likely to gain more qualifications and develop more skills and so, as indicated above, are

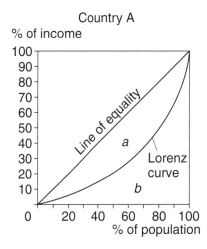

Country A

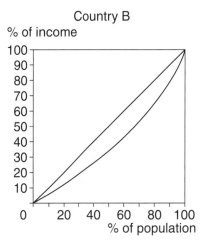

Country B

Figure 1: Comparative levels of inequality

Hot potato

The family of the Duke of Westminster stand to inherit £1,750 million. Is this socially acceptable?

Region	Average gross weekly income
	(UK Index = 100)
North East	165
North West	183
Yorkshire and Humberside	182
East Midlands	191
West Midlands	189
East	218
London	264
South East	258
South West	194
England	212
Wales	158
Scotland	183
Northern Ireland	142

Table 3: Average gross weekly income for the period 1998–2001 in the different regions of the UK
Source: *Regional Trends 2003*, Office for National Statistics

Thinking like an economist

Assess the effect a rise in wealth is likely to have on consumption.

likely to increase their earning potential. Indeed, lifetime earnings of graduates are noticeably higher than those of non-graduates.

- Discrimination. The income of some groups is adversely affected by discrimination in terms of employment, pay and promotion opportunities.
- Differences in hours worked. Most full-time workers earn more than part-time workers, and those who work overtime earn more than those who work the standard hours.

Geographical distribution of income

Income is unevenly distributed between the regions of the UK. For example, in 1997 the average disposable income per head was £11,084 in London, £8,661 in Scotland and only £8,464 in Northern Ireland. Table 3 shows average gross weekly income for the period 1998–2001 in the different regions of the UK.

However, there are variations within regions not illustrated in this data. Thus, London as a whole has a high income per head, but also includes some of the most deprived districts in the UK.

Summary

For many people, the most important forms of wealth they hold are their homes and their pension rights. Wealth is very unevenly distributed in the UK. The most wealthy ten per cent of the population own fifty per cent of the wealth. The main cause of this inequality is inheritance. Differences in holdings of wealth give rise to differences of income. Other causes of the inequality of income are differences in earnings ability (which, in turn, reflect differences in skills and qualifications) and differences in the composition of households. Income is more evenly distributed than wealth, although the last two decades have witnessed a rise in inequality.

Quickie

Using the information given in Table 1, plot Lorenz curves for the distribution of marketable wealth between 1976 and 2000.

I n the last two decades, the number of households with incomes below 60 per cent of average income has risen. It is estimated, for example, that in the UK a third of children (4.5 million), live in poverty. This section discusses the meaning, measurement and consequences of poverty.

Absolute poverty

Economists distinguish between **absolute poverty** and **relative poverty**. People are said to be in absolute poverty when their income is insufficient for them to be able to afford basic shelter, food and clothing. Even in rich countries, there are some people who still do not have any housing. It has been estimated that in England in 2000 there were 1,600 people sleeping rough. Of course, the problem of absolute poverty is more extensive in poor countries.

Relative poverty

While people in the UK may consider themselves poor if they are living in poor accommodation, have a television but no video recorder and can only afford to go out once a week, people in, say, Mali might regard themselves as well off if they had the same standard of living. This reflects the difference between absolute and relative poverty.

People are relatively poor when they are poor in comparison to other people. They are those who are unable to afford a certain standard of living at a particular time. As a result, they are unable to participate in the usual activities of the society in which they live.

Table 1 is based on three items that most people in the European Union (EU) might have expected to be able to afford in 1995, and gives some indication of differences in living standards across the EU. The UK does not compare well with the other countries. The UK, Portugal and Greece had a relatively high percentage of households who did not appear to be enjoying a high living standard. Of course, if the same items were considered for most developing countries, the figures would be much higher.

Relative poverty varies between countries and over time. Someone who is regarded as poor in the USA might be regarded as relatively rich in, for example, Ethiopia. Fifteen years ago in the UK, a personal computer might have been regarded as something of a luxury for a household. However, these days it might be viewed as necessary to participate in the activities of society.

If a country experiences a rise in income, absolute poverty may fall. However, if those on high incomes benefit more than those on low incomes, relative poverty may rise.

Synoptic link

Section 5.15 discussed how income and wealth are unequally distributed. This section examines the position of those who are at the bottom end of the distribution.

Definitions

Absolute poverty: the inability to purchase the basic necessities of life.
Relative poverty: being poor in comparison to others.

Hot potato

Which is the more useful concept, absolute or relative poverty?

	Eat meat every other day	New clothes	A week's holiday
	%	%	%
Portugal	6	47	59
Greece	35	32	51
Spain	2	9	49
United Kingdom	10	15	40
Irish Republic	4	7	38
Italy	6	15	38
France	5	10	34
Belgium	4	10	26
Austria	8	10	24
Denmark	2	5	16
Netherlands	2	13	15
Luxembourg	3	5	14
Germany	5	15	12

Table 1: Percentage of households that did not feel that they could afford certain items: EU comparison, 1995
Source: *Social Trends 29*, 1999, Office for National Statistics

Measuring poverty

To assess the extent to which poverty is a problem, it has to be measured. Economists often define as poor those whose income is less than 60 per cent of the average income (adjusted to take account of family size).

The current Labour government (first elected in 1997) has set itself the task of eradicating child poverty within a generation, and now publishes a poverty audit. This includes poverty statistics and assesses the government's performance against a set of indicators in the form of targets. The first poverty audit came out in September 1999. It found that:

- one-quarter of the population were living in households with incomes below the poverty line of £132 a week – half the national average income
- one-third of all children (4.5 million) lived in poverty – three times the number in 1979
- more than half of the 5.6 million people claiming income support, Jobseeker's Allowance and incapacity benefit had been on benefits for more than two years
- one-fifth of children lived in households where nobody worked – which was twice the 1979 level
- the proportion of families with dependent children that are headed by lone parents increased from eight per cent to twenty-one per cent in 1996.

Research task

Investigate the incidence and causes of poverty in your area.

Among the targets included are:

- an increase in the proportion of working-age people with a qualification
- improving literacy and numeracy at age eleven
- reducing the proportion of older people unable to afford to heat their homes properly
- reducing the number of households with low incomes
- reducing homelessness
- reducing the number of children in workless households.

The poor

Particular groups are more prone to poverty than others. These include the old, the disabled, the sick, lone parents with children, the unemployed and those from ethnic minorities. For example, in 1995/96 66 per cent of Pakistani/Bangladeshi households were in the bottom fifth, and in 1996/97 42 per cent of lone parent families were in the bottom fifth of the income distribution.

Causes of poverty

Essentially, the amount of poverty experienced depends on the level of income achieved and how it is distributed. The reasons why particular people are poor include the following.

- Unemployment. This is a major cause of poverty, with some households having no one in employment.
- Low wages. Some workers in unskilled, casual employment earn very low wages. For example, a significant proportion of workers in Northern Ireland and the north-east are on low wages. However, just because someone earns low wages does not necessarily mean he or she is poor. It is possible that this person could live in a household with a high-income earning partner or parents.
- Sickness and disability. Most of the long-term sick and disabled are dependent on benefits and this takes them into the low-income category.
- Old age. For pensioners, state benefits are the largest source of income. However, occupational pensions and investment income are forming an increasing proportion of the income of some of the old.
- The poverty trap. This arises when the poor find it difficult to raise their disposable income because any rise in gross income results in them having to pay more in taxes and receiving less in benefits.
- Being a lone parent. Not having a partner to cope with the raising of a child may make it difficult for someone to obtain full-time employment.
- Reluctance to claim benefits. A number of people do not claim benefits that could help to supplement their incomes. This is because either they are unaware of their entitlements or they fear social stigma.

Exam hint

Human poverty, a concept introduced in the Human Development Report 1997, sees impoverishment as multi-dimensional. More than a lack of what is necessary for material well-being, poverty can also mean the denial of opportunities and choices most basic to human development: to lead a long, healthy, creative life; to have a decent standard of living; to enjoy dignity, self-esteem, the respect of others and the things that people value in life. Human poverty thus looks at more than a lack of income. Since income is not the sum total of human lives, the lack of it cannot be the sum total of human deprivation.
(Source: United Nations, *Human Development Report 1998*, Oxford University Press)

The effects of poverty

Poverty, especially absolute poverty, has a number of serious adverse effects on those who experience it. The poor tend to suffer worse physical and mental health and indeed have a lower life expectancy.

The children of the poor suffer in terms of receiving less, and often a lower quality of, education. They are less likely to stay in full-time education post-sixteen, have few books at home and attend low-performing schools. They are also less likely to have a personal computer in the home and to travel abroad. All these factors tend to result in them gaining fewer qualifications and a vicious circle of poverty developing.

The poor can also feel cut off and even alienated from society, unable to live the type of life that the majority can experience.

Summary

Absolute poverty is experienced by those whose income is below that needed to achieve a minimum standard of living, whereas people experience relative poverty when they are poor relative to others. Most economists define as poor those whose income falls below half of average income. Most of the poor are dependent on benefits and a major cause of poverty is that no one in the household is in employment. The poor are less healthy and their children's educational prospects are adversely affected.

Quickies

1   Is poverty in the UK growing?
2   What are the main causes of poverty?
3   Will an increase in real GDP reduce poverty?
4   What is the connection between education and poverty?

Puzzler

1   Explain how the definition of human poverty above differs from absolute poverty as it is usually defined.
2   Evaluate the difficulties in measuring human poverty and absolute poverty.

This section helps you to understand the broader context in which economists consider market failure and government intervention (social efficiency). It also explains the significance of property rights and gives further consideration to the possibility of government failure.

Social efficiency

In your AS course you will have assessed the effectiveness of the price mechanism as a means of allocating resources. You will have also learned that if markets are not competitive and/or if there are no externalities, the price mechanism will achieve an optimal allocation of resources. In other words, the world's resources will be used as efficiently as possible to meet the demands of customers in the marketplace. This theoretical state is know as Pareto Optimal.

Pareto Optimal

Vilfredo Pareto (1848–1923) was an Italian economist who argued in favour of positive economics. He contended that social efficiency was reached in an economy when it was not an improvement to make an individual better off at the expense of making someone else worse off. Conversely, if it was possible to make someone better off without making someone worse off, an economy would be described as operating sub-optimally – that is, it would be socially inefficient.

This analysis depends on consumers and producers behaving in a rational way, which means that consumers will go on consuming, say, cola, as long as the marginal benefit (the satisfaction gained from the last mouthful) is greater than the marginal cost (the cost of that last mouthful). If, on the other hand, the additional cost is greater than the additional pleasure, the rational consumer will cut down the consumption of cola. Thus, the rational consumer will stop consuming cola when its marginal cost is equal to its marginal benefit.

You will also be familiar with the behaviour of a competitive firm wishing to maximise profits. It will go on producing until the marginal cost of production is the same as the marginal revenue gained from sales. If marginal cost is less than marginal revenue then production will be expanded, whereas the profit-maximising firm will cut output if marginal costs exceed marginal revenue.

Finally, in the section on the labour market (5.12) you learned that in a competitive labour market, a profit maximising employer will go on employing more of an individual factor of production until the last unit adds as much to marginal revenue product as it does to costs.

Still with it? This is meant to be a gestalt moment in your understanding of economics. If all economic agents are rational, and all attempt to equate marginal benefits with marginal costs, private efficiency will be maximised – that is, it would not be possible to make someone better off without making someone else worse off.

Synoptic link

You looked quite a lot at market failure and government intervention for the AS part of your A level. You need to ensure that you are comfortable with:
■ positive and negative externalities
■ public goods
■ merit and demerit goods
■ market imperfections – monopoly power, imperfect knowledge, factor immobility
■ government use of indirect taxation, subsidies, price control, buffer stocks, pollution permits, state provision
■ government failure – for example, imperfect knowledge, conflicting objectives and administrative costs.

In addition for A2, before tackling this section you need to make sure that you understand:
■ monopoly
■ oligopoly
■ labour markets
■ inequalities in the distribution of income and wealth
■ poverty
■ cost benefit analysis.
This section is designed to help you to bring all this knowledge and understanding together and also to try to make sure that you are familiar with how economists might tackle some of the difficult issues linked to the whole issue of government intervention in markets.

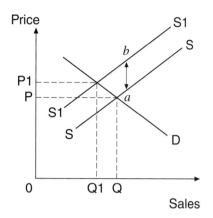

Figure 1: Taxing away negative externalities

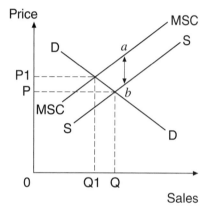

Figure 2: Marginal social cost analysis

This analysis can be extended to considering social efficiency – that is, if the marginal social benefit of any activity is equal to the marginal social cost, then society as a whole is achieving Pareto optimality. You may find this hard going, but you should have undertaken very similar analysis for AS. Do you remember Figure 1?

This uses an extra supply curve to represent a negative externality and indicates that if the government were to introduce a tax equivalent to the vertical distance **ab** it would be able to ensure an optimum allocation of resources because at **P1** and **Q1** an equilibrium is reached at which customers are paying the total cost to society of what they are consuming. The same analysis can be used, but for A2 you need to get used to calling S1 in this context the marginal social cost curve (MSC), which shows the full cost to society of providing a particular good or service – see Figure 2.

Property rights

You will have learned for the AS part of your A level that one way of dealing with negative externalities is by introducing tradable permits whereby governments can encourage individual firms to reduce pollution by creating a market in which those firms that cut pollution the most have the most to gain.

This is an extension of one approach of dealing with externalities without the necessity of government intervention. This approach is associated with an American economist, Ronald Coase. In 1960, Coase argued that government intervention was not required to deal with negative externalities as long as property rights are well defined and transaction costs are relatively low.

Coase argued that if it is possible to extend rights to define who owns what property, to what uses it can be put and what rights others have over it, then the owners would have an incentive to ensure that the value of their property was protected. Thus, if something that I own is damaged it would be logical for me to sue the person who caused the damage. Clearly, if the legal or transaction costs to this action were relatively large, I might be dissuaded from seeking compensation.

The difficulty of applying this approach to internalising external costs is that it is hard to establish property rights in relation to many environmental resources. Who owns the air above my house and the water that flows from mountains to sea? And what happens when it is difficult to identify the perpetrator of some perceived negative externality?

It is clear that the development of legal systems that include establishing the terms and conditions associated with contract law, the rights of buyers and sellers, the liability of particular types of businesses and the importance of insurance have all contributed to the development of economic systems that at least go some way to try to ensure that resources are used effectively. Indeed, great damage has been done to less developed and formally communist countries in applying market-led solutions in contexts where property rights were both ill-defined and ill-protected.

Government failure

In the AS sections on markets and market failure you were introduced to the concept of government failure. This concept recognises that government intervention in markets may lead to unintended outcomes. Misplaced price intervention may create surpluses or shortages. Direct government controls can lead to the creation of new unregulated markets. Taxes and subsidies may distort the signals given by the price mechanism. Such arguments are often used by economists who favour the working of free market forces, who sometimes suggest that there is a straight choice to be made between free market or capitalist solutions and interventionist or socialist solutions.

The winner of the Nobel Price for Economics in 2001, Joseph Stiglitz, has suggested that much of this debate is misplaced. He has argued that free market ideology is fundamentally flawed as 'whenever information is imperfect and markets incomplete, which is to say always, then the invisible hand works most imperfectly'.

Stiglitz goes on to argue that government interventions 'can improve upon the efficiency of the market' and that if information were perfect there would be little role for financial market regulation. He suggests that the failings of the market system 'from massive inequity to unliveable cities marred by pollution and decay' has led to the rejection of free market policies by all advanced industrialised countries. He suggests that it is more useful to discuss the appropriate balance between governments and markets.

Hot potato

Do you agree with Joseph Stiglitz that markets are always imperfect and incomplete? Give reasons for your answer.

Exam hint

It has been said a number of times, but forget at your peril the things you learned for AS. The examiners can set questions on anything you did for AS as well as for A2.

Quickie

What assumptions have to be made for the free market system to ensure the optimum allocation of resources?

5.19 Competition policy

Synoptic link

In the AS part of this A level, you learned about the different forms and effects of market failure. This included consideration of:
- monopoly power
- externalities
- public and private goods
- market imperfections.

For A2 you need to build on this work. You are expected to know a little more in terms of the detail of various measures that governments can undertake to try to remove some of the adverse effects of market failure.

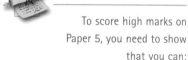

Exam hint

To score high marks on Paper 5, you need to show that you can:
- evaluate the use of economic models to explore economic behaviour
- assess the impact of government policies on economic performance.

The more detailed theoretical treatment of the significance of market structures tends to indicate that, subject to crucial assumptions, customers and societies will be better off if markets are competitive rather than monopolistic. However, there is growing evidence that concentration ratios in key industries tend to be increasing and that many firms develop strategies to avoid competitive pressures. This divergence between what might be seen as socially desirable and the actual behaviour of an increasing number of larger firms provides a challenge both to economists and to governments. This section explores how governments have attempted to promote competition and limit the adverse effects of firms able to exercise monopoly power. The case against monopolies is summarised below. This is followed by consideration of anti-monopoly policies, those to promote competition, and a review of policies towards public ownership and privatisation.

The case against monopoly

Economic theorists have argued that monopoly power can result in:
- higher prices
- lower outputs
- less customer choice
- fewer innovations
- less efficient production – both allocatively and productively.

On the other hand it can be argued that firms with large market shares:
- are able to exploit economies of scale
- can compete more effectively in the global marketplace
- have the resources to devote to research and development
- can be socially responsible.

The economic arguments against monopolistic power are not conclusive. They provide a particular challenge to governments in developing policies that guard against the potential excesses of monopolistic power while trying to ensure that possible benefits are not lost.

UK government policies on monopolies

The UK government has not always been suspicious of the motives and behaviour of firms perceived to have monopoly power. In the 1930s the government promoted development of larger and more powerful companies, because it was considered that they would provide a more secure business environment. However, since the Monopolies and Restrictive Practices Act was passed in 1948, successive governments have looked more critically at the activities of large firms.

This Act, which has been amended and strengthened by additional powers, has provided the basis of government control that continues today. The government trade Minister, the President of the Board to Trade, is advised by what is now known as the Office of Fair Trading. In particular, the Office of Fair Trading recommends cases of possible abuse of monopoly power that should be investigated more fully.

This function is carried out by the Competition Commission (formally known as the Monopolies and Mergers Commission). The Commission is a quasi-legal body that hears evidence prior to coming to a judgement about suspected abuses of monopoly power. Its findings are reported to the Minister, who has the final say about whether or not to take action.

The law defines a monopoly as being any firm that has a twenty-five per cent or greater share in a local or national market, or two or more firms supplying twenty-five per cent of the total market if it is suspected they are colluding informally. The 1980 Competition Act identified various types of uncompetitive behaviour, which included:

- price discrimination
- selective distribution where a firm refuses to supply particular companies
- predatory pricing, when firms deliberately cut prices below costs in an attempt to force competitors from a market.

The job of the Competition Commission is to establish whether or not uncompetitive behaviour is taking place and to balance this against possible benefits in order to make a judgement as to whether or not the firm in question is acting in the public interest.

The Commission and its predecessor have investigated many different possible instances of the abuse of monopoly power. These include the control of public houses by major breweries, high profit levels earned by the major supermarkets, selective distribution by Bird's Eye Walls and retail only agreements by Rank Xerox. Various recommendations have been made which have included price cuts, reduced expenditure on advertising and reducing barriers of entry.

Web link

Check out some recent Competition Commission investigations by going to the following website and entering express code 0181OP: www.heinemann.co.uk/hotlinks.

Control over mergers

In 1965, Parliament enacted legislation that strengthened government controls over the potential abuse of monopoly power by compelling companies to give notice to the Office of Fair Trading of any proposed merger resulting in the creation of a monopoly as defined by the legislation.

The Office of Fair Trading can recommend to the Minister that conditions may be attached to giving permission for the merger to take place or reference can be made to the Competition Commission to investigate the likely outcomes of the merger in terms of the framework developed for investigating the abuses of monopoly power. The Commission, having considered evidence, recommends to the Minister whether or not the merger should proceed. In practice, only a tiny minority of mergers have been referred to the Commission. Practically all of these proposals have been rejected by the Minister or abandoned by the companies in question. This apparent contradiction may indicate that government policies towards mergers has lacked consistency. It is not clear on what basis referrals are made to the Minister and analysis of the outcomes indicates that mergers tend not to be in the public interest.

The Labour government (first elected in 1997) gave greater powers and independence to the Office of Fair Trading. Its Director is empowered to decide which mergers be investigated by the Competition Commission and the Director General of the Office of Fair Trading takes responsibility rather than the Minister in making the final decision as to whether or not a proposed merger should take place.

Control over monopolistic and oligopolistic abuses

The legal framework used to curb the abuse powers of monopolists and oligopolists is tougher than that relating to their existence and creation. Restrictive Trade Practices is the legal terminology used to describe various forms of collusion. All such agreements have to be registered with the Office of Fair Trading and are banned unless participants can prove that they are in the public interest. The law recognises that collusion can bring benefits such as protecting employment, promoting exports and ensuring safety standards are met.

But even if it is possible to prove the existence of such benefits before the Restrictive Practices Court, firms still have to demonstrate that possible benefits outweigh any harmful effects.

Similarly, a tough stance is taken towards limiting the power of manufacturers to set and enforce minimum retail prices for their products. Over the years, formal price-fixing agreements have been ended and only currently exist for some medical products.

Thinking like an economist

What can the government do to protect consumers from monopolists?

Research task

Use this section and other sources to plan and research an essay in which you assess the effectiveness of government attempts to limit the harmful economic effects of the abuse of monopoly power.

European Union legislation

The development of the single European market has meant that member states have been forced to adopt a common approach to competition policy, especially in respect of those firms that have monopoly power within the EU. There is no minimum market share that triggers investigation. Firms that behave unfairly towards consumers by their pricing policies or other activities can be referred to the European Court of Justice. If found 'guilty', they can be fined as well as being debarred from acting uncompetitively.

EU policies towards mergers and collusive behaviour are similar. The focus is on investigation of uncompetitive behaviour rather than market share.

Quickies

1   What is meant by the abuse of market power?
2   Will consumers suffer if a market is supplied by a monopolist?
3   What are the roles of the Competition Commission and the Office of Fair Trading?

The Conservative government under Margaret Thatcher (elected in 1979) favoured market-based strategies in an effort to improve the performance of the UK economy. Two aspects of their polices related to the control and influence of monopolistic and oligopolistic power:

- privatisation and the transfer of the ownership of some firms from the public to the private sector
- the introduction of competitive forces with those organisations that remained in the public sector.

Privatisation

First, businesses such as BP, ICL (Computers) and British Sugar operating in competitive markets were transferred from public to private ownership. In the mid-1980s, Sealink, Jaguar, British Telecom and British Gas were sold. At the end of the decade and in the early 90s, more complicated sell-offs such as the water, electricity and rail industries were undertaken. The Labour government elected in 1997 has indicated that it will continue these Conservative policies by privatising Air Traffic Control. However, it has now backed away from selling off the Post Office.

In addition to fitting in with the overall policy of promoting the private sector and the expense of the public sector, privatisation created additional government revenue estimated to have exceeded £60 billion.

The privatisation process

Transferring ownership from the public to the private sector usually takes place in the following way:

- assets to be sold off are valued
- a prospectus is published detailing the form and nature of the share offer – including the determination of a number of shares to be issued
- individual share prices are set
- the sell-off is publicised
- the shares are floated – that is, made available for sale.

From the government's point of view, the third stage is crucial. If the business is undervalued, the government loses potential revenue; if it is overvalued, the actual flotation could fail.

The Conservative governments in the 1980s recognised that the transfer of ownership from the public to the private sectors would not be sufficient to protect the public from the abuse of monopoly power. In order to safeguard the public interest, legislation to permit privatisation also contained provision for the creation of regulators. These are independent bodies such as Ofcom (media and telecommunications), Ofwat (water) and Ofgem (gas and electricity) with powers to regulate the actual behaviour of these industries by imposing pricing formulas, insisting on customer service targets and levels on investment.

Synoptic link

Industrial relations, production and the international competitiveness of the UK economy in the late 1970s were seen to be poor. Conservative prime minister Margaret Thatcher came to power in 1979 with the slogan 'Getting Britain back to work'. She was strongly influenced by 'right wing' economists, who argued that the performance of UK economy would improve if:

- monetarist polices were followed
- trade union power was reduced
- government intervention in markets was reduced
- enterprise and market-based strategies were encouraged.

The most important sanction available to most regulators is over-pricing. In many cases, the freedom of newly privatised firms to raise prices is limited by formulae. Although its application varies between industries, the regulator's formula can be represented as RPI = X + Y + K, in which:

- RPI stands for the retail price index
- X is a percentage representing costs saving that the regulator expects to be reflected in lower customer prices
- Y stands for unavoidable cost increases
- K applies to, for instance, the water companies as an allowance to cover the costs of environmental improvements – for example, cleaner rivers.

These regulatory powers are in addition to the legal constraints outlined earlier, and are particularly relevant in the case of natural monopolies.

Natural monopolies

Definition

Natural monopoly: a market in which full advantage of economies of scale can be achieved only if there is one firm.

Industries such as water, electricity supply and the railways can be described as **natural monopolies**. It has been more difficult to sell them off in such a way as to promote competition and the other benefits that private ownership is meant to bring.

Privatising British Rail

This was one of the Conservatives' last privatisations, which turned out to be especially problematical. On the advice of economists, the Conservative government created an imaginative plan to try to introduce competition into this natural monopoly. It split the industry into three:

- the railway and station network
- rolling stock provision
- rail operating companies.

Each section was privatised differently.

- Railtrack (now Network rail): the government accepted that this was a natural monopoly that could not be broken up. In 1996, it was sold into private ownership for slightly less than £2 billion. Its market value in January 2000 was £3.25 billion.
- Rolling stock: three rolling stock companies were created whose job was to compete in order to supply engines and carriages to the train operating companies.
- Train operating companies: investors were encouraged to bid for franchises to run trains over regional and inter-city routes. Successful companies would then pay Railtrack to use 'their' stations and track, and lease rolling stock as required. At the end of seven to fourteen years, new bids would be invited to run services in the future.

Privatised rail companies: better or worse?

Regulation

A powerful independent regulatory regime was introduced to ensure that minimum service levels were met, that profits were not excessive and that government guidelines were followed.

Assessing performance of the privatised rail network

The general perception of the public as revealed in surveys is that the privatisation of the railways has yet to be successful.

- Train operating companies have used their market power to introduce complicated discriminatory pricing policies.
- Prices on some services have been dramatically increased.
- Punctuality and customer service are thought to have deteriorated.
- Safety may have been given less priority.

The long-term test of the success of this particular privatisation will be the degree to which a natural monopoly re-establishes itself through merger and takeover within the industry. This has already started to occur in the electricity generation and supply industry.

Competition within the public sector

In the 1980s, the Conservative government realised that the total privatisation of the public sector would be both politically unacceptable and very difficult to implement. It chose instead a variety of strategies designed to introduce or mimic market forces within industries and organisations. These included:

- the creation of internal markets in the British Broadcasting Corporation (BBC) and National Health Service (NHS)
- compulsory competitive tendering for a range of central and local government functions
- greater freedom for educational institutions to control their own budgets.

Summary

Public policy associated with trying to prevent the abuses of monopolistic and oligopolist power has traditionally been based on a legal framework that has focused attention on ownership and structural aspects of large companies. Merger and monopoly policy has not been strictly or consistently applied in the UK, and few sanctions have been used against firms whose actions have been judged to be against the public interest. More recent developments in European law and the developing role of regulatory bodies places greater emphasis on examining unacceptable behaviour by large firms, backed up by the use of fines and direct controls.

Research task

Investigate a privatisation.

In recent years, governments in the UK have also attempted to encourage the development of more competitive markets through privatisation and the introduction of internal markets and other structures within the public sector. Some of these policies appear to have been more successful than others, but it is too early to assess the long-term impact of these changes on society as a whole.

Hot potato

Will competition increase health care and educational standards?

Quickie

Select an industry that has been privatised or an area of the public sector that has been opened up to competitive forces and evaluate the effectiveness of these changes.

Section 5.19 examined government policies designed to limit the abuses of market power by monopolists and oligopolists. Using privatisation to transfer economic functions from the public to the private sectors has also been described. Governments have realised that for political and social reasons it may be inappropriate to privatise some functions. An alternative policy is to try to create more competitive structures within the public sector. This has involved:

- the creation of internal markets
- compulsory competitive tendering
- league tables
- public finance initiatives (PFIs).

Evaluating the performance of the public sector

It was, and still is, hard to assess the performance of the public sector. Some elements, such as public libraries, have always been run as 'public services'; others, such as British Rail, were expected to 'break even' (that is, make neither a profit nor a loss). Yet others – for example, the NHS – were expected to meet any demands. Some, like the Coal Board, found it difficult to make a profit, whereas British Gas was highly efficient. It is clear, however, that firms operating in the public sector:

- were insulated from market pressures
- suffered varying degrees of political interference.

Market pressures

Managers of firms operating in the private sector need a high regard for the profitability of their businesses. Those who ignore **the bottom line** are unlikely to keep their jobs, and privately owned businesses that consistently make loses will go out of business, be taken over or reorganised.

Those working in the public sector have traditionally been insulated from concerns about profitability. They have been able to take decisions without reference to revenue, costs and profit. In the past, schools, hospitals and other public services were run with little control over expenditure. Instead, local authorities and central government provided funding to ensure that each covered its costs.

Employees in the public sector considered that their jobs were secure and there was, therefore, less incentive for them to be productive and cost efficient. These factors have been called 'x inefficiencies' and could be represented by the higher average costs of production that can occur if firms are insulated from competitive or market pressures.

Definitions

The bottom line: the ultimate profitability of providing a product or service.

Political interference

Although firms in the public sectors were theoretically given varying degrees of independence from government interference, it was inevitable that politicians had some say in key decisions.

- Major spending decisions had a direct effect on jobs and the popularity of both MPs and the government. Many firms in the public sector found government finance more generous immediately before elections than after.
- Some MPs were more effective than others in lobbying for government support for particular industries – for example, major steelworks were built at Newport and Port Talbot.
- Profits from the public sector were taken by the Treasury to boost government revenues.

All the above could have contributed to government failure in the sense that government intervention might make a bad problem worse.

Internal markets

In the 1980s, the Conservative government realised that the total privatisation of the public sector would be both politically unacceptable and very difficult to implement. One way of trying to introduce competition was by the creation of internal markets, involving the creation of individual cost centres and greater independence in financial decision-making.

Thus, in the NHS, budget-holding doctors were given the freedom to purchase medical care from those hospitals providing the most attractive service. Hospitals were expected to compete for business from GPs. This represented a radical change in established procedures, which could have had devastating political effects had the government been prepared to allow failing hospitals to go 'bust' and close. The incoming Labour government abandoned these policies in 1997.

A version of an internal market still exists within the BBC, in which independent programme makers have the freedom to employ camera operators, directors, costume designers and so on from within the BBC or from outside contractors.

Compulsory competitive tendering

Local and central government departments were compelled by legal changes to put the provision of services out to tender. This meant that, rather than a council employing refuse collectors, it was required to invite private companies to bid for contracts to collect domestic and commercial refuse. The rules relating to tendering have now been relaxed to permit councils to tender for the provision of their own services.

The impact of these policies is difficult to measure. Who supplies food and drink in your school/college? Have prices changed? Is there more choice? Has the quality of service increased?

There is some evidence to suggest that the use of outside contractors in the health service has contributed to a decline in hygiene standards, while in other services greater competition has had the effect of driving down the relative wages of the less skilled and worsening working conditions. On the other hand, some local government functions have been characterised by very poor levels of service. It might be fair to say that more competition creates more efficient outcomes, but these greater efficiencies might carry additional costs or externalities with them.

League tables

As we saw on page 119, the Conservative governments in the 1980s also tried to apply market disciplines to education. One aspect of these policies has been to publish league tables to compare the performance of different schools, hospitals and local councils. Those scoring well could be rewarded with additional resources or greater freedom from central government control.

Again, it is hard to assess the impact of these reforms. Competition implies winners and losers, and thus we might expect to see improvements in some schools, colleges and hospitals – but possibly only at the expense of failure and closure of others. The Labour government first elected in 1997 has tried hard to improve education and health standards by applying these principles of greater competition, but it may have created government failure – for example, the short-term switching of resources in hospitals away from general patient care to dealing with accident and emergencies to meet government-imposed targets. Similarly, there has been greater pressure on some schools to exclude difficult students, thus boosting league table performance.

Public finance initiatives

Finally, the Labour government has placed considerable priority on PFIs to provide much needed new capital spending. Although the detail of such schemes to build hospitals, schools, roads and even to renew London's underground are complicated, the key concept is simple. The government reaches agreements for capital spending projects to be completed for agreed amounts, to a required standard and by a given deadline. It is argued that private sector entrepreneurial skills are better than those of managers in the public sector, and that this strategy should ensure projects are completed on time and to budget.

Research task

Investigate the impact of 'outsourcing' catering in your school or college.

As discussed previously, evaluation of the success of these policies is difficult. The National Audit Office has indicated that PFIs can be less efficient and more costly. Much depends on the ability of public sector organisations like health trusts and local education authorities (LEAs) to manage and oversee the running of such projects.

Summary

In recent years, governments in the UK have attempted to encourage the development of more competitive markets through privatisation and the introduction of internal markets and other structures within the public sector. Some of these policies appear to have been more successful than others, but it is too early to assess the long-term impact of these changes.

Quickie

1   Are foundation hospitals a good idea?
2   Why might a firm in the public sector be inefficient?
3   What is the purpose of school league tables?

Puzzler

How would you go about assessing the effectiveness of government policies to promote greater competition in the public sector?

The extent to which a government intervenes to affect the distribution of income and wealth depends on the extent to which it believes that the free market distribution would be inequitable, the effects such inequality will have on society, and the effects it believes any intervention will have on incentives and efficiency.

New classical economists do not favour significant intervention. This is because they believe that differences in income act as signals encouraging workers to move jobs, and differences in wealth promote saving and investment. They also argue that the provision of benefits above a minimum level for those who cannot work – for example, the disabled and sick – can encourage voluntary unemployment.

In contrast, **Keynesians** believe that intervention is justified because market forces will not ensure an efficient allocation of income and wealth, and that low levels of income and wealth can cause considerable problems for the households involved – including having a detrimental effect on the educational performance of the children. They also think that significant differences in income and wealth can cause social division, with the poor feeling socially excluded.

Conservatives and other right wing parties tend to regard the existence of inequalities as a necessary characteristic of the free working of markets. Labour and the Liberal Democrats are more likely to favour redistributative policies. But even within these parties there is no clear consensus regarding the importance of such policies compared to other policy objectives.

Ways in which governments affect the distribution of income and wealth

Governments can influence the distribution of income and wealth in a number of ways, including:

- taxation
- cash benefits
- benefits in kind.

Taxation

The UK government uses eight main sources of government tax revenue. The relative importance of each is shown in Table 1. Those marked with an asterisk, such as income tax, are relatively more progressive. They take a higher percentage of the income or wealth of the rich, which reduces inequalities in income and wealth. On the other hand, regressive taxes, such as VAT, take a higher percentage of the income of the poor, making the distribution more unequal.

The most effective means of redistributing wealth and therefore affecting the distribution of income is by the use of inheritance tax. However, this only applies to people leaving more than £250,000, and thereafter applies as a simple percentage of the value of the estate of someone who has died. There

Synoptic link

This section follows on from section 5.16 on the distribution of wealth and income and section 5.17 on poverty. It also links with AS sections on government intervention. Additionally, there are overlaps with consideration of macroeconomic policies.

Definitions

Keynesians: a group of economists whose ideas are based on the work of the economist John Maynard Keynes. They believe that government intervention is necessary to correct market failure and ensure full employment.

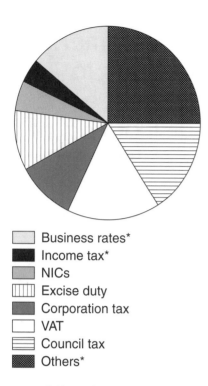

- Business rates*
- Income tax*
- NICs
- Excise duty
- Corporation tax
- VAT
- Council tax
- Others*

Table 1: Sources of government revenue, 1999–2000

Hot potato

Do you agree that poverty is a necessary incentive for economies to work well?

are also many ways in which the impact of inheritance tax is minimised, which means that this is a very under-used means of redistributing wealth.

The overall effects of taxation on the distribution of wealth can be assessed by comparing pre- and post-tax distribution. In the UK, because of the significance of income tax, the overall effect of the tax system is to reduce inequality.

Cash benefits

There are two types of cash benefits – means tested and universal. Means-tested benefits – for example, family credit – are available to those who claim them and who can prove their income is below a certain level. Universal benefits are available to everyone in a particular group regardless of income – for example, families with young children receive child benefit.

There is great debate about the effectiveness of these two kinds of benefits. It has long been argued that child benefit, which is paid to all mothers at the same rate regardless of their income, should be replaced by benefits specifically targeting the poor. The problem is that not everyone who is entitled claims non-universal benefits. Old people, in particular, do not claim all those benefits to which they are entitled.

Benefits in kind

These include the provision of, for example, health care, education and school meals. The take-up of these benefits depends on the age composition of the household (for example, the elderly make the most use of the NHS) and attitudes and opportunities to access the provision (for example, more middle-class children stay in education after sixteen than working-class children).

Other polices designed to redistribute wealth and income

There are many other ways in which the government can use its spending to promote greater equality – including the following.

- Labour market policy. The Minimum Wage Act of 1999, anti-discrimination acts and government subsidising of training reduce income inequality.
- Macroeconomic policy influences the distribution of income and wealth in a number of ways. For example, measures to reduce unemployment may benefit low-income households and regional policy reduces geographical inequalities of income and wealth.
- The amount spent on education and training to increase the skills of the least well off.
- Similarly, the amount of spending targeted at the least healthy or the worst housed to promote greater equality – especially if it is financed by taxation of the better off.

	£ per year					
	Quintile group of households					
	Bottom fifth	Next fifth	Middle fifth	Next fifth	Top fifth	All households
Average per household						
Wages and salaries	1,510	4,680	12,090	20,780	35,110	14,830
Imputed income from benefits in kind	10	30	90	320	1,010	290
Self-employment income	320	570	1,070	1,700	5,580	1,850
Occupational pensions, annuities	300	940	1,500	2,060	2,770	1,520
Investment income	220	340	610	920	2,980	1,020
Other income	160	210	170	180	160	170
Total original income	2,520	6,780	15,530	25,960	47,610	19,680
plus Benefits in cash						
Contributory	2,010	2,510	1,910	1,150	760	1,670
Non-contributory	2,770	2,490	1,680	900	360	1,640
Gross income	7,300	11,780	19,120	28,000	48,720	22,980
less income tax and national insurance contributions	320	960	2,710	5,090	10,530	3,920
less local taxes (net)	430	540	660	770	910	660
Disposable income	6,550	10,280	15,760	22,140	37,280	18,400
less indirect taxes	2,010	2,550	3,570	4,680	5,770	3,720
Post-tax income	4,540	7,730	12,180	17,460	31,520	14,690
plus benefits in kind						
Education	1,750	1,280	1,190	1,040	640	1,180
National health service	1,910	1,870	1,850	1,530	1,320	1,700
Housing subsidy	90	80	40	20	10	50
Travel subsidies	50	60	60	70	110	70
School meals and welfare milk	80	20	10	–	–	20
Final income	8,430	11,030	15,330	20,120	33,590	17,700

Table 2: Redistribution of income through taxes and benefits, UK, 1997/98
Source: Table 5.18, *Social Trends 30*, 2000, ONS

Assessing the impact of government measures to promote greater equality

Table 2 shows that income tax and benefits in kind reduced income inequality in the UK in 1997/98.

Government policy measures to reduce poverty

In addition to policies designed to reduce inequalities in wealth and income, governments may seek to reduce absolute poverty by introducing measures that raise the income of the poorest groups. They may also try to reduce relative poverty by introducing measures that also reduce the gap between the rich and the poor. The following are among the various measures they might use.

- Operating a national minimum wage. If set above the equilibrium rate, this will help the low paid who stay in employment. However, there are disputes about the effect that such a measure may have on the employment of unskilled workers. Also, as mentioned on page 119, not all low paid workers are poor and, of course, not all the poor are in low-paid jobs – for example, the old and the disabled. In addition, if over time the minimum wage is not raised in line with earnings, it will cease to have any effect.
- Increasing employment opportunities. This is thought to be significant as a major cause of poverty is unemployment. However, economists disagree about the best methods of increasing the number of jobs on offer. This can be achieved by managing aggregate demand to try to maintain full employment.
- Removing the **poverty trap**. The Labour government of 2003 has tried to remove this incentive not to work by introducing working families' tax credits to ensure that people are better off if they work. Similar changes have been introduced through children's tax credits.
- Making use of the trickle-down effect. This is a more controversial measure favoured by some supply-side economists. The idea is to cut the rate of corporation tax and the high rates of income tax, with the intention of encouraging entrepreneurs to expand and thereby create employment for the poor. It is also thought that the higher spending the rich may undertake may also stimulate the economy. However, it can be debated how the rich will react and whether the poor will benefit from any expansion that does occur. For example, will they have the skills for any new jobs created and what about the poor who are unable to work?

Summary

There are fundamental differences of opinion between economists as to how governments should respond to inequalities in wealth and income. There are those who believe that inequalities provide incentives for us all to work harder and that, in the long run, everyone benefits from the trickle-down effect. On the other hand, some economists argue that governments should intervene more directly to create more equality.

Definitions

The poverty trap: a situation in which an individual is better off not working and claiming welfare benefits than he or she would be in work and not eligible for benefits.

Hot potato

Why did inequalities in income increase in the UK in the 1980s and 1990s?

Quickie

What would be the effects of increasing inheritance taxes in the UK?

Cost benefit analysis is one of the statistical techniques developed by government economists to try to quantify both negative and positive externalities, determine possible levels of government subsidy, establish levels of taxation and help to reconcile the interests of different stakeholders.

Cost benefit analysis and market failure

Cost benefit analysis can be applied to new investments and also to existing markets. For example, there has been a long-running enquiry into the building of a new terminal at Heathrow Airport. Supporters claim that it will aid economic growth, not just of those directly concerned but also for firms and employees dependent on the continued growth and expansion of Heathrow. On the other hand, a range of interests opposed to the development have argued that noise pollution, congestion and so on will impose additional costs on the local community.

As part of the process to decide whether or not permission should be given for this new development, cost benefit analysis was undertaken. In this case, the purpose was to identify both the positive and negative externalities. A public enquiry was set up to reveal the full costs to society (that is, **social cost** of the new development) and the full benefits (that is, **social benefit**).

The government eventually decided that the social advantages outweighed the social disadvantages, and gave the go-ahead to one of the largest civil engineering projects ever undertaken

The cost benefit process

Undertaking cost benefit analysis usually involves the following.

- Identification and quantification of all private costs. These are the fixed and variable costs the company or organisation undertaking the project would normally be expected to pay. In the case of the Heathrow terminal, this might involve the cost of land, design, building, labour costs and many others.
- Identification and quantification of all external costs – in other words, putting a monetary value to all the negative externalities. It is relatively straightforward to estimate the additional costs to those living in the vicinity to improve soundproofing. However, it is much more difficult to find monetary values for matters relating to environmental damage and degradation.
- Calculation of social cost. This simply involves adding the private and external costs together to estimate the full cost to society of the project in question.
- Identification and quantification of all private benefits. These are all the benefits that customers are prepared to pay for. Sometimes such calculations are straightforward if the people who benefit actually have to pay for a new service.

Synoptic link

Your AS course – especially the sections on market failure – should have given you a good understanding of why, in most economies, there is a mix of private and public sector provision. In theory, governments intervene to try to ensure that the market system works more effectively or more in line with what a particular society wants. You will also have learned that government intervention does not always succeed and that it is possible for governments to make a bad situation worse. In 2003, the Labour government is committed to projects that involve partnership between the private and public sectors.

Definitions

Social cost: both the private costs and negative externalities attributed to a particular use of economic resources.

Social benefits: the private benefits and positive externalities attributable to a particular use of economic resources.

- Identification and quantification of all external benefits. As with negative externalities, this is more tricky because it involves identifying all those who are likely to benefit in some way and putting a monetary value on their benefit. What is the benefit of a business person arriving at a foreign appointment on time? How do you assess the positive effects on the local economy?
- Calculation of social benefit. These are the private and external benefits added together.

When all this has been undertaken, it is possible to make a direct comparison between the social costs of a project and the social benefits. In theory, if the social benefit exceeds the social cost, society as a whole would benefit from the development. If this relationship were reversed, society would be economically worse off.

Problems with cost benefit analysis

The big challenge to those undertaking cost benefit analysis is to put a financial valuation on external costs and benefits, and this requires a mixture of approximations, forecasts and guesswork.

Calculation problems are especially difficult when it comes to dealing with the costs faced by people. For example, what would be the value of building a road that cuts five minutes off the typical journey time of n thousand road users per week? If improvements to road safety demonstrate that fewer accidents will occur, it is reasonably easy to put a value to the lower demand for hospital and medical care, but what value should be given to a saved limb or even a saved life?

These practical difficulties are made harder as cost benefit analysis is often used to assess the economic impact of controversial proposals. This was the case with the Heathrow extension mentioned earlier, in which rival stakeholders challenged the data that each side and the inspector were using.

Using cost benefit analysis

Cost benefit analysis is used in a number of ways. These include:
- public subsidy
- regulation
- planning.

Public subsidy

If cost benefit analysis demonstrates that there will be greater social benefit than social cost – that is, there is a net social benefit – then this analysis might be used to justify government subsidy to ensure that resources are used in such a way as to maximise public welfare.

Regulation

Similarly, if cost benefit shows that negative externalities outweigh positive, a rationale is provided for government intervention to limit or control such outputs. This could involve direct controls, pollution taxes or the introduction of tradable permits.

Planning

As in the case of the expansion at Heathrow, cost benefit analysis can be used to try to resolve the competing claims of different stakeholders. It can provide a more rational way of resolving controversial issues. It also provides government bodies such as the NHS and the Department of Environment with a means of deciding which investments in the public sector should be selected and which rejected.

Summary

Cost benefit analysis is a good topic for coursework. The principles are relatively easy to understand and there is lots of scope for primary and secondary research. You might start by picking a market in which you consider there are significant positive or negative externalities. You would need to try to put a monetary value on such externalities and suggest possible government intervention strategies. You will need to consider the strengths and weaknesses of the technique, the data that you collect and any analysis undertaken. Do not rely on one source for your information, and do not get public and private costs and benefits muddled up.

Hot potato

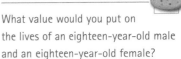

What value would you put on the lives of an eighteen-year-old male and an eighteen-year-old female?

Quickie

List three advantages and three problems associated with cost benefit analysis.

Puzzler

1. Assess the contribution that cost benefit analysis can make to rationing scarce resources in the public sector.
2. How would you go about undertaking a cost benefit analysis on the building of the new Wembley Stadium?

Activities

Business economics

1 Explain the difference between diminishing returns (in the short run) and decreasing returns to scale (in the long run).

2 Explain the difference between increasing returns (in the short run) and increasing returns to scale (in the long run).

3 The table below shows how output varies in a certain production unit when an increasing amount of labour is used with a fixed amount of other factors.

No. of workers	Total product	Average product	Marginal product
1	2		
2	6		
3	16		
4	40		
5	60		
6	72		
7	80		

Complete the table and use it to find the number of workers employed at the point of:

a) diminishing average returns

b) diminishing marginal returns.

4 The table below shows how revenues change for a certain firm as sales are increased.

Units sold	Total revenue	Average revenue	Marginal revenue
1	50		
2	100		
3	150		
4	200		

Complete the table and use it to answer the following questions.

a) What sort of competition is faced by this firm? How can you tell?

b) What is the price charged per unit sold?

c) Why is it not worthwhile for the firm to either increase or reduce price?

The distribution of income

5 Are the employers of David Beckham able to pay the footballer high wages because they charge high admission prices to their stadium, or are they forced to charge high admission prices because of the player's ability to command high wages?

6   British workers have working hours that are among the longest in
    Europe. The productivity of French and German workers is
    approximately twenty per cent and thirty per cent higher respectively
    than that of British workers. What are the economic causes and effects
    of these differences?

7   Use supply and demand analysis to help you explain why the wages of
    airline pilots are substantially higher than the wages of bus drivers.

8   Explain why land prices are much higher in the City of London than
    they are in the Scottish Highlands.

9   Examine the Lorenz curve in Figure 1. It shows the cumulative
    percentage of a country's income earners (x) against the cumulative
    percentage of income earned (y).
    Does this curve show an equal or unequal distribution of income?
    Explain your answer carefully.

10 Examine these figures for male and female earnings in selected
    occupational groups in a certain country.

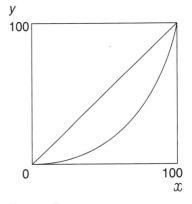

Figure 1 Lorenz curve

Occupational group	Proportion of female employment (see note 1)	Female–male differential (see note 2)
Selling	8.3	55.8
Repetitive assembling	8.1	72.7
Clerical	59.1	80.1
Catering, cleaning	12.4	82.4
All identified occupations	100.00	79.2

Notes

(1) Females in the occupational group as a percentage of all females in
    identified occupations.

(2) Average hourly earnings of adult women in full-time employment as a
    percentage of average hourly earnings of adult men in full-time
    employment.

a) What are the main problems involved in measuring earnings and
    comparing the earnings of men and women?

b) What are the economic reasons for the differences between male and
    female earnings? Can pure economics completely explain the
    differences?

c) Discuss the extent to which income inequalities can be reduced by:
    (i)   legislation
    (ii) trade union membership
    (iii) the tax and benefits system.

Exam practice

In Section A, answer all parts of the question.
In Section B, answer one question.

Section A

1 Study the extracts and answer all parts of the question.

Extract A: Five-firm concentration ratios for selected industries in Rubovia

Industry	Percentage market share of the five largest firms in the industry in Rubovia
Toys and sports goods	16
Footwear	37
Soft drinks	45
Bread, biscuits, cakes	55
Mobile phones	71
Brewing	78
Motor vehicles	92
Tobacco products	99

Extract B: Oligopolies rule in Rubovia

The concentration of industry in Rubovia is typical of many other countries in the world today, where oligopoly has emerged as the most prevalent market form in many industries. Why has this happened? It is partly explained by the existence of economies of scale, particularly in manufacturing.

The idea of 'minimum efficient scale' (MES) is relevant here (see Extract C). This is the point at which cost reductions achieved through larger size run out and firms experience constant returns to scale. After this point, it is just worthwhile for firms to increase their output if they wish to increase revenue and market share. However, they cannot reduce long-run costs beyond this point until some major technological or management change enables the whole long run cost curve to be shifted downwards. Empirical studies show that in Rubovia, as in many other industrialised countries, many firms are in the range of output where they are experiencing constant returns to scale.

The further to the right that the point of MES occurs, the less room there is in the world for rival firms to exist. Take the motor car industry for example. In a country such as Britain there used to be more than twenty car manufacturers. Today not even the largest British firm is large enough on its own to compete on world markets and trans-national companies are the norm. In Rubovia, which has never had a substantial car market of its own, large multinationals such as Ford and General Motors have always dominated the market, as the concentration ratio in Extract A indicates.

As time goes on, some industries become more concentrated as a result of deliberate pricing policy. Mobile phone companies, for example, have decided to sell handsets at prices below the cost of production. This business model has put some firms into financial difficulty and ultimately reduced the number of firms. Some other industries, however, have become less oligopolistic. Established airlines, for example, are facing more competition from companies with a low-cost business model.

There is some evidence that certain industries have five-firm concentration ratios that are larger than their MES would suggest is necessary. For example, there is probably room in the world for three or four more large oil-producing companies. The fact that Exxon, Shell and one or two others dominate the world market is due not just to economies of scale, but also to collusion and anti-competitive practices which have created markets that are more monopolistic than they would otherwise be.

Extract C: Minimum Efficient Scale

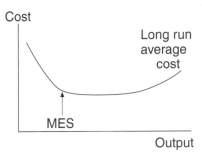

Source: The Rubovia Financial News, 1 October, 2003

Section A

1 a) Describe what the five-firm concentration ratio indicates about the structure of the mobile phone industry in Rubovia and suggest a reason why this is not in itself an adequate measure of oligopoly.
(4 marks)

   b) Explain why companies in the mobile phone industry might sell handsets at prices that are below the costs of production.   (6 marks)

   c) Analyse the types of competitive behaviour typically undertaken by firms in oligopolistic markets.   (10 marks)

   d) Suppose that the government decided to significantly increase taxes on the profits of companies identified as oligopolists. Discuss the possible impact of this policy.   (30 marks)

Section B

2 a) Explain why the idea of 'perfect competition' is important, even though competition can never actually be 'perfect'.   (20 marks)

   b) Discuss how changes in technology can make certain markets more competitive.   (30 marks)

3 'Where market failure exists, there is an argument for government intervention.'

   a) Using examples, explain this statement.   (20 marks)

   b) Company A is considering a takeover of Company B. Discuss why this might result in 'market failure', and assess whether the government should intervene to prevent the takeover.   (30 marks)

4 a) Why are there inequalities in the distribution of income and wealth?
(20 marks)

   b) Identify and evaluate government policies that are aimed at making the distribution of income and wealth more equal.   (30 marks)

Exam guidance

General hints

Modules 5 and 6 are synoptic modules: some of the tasks will assess your understanding of the relationship between different aspects of economics. In practice, this means that the previous work you have studied for units 1 to 4 should not be forgotten. This synopticity is nothing to worry about, as economics topics tend to link together in a chain quite naturally, and the understanding of one concept will depend on the understanding of a previous concept. The best way to learn economics is therefore step by step and link by link: break a link in the chain and understanding is lost.

Specific hints

Section A

1   a)   Explain the meaning of a five-firm concentration ratio: it is the total percentage market share of the five largest firms in the industry. Remember that under UK law, a firm is regarded as a monopoly if it controls 25 per cent of the market. If oligopolists collude (i.e. fix output and prices together) then they can act as a 'complex monopoly'. It follows that any concentration ratio above 25–30 per cent indicates a potential problem with monopoly. A ratio above 50–60 per cent shows that there is comparatively little room left for smaller competitors. On this basis, the mobile phone industry (71 per cent) appears to be oligopolistic. However, this information by itself does not tell us whether the five firms are of equal size, or whether there is one dominant firm and four smaller ones.

b)   In business, this is known as a 'loss leader'. Marketing people talk about 'predatory pricing'. A useful economic concept here is the idea of 'barriers to entry and exit'. Once a handset has been sold and a contract signed the company providing the network has a 'captive' customer who cannot respond to price incentives from competing firms, at least for the duration of the contract.

c)   The key concepts here are 'interdependence', 'uncertainty', and 'price stickiness'. The kinked demand curve is a useful diagram for explaining the pricing behaviour of oligopolists. However, it does not explain how oligopolistic prices are decided in the first place. For this you need to discuss the possibilities of collusion over prices (which is illegal) and different types of price leadership, for example, barometric and dominant firm. Price elasticity of demand could also be discussed.

d)   Taxes affect both supply and demand. If a competitive firm is already maximising profits and has no power over the consumer, then a percentage tax on profits is likely to leave price and output unchanged, since receiving profits which are a percentage of a maximum is better than receiving the same percentage of less than a maximum. You could therefore consider the nature of indirect taxes and distinguish between 'flat rate' and 'ad valorem' (percentage rate) taxes. Oligopolists have some market power and will try to transfer the burden of taxes to the consumer. The theory of the incidence of tax is relevant here.

Section B

2 a) Explain the meaning of perfect competition, by explaining its features and the idea of 'price taking'. Relate this to productive and allocative efficiency. This market model is described as 'perfect' because it is the only theoretical model that results in both types of efficiency at the same time. 'Perfect' does not necessarily mean 'best', however. Sometimes, in the case of public goods or markets with strong externalities, competition is not the most efficient way of producing a good or service: look at the railways or the water industry, for example.

  b) Following on from that point, technology can change in such a way as to make a market more divisible. The fact that telecommunications, for instance, no longer requires a massive investment in underground copper wires, but depends on a 'lighter' and more flexible infrastructure of radio masts and satellites, has opened the way for more competition to replace a natural monopoly.

3 a) Explain the meaning of market failure and suggest some causes (externalities) and examples (public goods).

  b) This is essentially an argument about market failure versus government failure. You could mention efficiency versus economies of scale; competition versus monopoly; costs versus benefits; market forces versus government intervention; private versus public interest arguments.

4 a) Distinguish between income (a flow concept) and wealth (a stock). Refer to the AS book if you are unsure of this distinction. You could use supply and demand analysis to explain why, for example, airline pilots earn more than bus drivers (you did a similar exercise in section 5.24). You can then point out that income and wealth are closely related, because:
    (i) a person's stock of wealth is an accumulation of past flows of income (income can be used to create wealth)
    (ii) wealth can be used to create incomes (for example, if you inherit land or capital from your parents you can put it to work as an income earner).
  Therefore high income earners tend to be wealthy, and wealthy people tend to have high incomes.

  b) Governments can adopt various strategies for making incomes more equal. These strategies might be based on using welfare benefits or progressive taxation. They can also be based on government spending. Because governments provide public or merit goods, which everyone benefits from, we can regard everyone as receiving a 'social wage' which represents the value of these government services (defence, health, education and so on). Progressive taxation means that higher income earners contribute more towards this 'social wage' than lower income earners, and the effect is therefore to redistribute incomes from the better off to the less well off. An important point is that an actual money transfer need not accompany this. Progressive taxation is, in itself, automatically redistributive if there is a substantial 'social wage'. Additional welfare benefits, especially if they are means tested will re-enforce this redistribution. Current welfare policy focuses neither on taxes or benefits, but on 'welfare to work', with schemes like the New Deal attempting to redistribute incomes by upgrading people's skills and getting more people into work. You should consider the possible advantages and disadvantages of these different policies.

5.2

A. Griffiths & S. Ison. *Business Economics*. Heinemann, 2001. Chapter 2.

5.3

C. Bamford & S. Munday. *Markets*. Heinemann, 2002. Chapter 4.
C. Bamford. *Transport Economics*, 3rd edition. Heinemann, 2001. Chapter 3.
A. Griffiths & S. Ison. *Business Economics*. Heinemann, 2001. Chapter 1.

5.4

C. Bamford. *Transport Economics*, 3rd edition. Heinemann, 2001. Chapter 3.
A. Griffiths & S. Ison. *Business Economics*. Heinemann, 2001. Chapter 2.

5.5

A. Griffiths & S. Ison. *Business Economics*. Heinemann, 2001. Chapter 1.

5.6, 5.7

C. Bamford & S. Munday. *Markets*. Heinemann, 2002. Chapter 4.
A. Griffiths & S. Ison. *Business Economics*. Heinemann, 2001. Chapter 3.
S. Munday. *Markets and Market Failure*. Heinemann, 2000. Chapter 3.
I. Wilson. *The Economics of Leisure*. Heinemann, 2003. Chapter 5.

5.8

C. Bamford & S. Munday. *Markets*. Heinemann, 2002. Chapter 7.
A. Griffiths & S. Ison. *Business Economics*. Heinemann, 2001. Chapters 2 and 4.
S. Munday. *Markets and Market Failure*. Heinemann, 2000. Chapter 4.
I. Wilson. *The Economics of Leisure*. Heinemann, 2003. Chapter 5.

5.9

C. Bamford & S. Munday. *Markets*. Heinemann, 2002. Chapter 7.
A. Griffiths & S. Ison. *Business Economics*. Heinemann, 2001. Chapter 6.
I. Wilson. *The Economics of Leisure*. Heinemann, 2003. Chapter 5.

5.10

C. Bamford. *Transport Economics*, 3rd edition. Heinemann, 2001. Chapter 5.
C. Bamford & S. Munday. *Markets*. Heinemann, 2002. Chapter 7.
A. Griffiths & S. Ison. *Business Economics*. Heinemann, 2001. Chapter 7.

5.11

C. Bamford & S. Munday. *Markets*. Heinemann, 2002. Chapter 6.
G. Hale. *Labour Markets*. Heinemann, 2001. Chapter 2.

5.12
C. Bamford & S. Munday. *Markets*. Heinemann, 2002. Chapter 6.

G. Hale. *Labour Markets*. Heinemann, 2001. Chapters 1 and 4.

5.13
G. Hale. *Labour Markets*. Heinemann, 2001. Chapters 3 and 4.

5.14
G. Hale. *Labour Markets*. Heinemann, 2001. Chapter 3.

5.15
G. Hale. *Labour Markets*. Heinemann, 2001. Chapter 6.

D. Smith. *UK Current Economic Policy*, 3rd edition. Heinemann, 2003. Chapter 2.

5.16
G. Hale. *Labour Markets*. Heinemann, 2001. Chapter 7.

5.17
S. Munday. *Markets and Market Failure*. Heinemann, 2000. Chapters 6–8.

5.18
A. Griffiths & S. Ison. *Business Economics*. Heinemann, 2001. Chapter 9.

5.19
C. Bamford. *Transport Economics*, 3rd edition. Heinemann, 2001. Chapter 5.

A. Griffiths & S. Ison. *Business Economics*. Heinemann, 2001. Chapter 9.

5.20
S. Munday. *Markets and Market Failure*. Heinemann, 2000. Chapter 6.

5.21
G. Hale. *Labour Markets*. Heinemann, 2001. Chapters 6 and 7.

5.22
C. Bamford. *Transport Economics*, 3rd edition. Heinemann, 2001. Chapter 4.

S. Munday. *Markets and Market Failure*. Heinemann, 2000. Chapter 6.

PART 6

Government policy, the national and international economy

Government policy, the national and international economy

This module develops and extends the knowledge and understanding of macro economics you gained in AS module 2. As the examiners recommend that developments in the UK should be seen in the context of both the world economy and the UK's membership of the EU, module 6 is obviously closely linked to module 4.

The nature of the module

The module covers four main areas:

- growth of the economy and cyclical instability
- inflation and unemployment
- managing the national economy
- the international economy.

You will already have some background knowledge on these areas from your AS studies. At A2 level you will explore them in more depth and apply additional theories and concepts including the natural rate of unemployment hypothesis, the Phillips curve and the law of comparative advantage. You will be able to make considerable use of aggregate demand and aggregate supply analysis, and your understanding of the effectiveness of fiscal, monetary and supply-side policies will prove to be very useful. The area which is probably most developed from AS to A2 level is international trade. At this higher level, the skills of analysis and education are given greater weighting. Part 6 reflects this emphasis, frequently analysing and assessing different views on economic relationships, causes of economic problems and what are appropriate government policies.

The examination

This module is assessed in a one and a half-hour unit paper. The examination counts for fifteen per cent of the total A level marks. It consists of one compulsory data response question and one essay chosen from three.

Maximising your grade

You can do well in this module if you:

- show an awareness of recent changes in the UK economy
- interpret macro economic data accurately
- apply relevant economic concepts to analysing macro economic issues
- make judgements about the causes, consequences and possible solutions to macro economic problems
- write clearly.

You should have some knowledge of changes in government policies and trends in economic growth, inflation and unemployment over the last ten years. You need to know how key macro economic indicators are measured, be able to interpret trends in data and note any limitations of the data.

In analysing economic issues you should make use of aggregate demand and aggregate supply analysis and the new concepts you will learn in this module, for instance, the Quantity theory of money. You should show the ability to assess information critically and to decide on appropriate policies to tackle particular economic problems.

You must select the essay question carefully. Make sure that you can do well on both parts of the question. Once you have selected the question, spend time planning your answer. Then answer it directly, supporting your answer with relevant economic theory, awareness of recent events and appropriate evaluative comments.

Figure 1: An overview of Part 6

Fluctuations in economic activity

Synoptic link

This section builds on AS sections 2.4, 2.10 and 2.17. Before you start this section, check your understanding of the causes of changes in aggregate demand and aggregate supply, the multiplier effect and policies to promote economic growth.

Definition

Economic cycles: fluctuations in economic activity.

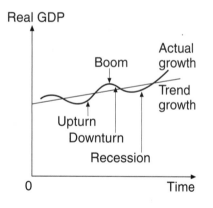

Figure 1: The four phases of the economic cycle

Economic cycles are sometimes referred to as trade cycles and business cycles. They describe the tendency for economic activity to fluctuate outside its trend growth rate, moving from a high level of economic activity to negative economic growth. The last two decades of the twentieth century witnessed two recessions in the UK: 1980–1981 and 1990–1992. There were also periods of rapid economic growth and falling unemployment – for example in 1987–1989, when a consumer boom took place.

Phases of the economic cycle

The economic cycle comprises four recognisable phases:

- upturn
- boom
- downturn
- recession.

Upturn

This can also be referred to as the upswing or recovery phase. At this time, economic activity is increasing because of a rise in optimism about the future. Consumers increase their spending and entrepreneurs increase their investment. As a result, employment rises, which further stimulates spending and output. Bank lending will increase to finance some of this extra consumption and investment.

Boom

During this phase, which can also be called the peak, economic activity reaches its highest point. Unemployment is low and economic growth is high, as existing firms expand and new firms are set up. However, a point comes where it is not possible for output to continue to rise to meet the increasing levels of aggregate demand. A supply constraint is met, the economy overheats, and the excess aggregate demand results in inflation and balance of payments difficulties.

Downturn

This can also be called a downswing. It is the period during which economic growth starts to slow below its trend growth rate.

- The high level of inflation will result in a loss of international competitiveness, causing some domestic firms to cut back their output and some to go out of business.
- The government may respond to the problems of inflation and balance of payments deficit by introducing policies to cut back on aggregate demand.
- The fall in economic growth and rise in unemployment is likely to make households and firms more pessimistic about the future, and so reduce their consumption and investment plans.
- This will further contribute to the slow down in economic activity.

Recession

A recession, which can also be referred to as a trough, is a period with a negative economic growth rate, which lasts for at least six months. In this period, aggregate demand falls and unemployment reaches high levels. The economy may even move into a depression or slump, which is a prolonged period of falling output. This decline in economic activity comes to an end and the economy moves into an upward phase.

There are two main reasons why this reversal in economic activity occurs.

- One is that the demand constraint is likely to be broken. However pessimistic consumers and firms are about the future, a point comes when they have to raise their spending in order to replace such items as worn-out washing machines, cars, office equipment and machines.
- Another is the role of the government. During a recession, net government spending is likely to rise. This may occur automatically, as the lower level of economic activity will cause tax revenue to fall while government spending, especially on unemployment benefit, rises. It may also be the result of a deliberate rise in government spending and/or cut in tax rates designed to stimulate economic activity.

Consumers will increase their spending during an economic upturn

Explanations of economic cycles

A number of explanations are advanced to explain fluctuations in economic activity. These include:

- the Keynesian explanation
- the **monetarist** explanation
- political cycles
- shocks.

The Keynesian explanation

This suggests that economic cycles arise because of the multiplied effects of changes in spending and investment. A small change in spending has a knock-on or multiplied effect on national income, as the extra spending generates a rise in incomes, some of which, in turn, is spent creating more income. The higher level of demand encourages consumers and firms to be more optimistic. Firms increase investment by a greater percentage. When full employment is reached and the government introduces measures to restrict aggregate demand, spending starts to slow down, causing firms to cut back on their investment plans and a downward process occurs. In this Keynesian explanation, changes in investment and expectations play a key role.

The monetarist explanation

Monetarists believe that fluctuations in economic activity arise because of fluctuations in the money supply. They argue that if the money supply grows faster than output, consumption will rise as people feel better off.

This extra spending causes inflation. As consumers realise they are not better off in real terms, they reduce their spending and demand from abroad declines due to the reduction in international competitiveness.

Political cycles

A government may raise its spending and cut tax rates before an election to win political support. Such reflationary policy is likely to stimulate economic activity. However, after the election, if its pre-election policy measures have resulted in inflation and balance of payments difficulties, it may introduce measures to reduce aggregate demand. This explanation can be linked to the monetarist explanation, since changes in government spending and taxation can result in changes in the money supply.

Shocks

Unanticipated changes in aggregate demand and aggregate supply can set off an economic cycle. Shocks are sometimes called real shocks. They are independent of changes in government policy. They may be internal (arising in the country) or external (arising outside the country). They may also be positive or negative and may be supply-side or demand-side in nature. An example of an external, negative, demand-side shock would be a fall in UK aggregate demand resulting from a recession in the USA. Advances in technology in the country may provide an internal, positive, supply-side shock.

In recent years, the role of shocks has been given more prominence in the explanation of economic cycles. It is thought that a number of recent fluctuations in economic activity have been caused by unexpected changes. For instance, the fall in world oil prices in the mid-1980s is thought to have been an important factor behind the increase in output and employment in the USA, and the financial crisis that occurred in East Asia in the late 1990s contributed to an economic downturn in a wide variety of countries including Russia, Brazil and Argentina.

Thinking like an economist

Using an aggregate demand and aggregate supply diagram, explain the effect of a prolonged strike in the electricity industry on the economy.

Definition

Counter cyclical policies: government policies designed to offset fluctuations in economic activity by stabilising aggregate demand.

Economic cycles and government policy

The traditional policy response to the existence and potential existence of economic cycles has been to operate **counter cyclical policies** in a bid to maintain the economy on the trend growth path. This could be by the deliberate increasing of government spending and/or cutting taxation during a recession, and cutting government spending and/or increasing taxation during a boom. It might also be by allowing:

- government spending to rise on benefits (particularly unemployment benefit) and tax revenues to fall automatically during a recession
- government spending to fall and tax revenue to rise automatically during a boom.

In recent years, governments have taken steps to try to prevent economic cycles occurring, or at least to flatten them out. One way the Labour government of 2003 is seeking to achieve greater economic stability is by creating greater stability of government policy. It:

- has given the Bank of England independence to determine interest rates (subject to its need to meet the government's inflation target)
- sets three-year spending plans for government departments
- has put limits on government borrowing.

Effects of economic cycles

Governments seek to dampen down cyclical fluctuations because of the harmful effects they can have on the performance of the economy. For instance, fluctuations in aggregate demand and unexpected rises in costs of production make it difficult for firms to plan, and tend to discourage both domestic investment and foreign direct investment (FDI). It may also mean that some firms do not employ the optimum number of workers.

Quickies

1 Identify the four phases of the economic cycle.
2 Explain how a recession may come to an end.
3 Distinguish between supply-side and demand-side shocks.
4 Why would the elimination of economic cycles be beneficial?

Puzzler

Would good weather, which leads to better harvests, be a positive or negative shock and would it be a demand-side or a supply-side shock?

Research task

Compare annual economic growth rate figures for the UK in the 2000s with those of annual economic growth rates in the 1990s. Decide whether cyclical fluctuations were greater in the 1990s or 2000s to date.

Exam hint

Use AD and SRAS diagrams to illustrate supply-side and demand-side shocks.

6.3 The trend rate of economic growth

The trend rate of economic growth is the expected increase in productive potential over time. It is influenced by supply-side factors including education, training, investment and technological change. In recent years there has been some optimism that the UK's trend rate of economic growth has increased.

Synoptic link

This section builds on AS section 2.4. Before you start this section, check your understanding of economic growth, including trend growth.

Determinants of trend economic growth rate

The trend economic growth rate will rise if the quality and/or quantity of factors of production increase. So the determinants include:

- education and training (over time educational and training standards tend to rise, leading to a more educated labour force)
- advances in technology often arising from investment
- more investment which can be encouraged by, for example, greater stability of economic policy
- increases in the size of the labour force arising, for instance, from increases in economic activity rates.

Improved education and training, advances in technology and more investment will raise productivity. It has been estimated that increases in productivity account for more than 80 per cent of the trend growth rate with the rest coming from an increase in the quantity of resources.

New economic paradigm

Definition

New economic paradigm: the view that economies are entering a new era of high, sustained economic growth, low unemployment and low inflation.

The **new economic paradigm**, sometimes called the new economy, holds out hope that the trend growth rate will be higher and the economic growth rate will be more stable in the future. This belief that economies may be entering a new era in which it is possible for output to rise at a high rate without encountering a supply constraint and without provoking inflationary pressures was based largely on the performance of the US economy in the mid and late 1990s. In this period, the US economy grew at a rapid rate with both unemployment and inflation falling to low levels. Then it was found that other industrialised economies, including the UK, were also improving.

Reasons for improved performance

The main reasons given for the belief that the underlying performance of economies is improving include:

- improvements in information technology and communications (these have increased productivity and, as with the introduction of electrical power and the car in the past, have created new products, new industries, new methods of production and new management techniques)
- **globalisation**, which has increased competition and facilitated the spread of new technology
- reduced expectations of inflation following a period of low inflation

Definition

Globalisation: the development of the world into one marketplace.

- more flexible labour markets in which the hours worked can be adjusted smoothly to changes in aggregate demand
- an increase in the participation rate of previously marginal workers, including lone parents, college students, older workers and married women (the USA in particular has been successful in increasing not only the number of jobs but also the supply of labour; in the period 1996–2000, the US economy grew on average by four per cent – two-thirds of which was attributed to increased productivity and one-third to increases in the number of workers)
- increased growth and flexibility of venture capital (finance for new high risk firms) markets, again particularly in the USA. This has facilitated the start-up of new firms that are exploiting new technology.

Thinking like
an economist

Using an aggregate demand and aggregate supply diagram, explain the effect of advances in technology on an economy.

Views on the new economic paradigm

Some economists believe that economies have really changed and have entered a 'golden age' of high economic growth, low inflation and low unemployment. They think that the advances in information and computer technology will have a larger and more prolonged impact than previous periods of significant innovations.

Others are more cautious and some are openly sceptical. The latter raise questions about the accuracy of productivity figures, question whether inflationary pressures are likely to remain low, and argue that economies in the mid and late 1990s were experiencing a short run increase in economic activity and not a rise in the trend growth rate.

Implications of the new economic paradigm

The debate about the new economic paradigm is an important one since if the way in which economies work has changed, it will have a number of significant implications. The four main ones are as follows.
- The trend economic growth rate will increase.
- Government spending can be higher and/or tax rates lower since government revenue will rise and government spending on unemployment benefit and other benefits will fall with increases in output.
- The need for governments to restrain rises in aggregate demand to counter inflationary pressures will be removed or reduced.
- Living standards will rise.

New economic paradigm and the 2000s

The early 2000s saw the economic growth rate in a number of industrialised countries slow down and in some cases even become negative. This change in economic performance threw doubt on the new economic paradigm.

Thinking like an economist

Using recent newspaper and economic magazine articles, assess how optimistic economists now are about the prospects of the UK economy.

However, its supporters claim that the underlying performance of a number of economies, including the USA and UK, remains good. What they claim happened was that much of the world was affected by a number of negative economic shocks, including the terrorist attack on the World Trade Center on 11 September 2001 and its aftermath, and that the ability of the US and UK economies to grow remains high.

Quickies

1 Explain three factors that influence the long-term growth potential of an economy.
2 How are investment and technological change linked?
3 Identify three possible negative demand-side shocks.
4 What effect would an increase in the trend economic growth rate be likely to have on inflation?

Puzzler

How would you assess whether an economy's trend economic growth rate has increased?

I n the 2000s, the annual average growth rate in China was seven per cent. By international standards, seven per cent is a high rate and the increases in output increased the material living standards of many people in China. However, it is below the high rates China achieved in the early 1990s and is lower than the country's trend growth rate.

Some economists have expressed concern that if China's economic growth rate declines, it would mean that some of the ever-increasing numbers of school-leavers would not find jobs and the long-term unemployed would feel increasingly frustrated. There were also signs that the rapid industrialisation taking place in China was increasing levels of pollution.

Benefits of economic growth

Economic growth should enable people's material standard of living to rise. An increase in real gross domestic product (GDP) per head means that more goods and services are being produced. Poor countries are desperate to raise their output, so that their people have enough food, housing and other necessities. Rich countries have already seen most of their citizens obtaining not only basic necessities, but also an increasing range of luxury goods and services.

Economic growth enables poverty within a country to be reduced without having to redistribute existing income. Higher output raises tax revenue without having to increase tax rates, and some of this can be used to finance schemes to help the poor. Some of the higher tax revenue can also be used to improve public services such as education and healthcare, and to tackle pollution and improve the environment. When output is increasing at a relatively rapid rate, unemployment may be falling. Indeed, the absence of economic growth is likely to result in unemployment.

Economic growth raises the level of a country's real GDP, and can thereby increase its international status and power in organisations and negotiations. The USA, which has a very high level of real GDP per head, is a very powerful member of the United Nations (UN), the International Monetary Fund (IMF) and the World Trade Organization (WTO).

Costs

Economic growth can have costs. If an economy is currently using all its resources and so producing on its production possibility curve, the only way it can increase output is to switch resources from making consumer goods and services to making capital goods. So, in the short run, fewer consumer goods and services will be produced. However, in the long run the extra capital goods will enable more consumer goods and services to be made.

If economic growth is achieved in a way that is not sustainable – for example, by the expansion of heavy industry without regard to controls on pollution – there will be damage to the environment. There is also the risk that economic growth may result in the depletion of non-renewable

Costs and benefits of economic growth

6.4

Synoptic link

This section builds on your understanding of the benefits and costs of economic growth covered in AS section 2.4.

Thinking like an economist

Compare the benefits that economic growth may provide for the citizens of India and for the citizens of the UK.

resources. For example, in the 1990s and early 2000s the Malaysian economy grew quite rapidly, in part due to cutting down parts of its rainforests.

Economic growth may also reduce the quality of some people's lives. A growing economy is one that requires some people to adapt new skills and others to change jobs. The pace of work may also increase. Some people may find these changes stressful.

While economic growth has the potential to reduce poverty, it may make some of the poor worse off. This is because a more prosperous economy may produce fewer goods and services for the poor. The gap between the rich and the poor may also increase.

The quality of life of a range of people may be adversely affected by the increase in the quantity and range of goods and services. For example, the production and use of more cars has increased people's flexibility of travel but has also resulted in more accidents, an increase in breathing-related illnesses and has reduced the ability of children to play in their local streets. In addition, having more goods and services does not guarantee happiness. Indeed, it can create a desire for even more goods and services and a feeling of discontent. Some years ago, most households were happy with one television; now many have two televisions and would like more – for example, one for each child's bedroom, one in the main family room and one in the kitchen.

Sustainable economic growth

For output to continue to rise, it is important that aggregate supply rises in line with increases in aggregate demand. If it does not, the economy will hit a supply constraint and is likely to experience inflation and balance of payments difficulties.

It is also important that economic growth is sustainable in the even longer term – that is, it is achieved in a way that does not damage future generations' ability to produce more. For example, a country may, in the short term, grow very rapidly by using intensive farming methods that erode the soil and result in fertilisers being washed into rivers, causing pollution. However, these methods will reduce a country's ability to produce in the future.

Quickies

1   What effect is an increase in the economic growth rate likely to have on relative and absolute poverty?
2   Explain how education and economic growth are linked.

Puzzler

Will the introduction of genetically modified crops increase or reduce the rate of sustainable economic growth?

I t is not easy to measure living standards because it is difficult to assess what constitutes a good quality of life. One of the best-known indicators of living standards of residents of different countries is real GDP, but there are also a range of other indicators.

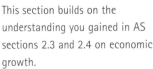

Living standards and real GDP

Increases in real GDP are usually associated with increases in living standards. When output rises, there are more goods and services for people to enjoy. Economic growth also tends to be associated with reduced levels of absolute poverty, reduced water pollution, improved education and increases in life expectancy. In turn, improvements in health, education and environmental standards can contribute to economic growth.

For the 2.4 billion people who live on less than US$2 a day, it is fairly clear that a rise in incomes is needed to improve their lives. However, in many industrialised countries, the quality of people's lives does not always seem to rise in line with real GDP. This is for a number of reasons, including the fact that high living standards require more than money.

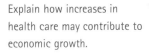

Synoptic link

This section builds on the understanding you gained in AS sections 2.3 and 2.4 on economic growth.

Making connections

Explain how increases in health care may contribute to economic growth.

Changes in real GDP and living standards

There are a number of reasons why an increase in real GDP may not raise living standards. One problem of interpretation that economists can eliminate is that a rise in output may be exceeded by a rise in population. If there is, for example, four per cent more output and seven per cent more people to share the output between, on average each person will be worse off. So what economists often assess is real GDP per head (or per capita). This is found by dividing real GDP by population.

However, there are other problems involved in comparing a country's real GDP over time and between countries. One is the existence of the unofficial (or hidden) economy. This term covers undeclared economic activity. The output of a country is likely to be higher than its official real GDP figure suggests. Some people selling goods and services may not include all the money they have earned on tax returns, and those engaged in illegal activities – for example, selling non-prescribed drugs – will not be declaring any of their income from such activities.

The size of the unofficial economy is influenced by social attitudes to tax evasion, penalties involved, the risk of being caught out, tax rates and the range of activities that are declared illegal. For example, in a country with high marginal tax rates, the size of the unofficial economy may be high.

It is also not just the size of real GDP and its increase that are significant. What is also important in deciding how the level and changes in real GDP affect people's living standards is the composition of real GDP. If more is produced but the extra output consists of capital goods, people will not immediately feel better off, although they will in the long run. If the rise in real GDP has been accounted for by increasing the police service to match rising crime, people may actually feel worse off.

A rise in real GDP may not benefit many of the population if income is very unevenly distributed. People may also not feel the quality of their lives has improved, despite higher incomes, if they are working longer hours or working under worse conditions. These are factors that the official figures do not take into account.

Also, the official figures do not include positive and negative externalities. So, for example, if pollution rises, real GDP does not fall, even though people will experience a lower quality of life. Indeed, if measures have to be taken to cope with the higher pollution – for example, extra cleaning – real GDP will rise.

Quality of life indicators

In 1998, the Labour government introduced a series of 13 new headline main indicators, covering 120 separate categories. These allow the government's performance to be judged, not only by economic growth rates but also by the effect of policies on the environment and social welfare. The thirteen indicators are:

- economic growth
- social investment (for example, investment in buses, hospitals and schools)
- employment
- health, including life expectancy
- education and training
- housing quality
- climate change
- air pollution
- transport
- water quality
- wildlife
- land use
- waste.

Human Development Index

The Human Development Index (HDI) is a measure of the quality of people's lives in the form of human development. It was first published by the UN in 1990. It takes into account longevity, knowledge and 'a decent standard of living', and is measured by life expectancy, educational achievement and real per capita GDP. Table 1 shows the 1999 worldwide HDI top twenty rankings.

1 Norway	11 Switzerland
2 Australia	12 Luxembourg
3 Canada	13 France
4 Sweden	14 United Kingdom
5 Belgium	15 Denmark
6 United States of America	16 Austria
7 Iceland	17 Germany
8 Netherlands	18 Ireland
9 Japan	19 New Zealand
10 Finland	20 Italy

Table 1: The 1999 Human Development Index top twenty rankings

Human Poverty Index

The Human Poverty Index (HPI) measures how progress is distributed in a country and takes into account the proportion of people who are left behind – the extent of deprivation.

HPI–1

This measures poverty in developing countries (see Table 2). It takes the following into account:
- the percentage of people expected to die before the age of 40 years
- the percentage of adults who are illiterate
- the percentage of people without access to health services and safe water
- the percentage of underweight children under the age of five years.

1 Sierra Leone	6 Mozambique
2 Niger	7 Guinea-Bissau
3 Burundi	8 Chad
4 Burkina Faso	9 Central African Republic
5 Ethiopia	10 Mali

Table 2: HPI–1 lowest ten countries, 1999 (starting with the lowest)

HPI–2

This measures poverty in rich, industrial countries and accepts that human deprivation varies with the social and economic conditions of the country. It takes the following into account:

- the percentage of people likely to die before the age of 60 years
- the percentage of people whose ability to read and write is far from adequate
- the percentage of people with disposable income of less than 50 per cent of the median (the average)
- the percentage of long-term unemployed (twelve months or more).

Life survey indicators

Surveys are now undertaken to assess what proportion of people are satisfied with life. In a survey of the EU 15 conducted in 2003, the UK came sixth. There was some correlation between happiness and income levels, as Denmark and Sweden (two of the richest countries) came top, while Portugal and Greece (the poorest two) were at the bottom. However, it was not a perfect fit, with the relatively rich countries of France and Germany coming quite low down the list. What has also been found is that experiencing a divorce, feeling in poor health, lacking job security and fearing crime are significant factors in reducing the quality of some people's lives.

Quickies

1 Identify two reasons why an increase in real GDP per head may not result in an increase in most people's living standards.
2 Distinguish between GDP and HPI.
3 What effect are mobile phones having on the quality of people's lives?
4 Explain the possible effect an increase in car production will have on real GDP and living standards.

Puzzler

UK citizens are richer today than ten years ago, but are they happier?

U nemployment can be caused by demand-side factors and supply-side factors. People may be without jobs because of a lack of aggregate demand. They may also be unemployed because they lack information about job vacancies, the incentive to work, the appropriate skills and/or the ability to move to where vacancies exist.

Demand-side causes

Unemployment that arises through a lack of aggregate demand can be called **cyclical unemployment,** or demand-deficient unemployment. It is linked to the business cycle, as it begins to develop during a downturn in economic activity and can grow to very high levels during a recession.

Another term that is sometimes applied to cyclical unemployment is disequilibrium unemployment. This term emphasises the fact that cyclical unemployment arises when there is disequilibrium in the labour market, with the aggregate supply of labour exceeding the aggregate demand for labour at the going wage. Figure 1 shows that the number of people wanting to work at the wage rate x is QS, while the number of workers firms want to employ is QD, resulting in unemployment of QD-QS.

When aggregate demand for labour falls, the real wage may not fall because workers are likely to resist cuts in wages. Indeed, if the wage rate *did* fall, it may actually make the situation worse. This is because a fall in wages is likely to reduce demand for goods and services that, in turn, will cause a further fall in demand for labour – in other words, there is a risk that a downward spiral may develop.

Keynesians favour trying to reduce cyclical unemployment by raising aggregate demand via increases in government spending and/or cuts in taxation or interest rates.

Supply-side causes

Unemployment may also arise because of supply-side problems. There may not be a lack of vacancies, but those people out of work may not be able or willing to fill the vacancies for a number of reasons. Economists identify a number of types of unemployment related to supply-side problems – the main three being voluntary, frictional and structural.

Voluntary unemployment

Voluntary unemployment occurs when there are vacancies, but the unemployed do not take them up because they are not prepared to work for the going wage rate. New classical economists argue that if unemployment benefit is high, some of the unemployed may take their time looking for a good job and some may decide they are better off being unemployed.

Synoptic link

This section builds on AS section 2.6. Before you start this section, check your understanding of the causes of unemployment.

Definitions

Cyclical unemployment: unemployment arising from a lack of aggregate demand.

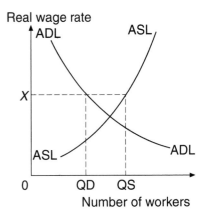

Figure 1: People wanting to work and firms wanting to employ

Thinking like an economist

Analyse the likely effect on UK unemployment of an economic boom in the USA.

Frictional unemployment

Definition

Frictional unemployment: unemployment arising because workers are in between jobs.

Frictional **unemployment** includes workers who are between jobs and young people seeking their first job. What determines how long these people are out of work is principally the mobility of labour. The more geographically and occupationally immobile workers are, the longer they are likely to be out of work.

There are three particular forms of frictional unemployment.

- Seasonal unemployment. The seasonally unemployed are people who are out of work for a short period because of falls in demand that occur at particular times of the year. For example, the hotel and catering industry and the construction industries tend to employ fewer workers in the winter than in the summer.
- Casual unemployment. Some people work on an occasional basis, most noticeably actors.
- Search unemployment. This is a form of frictional unemployment that economists pay particular attention to and which is related to voluntary unemployment. Some people who are out of work do not necessarily accept the first job on offer. Instead, they spend time searching for a congenial and well-paid job. The length of time people are prepared to remain unemployed is influenced by the savings they have, the level of benefits and how society views unemployment.

Structural unemployment

Definition

Structural unemployment: unemployment arising from changes in demand and supply affecting particular industries.

Structural unemployment is usually more significant than frictional unemployment as it is often more long run. Again, a key factor is immobility of labour, both geographical and occupational. It arises from changes in the pattern of demand or supply that cause a change in the structure of the economy's industrial base and a change in demand for labour.

At any time it is likely that some industries will be declining and some will be expanding. This will require workers to move from one industry to another. However, some of those workers may lack the necessary skills or may find it difficult to move from where they currently live to where the expanding industries are.

Web link

Go to the following website and enter express code 0810P to research more about unemployment: www.heinemann.co.uk/hotlinks.

The main forms of structural unemployment are as follows.

- Regional unemployment. This arises when declining and expanding industries are in different parts of the country. For example, some of the towns and cities in the south of the UK have shortages of labour, while some of the towns and cities in the north have significantly higher-than-average unemployment.
- Technological unemployment. This occurs when the introduction of new technology reduces demand for workers in particular jobs and industries. For example, the development of cash points and electronic banking have reduced the demand for bank cashiers. However, as well as

reducing demand for workers in certain industries and occupations, technological change can also result in an increase in demand for workers employed in other occupations and industries. For example, in recent years the mobile phone industry has expanded, taking workers on to, for instance, develop and market phones that incorporate facilities that give access to the Internet and transmit pictures.

- International unemployment. On a world scale, changes in comparative advantage can lead to changes in the demand for labour in terms of quantity and type in different countries. For example, while demand for British steel has declined in the last two decades, demand for steel from Brazil has increased as Brazil has become more efficient in its production.

Research task

Find out what is currently happening to national unemployment and unemployment in your area and the reasons why it is rising, falling or staying largely unchanged.

Supply-side problems and government policy

To reduce voluntary, frictional and structural unemployment, economists recommend measures that make work more attractive to the unemployed and that make the unemployed more attractive to employers – in other words, measures that increase the incentives to work, the ability of the unemployed to work, the skills of the unemployed, and the occupational and geographical mobility of the unemployed.

In recent years, particular attention has been paid to increasing the flexibility of the labour market. Firms are likely to take on more workers if it becomes cheaper and easier to hire and fire staff. The unemployed are also more likely to gain employment if they are willing to take on temporary work if necessary, are prepared to vary the hours they work, and are willing and able to adapt to new technology and new tasks (see section 6.8).

Quickies

1 Distinguish between frictional and structural unemployment.
2 What factors influence the level of voluntary unemployment?
3 Why might the aggregate supply of labour be greater than the aggregate demand for labour?
4 Why might a more flexible labour force reduce unemployment?

Puzzler

Why may workers be less keen than employers on flexible labour markets?

The consequences of unemployment

6.7

Synoptic link

This section builds on the understanding you gained about the costs of unemployment in AS section 2.6.

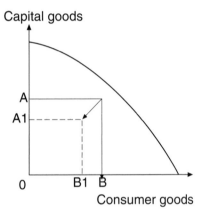

Figure 1: How an increase in unemployment makes an economy less productively efficient

Thinking like an economist

Use an AD/AS diagram to analyse the effect of unemployment on an economy.

The consequences of unemployment are influenced by the rate and the duration of unemployment. Obviously, a high rate of unemployment lasting for a long period of time will have more harmful effects than a low rate with most being of a short duration. The consequences of unemployment can be considered in terms of the effects on economic performance and on individuals.

Effects on economic performance

The most obvious cost of unemployment to an economy is the opportunity cost of lost output. If, for example, two million people are out of work, the output they could have produced is forgone for all time. When a country has unemployed workers, it is not using all its resources and so is not producing the maximum output it is capable of (not reaching its potential output). In this case there is an output gap.

Figure 1 shows that an increase in unemployment would make an economy even less productively efficient. Output of capital goods falls from A to A1 and the output of consumer goods from B to B1.

Unemployment has implications for fiscal policy. It automatically tends to push the government's budget position towards deficit. This is because it reduces tax revenue while increasing government spending. With income and spending levels being below those that would exist with full employment, tax revenue from income tax, corporation tax, VAT and excise duties is below its potential level. The existence of unemployment necessitates government spending on unemployment benefit (Jobseeker's Allowance) and on other benefits, including income support and housing benefit.

Government spending may also have to rise to deal with problems associated with unemployment, including health and crime. People tend to experience worse physical and mental health when they are out of work. There is also some evidence of a link between the level of unemployment and crime. Young men are particularly prone to unemployment. When they are out of work, they may feel alienated from society and turn to crime to gain a higher income and perhaps even a certain form of status. High levels of long-term unemployment may lead to social unrest, as was witnessed in some parts of the UK, including Liverpool, at the start of the 1990s. Unemployment is not evenly spread. It falls most heavily on unskilled, male workers from ethnic minorities. This can also cause social and racial tensions.

Additionally, unemployment reduces potential demand for firms' products. This, in turn, reduces potential profit levels and may discourage investment.

Cost of unemployment to the individual

The main cost of unemployment falls on those who are unemployed. A few people may be cushioned from the effects of unemployment if they have sufficient savings and are not out of work for long. However, most unemployed people experience a fall in income and often a fall in their self-esteem.

Unemployment usually involves financial costs. When people are out of work they may spend more time at home. This will increase, for example, their heating and lighting costs. Applying for jobs and going for interviews also involves paying out money. These costs build up the longer people are out of work.

The longer people are out of work, the more de-skilled they become. This is because they miss out on training and updating. They may also lose the work habit. Both of these effects make it more difficult for them to gain employment. Some unemployed people can become so dispirited that they give up looking for work. These people are sometimes referred to as **discouraged workers**.

Additionally, being unemployed places a strain on personal relationships. Indeed, in some cases it can contribute to physical violence in the home and divorce.

Benefits of unemployment

Being unemployed may enable some people to reappraise their skills and ambitions, and to gain a more rewarding job. Some people leave their jobs voluntarily in order to search for a better job.

The existence of unemployed workers enables firms to expand relatively quickly. Short-term unemployment may indicate a flexible labour force, with workers moving between jobs as demand and supply conditions change. Firms may also find that the existence of unemployed workers will keep wage rises down and make workers more willing to accept new production methods. From the economy's point of view, the existence of unemployment may keep inflationary pressures down.

However, most politicians and economists believe that the costs of unemployment, particularly long-term unemployment, outweigh any benefits.

Definitions

Discouraged workers: people who have given up looking for work.

Thinking like an economist

Explain why being unemployed tends to reduce a person's physical and mental health.

Quickies ✔

1 Explain three ways in which higher unemployment may increase government spending.
2 What effect would a decrease in unemployment be likely to have on the government's budget position?
3 Explain why a person's chances of gaining a job reduce the longer he or she is out of work.
4 In what ways will a reduction in unemployment improve a country's economic performance?

The natural rate of unemployment hypothesis

Synoptic link

This section builds on AS sections 2.6, 2.14 and 2.15. Before you start this section, check your understanding of the causes of unemployment, supply-side policies and policies to reduce unemployment.

Definition

NAIRU (the non-accelerating inflation rate of unemployment): the level of unemployment that exists when the labour market is in equilibrium.

N AIRU (the non-accelerating inflation rate of unemployment) is the level of unemployment that exists when the aggregate demand for labour is equal to the aggregate supply of labour at the going wage rate. This is why it is also sometimes referred to as equilibrium unemployment. As the name NAIRU suggests, it is consistent with the level of unemployment at which there is no upward pressure on the wage rate and inflation. If unemployment falls below this level, perhaps because a government raises aggregate demand in a bid to reduce unemployment, the rate of inflation increases. In contrast, if unemployment rises above NAIRU, this time perhaps because the government is seeking to reduce inflation, the wage rate and inflation will fall.

The nature of NAIRU

NAIRU consists of voluntary, frictional and structural unemployment (see section 6.6). These are the people who are out of work because they are:

- unaware of vacancies
- not suited to the vacancies
- unwilling to take up the vacancies.

Some economists argue that all these people are voluntarily unemployed because they could:

- put more effort into finding out about job vacancies
- be more prepared to move to find employment
- be more prepared to accept, for a period of time at least, a lower-paid job than they ideally would like.

NAIRU can be illustrated on a diagram that shows the aggregate labour force (ALF) but separates out from the labour force those prepared to work at the going wage rate (the aggregate supply of labour, ASL). The gap between the aggregate labour force and the aggregate supply of labour consists of NAIRU. The gap between ASL and ALF narrows as the wage rate rises as more of the labour force is prepared to work the higher the wage rate.

Figure 1 shows the labour market is in equilibrium at Q. However, there are still unemployed workers, Q–QZ, consisting of those not willing to work at the going wage rate.

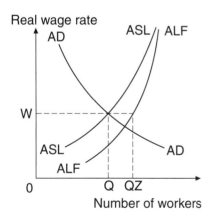

Figure 1: Equilibrium unemployment (NAIRU)

Views on NAIRU

NAIRU was originally referred to as the natural rate of unemployment and was almost exclusively associated with new classical economists. This group believes that the real wage rate adjusts quickly and smoothly to changes in labour market conditions so that any unemployment that occurs must be of an equilibrium level. It is now more frequently referred to as NAIRU, in part because the term 'natural' implies that a certain level of unemployment should exist and also because it emphasises the connection with inflationary pressure.

Keynesians also argue that while during a recession the main cause of unemployment is a lack of aggregate demand, at any time unemployment can include both equilibrium and disequilibrium forms, as illustrated in Figure 2. The figure shows that at the going wage rate, unemployment is QX–QZ, consisting of QX–QY disequilibrium unemployment and QY–QZ equilibrium unemployment.

However, Keynesians believe that real wages do not adjust smoothly to changes in labour market conditions to eliminate disequilibrium unemployment. They also argue that those experiencing frictional and structural unemployment may be experiencing real difficulties in gaining employment. For example, the longer people are unemployed, the more problem they may find in gaining a job because their skills have become out of date and perhaps because they lost the habit of working and some self confidence. This tendency for unemployment to generate longer-term unemployment and to push up NAIRU is called **hysteresis**.

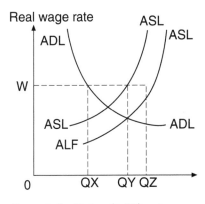

Figure 2: Equilibrium (Q-QY) and disequilibrium (Q4-Q2) unemployment

Factors affecting the NAIRU rate

A number of factors are thought to affect the rate of unemployment that is consistent with stable inflation, including the following.

- Hysteresis. This can be influenced by government policy. If a government seeking to reduce inflation reduces aggregate demand and causes a rise in unemployment, the level of unemployment may not return to the former NAIRU rate because of hysteresis.
- Educational standards, training and skills of the labour force. The higher the quality and quantity of education, training and skills, the more occupationally mobile workers are likely to be and the easier they will find it to move from one job to another.
- Unemployment benefits. New classical economists argue that if there is only a small gap between wages and Jobseeker's Allowance, there will be little incentive for the unemployed to seek work. So they favour widening this gap, which is called the **replacement ratio**, and tightening up the eligibility criteria for receiving benefit.
- Flexibility of labour. The more flexible labour is in terms of the hours worked, the length of employment contract, the types of tasks undertaken and location, the lower NAIRU is likely to be.
- Trade unions. New classical economists argue that trade unions can increase NAIRU by engaging in restrictive practices.
- Income tax rates. Lower income tax rates increase the return from working.
- Labour market regulations. New classical economists argue that the more government controls there are on the employment of workers, the higher NAIRU will be. This is why they opposed the signing of the Social Chapter of the EU which, for example, puts a limit on the number of working hours per week and gives male workers paternity rights.

Definitions

Hysteresis: the view that unemployment generates unemployment.

Thinking like an economist

Discuss whether a fall in wages will reduce or increase unemployment.

Definitions

Replacement ratio: the relationship between unemployment benefit and income from employment.

Policies to reduce NAIRU

New classical economists favour measures that:

- increase the flexibility of labour markets
- make work more attractive relative to unemployment by cutting income tax rates and Jobseeker's Allowance
- remove labour market regulations except essential health and safety rules
- reduce trade union power.

In contrast, Keynesian economists favour more interventionist policies, including increased government spending on education and training, and regional policies. The latter seek to reduce regional unemployment largely by moving work to workers. This policy approach is based on the view that:

- social ties can make labour immobile
- firms do not always seek the optimum location sites
- moving people out of areas of high unemployment can depress them further and waste social capital.

Recent labour governments have sought to reduce NAIRU by using interventionist and, to a greater extent, free market supply-side policies. These policies have included the following.

- Raising spending on education and setting higher performance standards.
- Widening the gap between the amount that low-paid workers receive and the amount that the unemployed receive. To date, it has done this by cutting income tax rates and introducing the working families' tax credit and the minimum wage. Cutting income tax rates raises workers' disposable income. The working families' tax credit is a top-up payment given to the low paid. Once in work, it is anticipated that most of the recipients will move into higher paid jobs and will therefore no longer require the subsidy.
- Introducing the New Deal. The intention is to reduce hysteresis by developing the skills and work experience of the unemployed. Initially, it was targeted at those aged between 18 and 24 years of age, then extended to most unemployed adults. Under the scheme, the unemployed have to take up the offer of a job subsidised by the government, a place on an educational or training course or on the government's environmental task force.
- Introducing compulsory job advice interviews for those receiving benefits, including those receiving income support and housing benefit.

Exam hint

The introduction of the national minimum wage has raised the income of the very low paid – although this is a measure opposed by many new classical economists who argue that it creates a labour market imperfection.

Exam hint

Lone parents are made aware of how they might be able to combine working with bringing up their children, including undertaking part-time employment. Again, the intention is to maintain the habit of work and keep skills up to date.

Thinking like an economist

It is claimed that the UK's NAIRU is now lower than it was in the 1990s, while Germany's NAIRU rate is higher. What could explain this?

Quickies ✔

1 What is the difference between the aggregate supply of labour and the aggregate labour force?
2 Who are unemployed at NAIRU?
3 Explain three factors that could result in an increase in NAIRU.
4 Explain why advances in technology may reduce NAIRU.

P**hillips curves** are used by economists to analyse the relationships between unemployment and inflation, and to assess the impact of changes in government policy on inflation and unemployment. In this section you will assess different views on the likely shape of the Phillips curve. You will also develop the ability to plot Phillips curves to assess current relationships between unemployment and inflation in the UK and other economies.

Origin of the short run Phillips curve

The Phillips curve is named after Bill Phillips, a New Zealander, who started his working life as an engineer. After the Second World War he moved to the UK to study sociology at the London School of Economics (LSE). During his course, he became interested in economics and, in particular, in studying the effect of changes in unemployment rates on money wages.

Phillips stayed on at the LSE, and studied unemployment rates and wage increases for the period 1861 to 1957. He found an inverse, non-linear relationship between unemployment rates and wage increases. This means that as unemployment falls, rises in wages increase but not at a proportionate rate – they accelerate. When unemployment falls to low levels money wages rise rapidly, whereas when unemployment rises to high levels, workers resist cuts in money wages.

Development of the short run Phillips curve

The Phillips curve was developed by two US economists, Paul Samuelson and Robert Solow, in 1960, with changes in money wages being taken as an indicator of inflation to show the expected relationship between unemployment and inflation. Figure 1 shows the inverse relationship between unemployment and inflation.

When demand for labour rises, unemployment is likely to fall. The increased competition for workers is likely to bid up wage rates. Higher pay for workers can increase the price level via increased costs of production and higher aggregate demand as the workers spend their wages.

Economists had drawn up Phillips curves for most countries by the mid-1960s (see Figure 2 as an example). In this period, the short run Phillips curve was interpreted by economists and politicians to suggest that policy makers could trade off inflation and unemployment to reach a desired combination. For example, a reduction in unemployment from, say, six per cent to four per cent might have to be 'bought' at the price of a rise in inflation from, for example, three per cent to five per cent.

Synoptic link

This section builds on the understanding you gained of inflation, unemployment and policies to reduce unemployment in sections 2.5, 2.6 and 2.15 of the AS book.

Definitions

Phillips curve: a graph showing the relationship between unemployment and inflation.
be given up as the result of a particular choice.

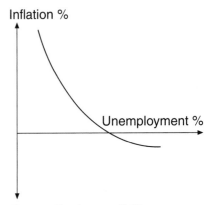

Figure 1: The short run Phillips curve

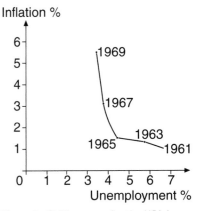

Figure 2: Phillips curve for the USA in the 1960s

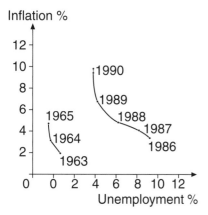

Figure 3: The rightward shift of the short run Phillips curve in the UK in the 1980s

Definition

Long run Phillips curve: a curve that indicates there is no long run trade off between unemployment and inflation.

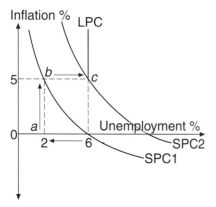

Figure 4: The long run Phillips curve

Changes in the relationship between unemployment and inflation

In the 1970s, the Phillips curve came in for criticism. Some economists argued that the relationship it predicted still existed, but that the curve had shifted to the right, indicating that a higher level of unemployment would be combined with any level of inflation. They suggested that in the 1970s workers had got used to higher levels of unemployment and so did not modify wage claims to the same extent when unemployment rose (see Figure 3).

Long run Phillips curve

Milton Friedman, the most famous monetarist economist, went further. He questioned the accuracy, in the long run, of the traditional Phillips curve in predicting the effect of changes in aggregate demand on the level of unemployment and inflation. He argued that while a Phillips curve relationship may exist in the short run between unemployment and inflation, in the long run changes in aggregate demand would influence inflation but leave output and unemployment unaffected. The **long run Phillips curve (LPC)** he developed is also sometimes referred to as the expectations-augmented Phillips curve (see Figure 4).

Explanation of the long run Phillips curve

Figure 4 shows the economy initially operating on the short run Phillips curve 1 (**SPC1**) with zero per cent inflation and six per cent unemployment.

An increase in aggregate demand may, in the short run, encourage firms to expand their output and take on more workers. Unemployment falls and the economy is at point *a*. However, the rise in demand for goods and services and the resources to produce them will result in inflation.

The economy now moves to point *b*. When producers and workers realise that inflation has eroded their real profits and wage levels, they adjust their behaviour. This, combined with some workers leaving their jobs because of the fall in real wages, causes unemployment to return to the NAIRU level.

The economy now moves to point *c* on the long run Phillips curve, where there is no trade-off between unemployment and inflation. However, the economy is also on a higher level short run Phillips curve since now expectations of inflation have been built into the system. Producers and workers have experienced five per cent inflation and so will base their future prices and wage claims on the assumption that the price level will continue to rise. Any future increase in aggregate demand not accompanied by an increase in long run aggregate supply will result in an acceleration in inflation.

Policy implications of the long run Phillips curve

The long run Phillips curve implies that there is no trade-off between unemployment and inflation in the long run and that governments are powerless to reduce unemployment by implementing expansionary fiscal and monetary policy.

The view that government attempts to reduce unemployment by increasing aggregate demand would not succeed in lowering unemployment but would increase inflation was expressed by James Callaghan, the Labour prime minister, in a speech to the Labour Party Conference in 1976. The Conservative government, which came to power in 1979, subscribed to this view, and the Conservative administrations of the 1980s and 1990s did not attempt to reduce unemployment by increasing aggregate demand.

> 'It used to be thought that a nation could just spend its way out of recession and increase employment by cutting taxes and boosting government spending. I tell you in all candour that that option no longer exists. In so far as it existed in the past, it had always led to a bigger dose of inflation followed by a higher level of unemployment.' *James Callaghan*

Relationship between Phillips curves and aggregate demand and aggregate supply

The long run Phillips curve is related to the long run aggregate supply curve. An increase in aggregate demand, caused by, for example, a rise in government spending, will, in the short run, increase real GDP and raise the price level. In the long run, there will be a decrease in short run aggregate supply due to the rise in production costs that occur when output is produced beyond the productive potential level.

Figure 5, which uses an aggregate demand curve, an aggregate supply curve and Phillips curves, shows how an increase in aggregate demand results in higher inflation but unchanged unemployment in the long run.

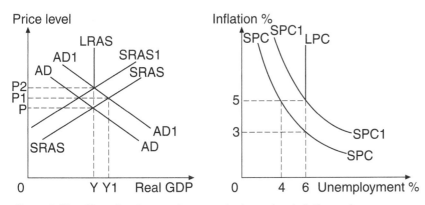

Figure 5: The effect of an increase in aggregate demand on inflation and unemployment

Recent relationship between unemployment and inflation

The late 1990s and early 2000s witnessed falls in both the unemployment rate and the inflation rate in the USA, the UK and a number of other European countries. Economic relationships appear to have changed in this period. Falling unemployment was not putting upward pressure on the inflation rate. There were a number of reasons advanced to explain why inflationary pressure may have fallen. These included:

- changes in labour markets (for example, reduced trade union power and increased labour market flexibility)
- advances in technology (which reduce unit costs)
- increased competition from abroad (forcing firms to keep down rises in prices).

Figure 6 shows an almost horizontal Phillips curve for the UK for the period 1993 and 2001. As the economy approached full employment, inflation remained low.

A horizontal Phillips curve is an ideal situation for a government, as it means that it can achieve both low unemployment and low inflation – that is, there is no policy conflict.

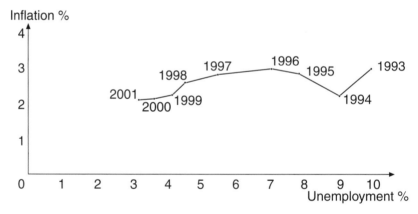

Figure 6: A Phillips curve for the UK economy 1993–2001

Quickies ✓

1 Why might a fall in unemployment cause an increase in inflation?
2 In what sense does the short run Phillips curve indicate a policy conflict?
3 Why in the long run might there be no trade-off between unemployment and inflation?
4 What could cause the long run Phillips curve to shift to the left?

To assess what is happening to prices, governments construct price indices (or indexes). These include producer price indices, which measure changes in the price of inputs and outputs, and the GDP deflator, which measures changes in the price of capital and consumer goods made in the home country. However, the price index that receives most media attention in most countries is the consumer price index. This shows changes in the price of consumer goods and services purchased in the UK.

Steps in constructing the RPI

The RPI is a weighted price index. This means that changes in the cost of goods and services on which people spend more money are given more importance than those on which they spend only a small amount.

Government officials first seek to find out what people spend their money on. They do this by carrying out a Family Expenditure Survey. This involves asking 7,000 households to keep a record of what they buy and which bills they pay over a two-week period, and to give details of their major purchases over a longer period.

From this, weights are given to different items of expenditure – for example, food, fuel and light, leisure goods and housing. If it is found, for instance, that ten per cent of people's expenditure goes on food, this will be given a weight of 10/100 or 1/10, whereas if five per cent is devoted to leisure goods, this category will be given a weight of 5/100 or 1/20.

Officials from the Office for National Statistics (ONS) then check how the prices of a variety of items have changed. To do this, each month they visit a number of shops throughout the country and gain information about changes in the prices of electricity, gas and rail fares from the headquarters of the companies and from the government. In total, they obtain more than 100,000 prices for approximately 600 types of goods and services.

The expenditure of two groups – low-income pensioner households and the households of the very rich – is omitted from the Family Expenditure Survey to make it more representative of the typical household. These omissions are made because it is thought their expenditure patterns are significantly different from the majority of the population.

The final stage is to multiply the price changes by weights in order to find the inflation rate, as shown in Table 1 on page 180.

Synoptic link

This section builds on AS sections 2.2, 2.3 and 2.5. Before you start this section, review your understanding of the meaning, measurement and causes of inflation.

Definitions

Retail price index (RPI): a weighted measure of changes in the prices of consumer goods and services.

Category	Weight	$\times$	Price change	$=$	Weighted price change
Food	3/10	$\times$	10%	$=$	3%
Housing	4/10	$\times$	20%	$=$	8%
Clothing	2/10	$\times$	5%	$=$	1%
Alcoholic drinks	1/10	$\times$	−15%	$=$	−1.5%
					10.5%

Table 1: Calculating the inflation rate using the Family Expenditure Survey

Other measures of inflation

The RPI aims to give a representative picture of what is happening to prices in the UK. However, there are several reasons for believing that it may not give a totally accurate picture. For example, some products improve in quality over time so that, although prices may rise, consumers may actually be gaining better value for money. Also, government officials do not monitor prices in all outlets (for example, charity shops). Additionally, one of the main categories in the RPI is housing. This includes mortgage interest repayments. When a central bank raises interest rates in a bid to lower inflation, this raises the cost of mortgage interest payments and so, at least in the short run, raises the inflation rate.

The government uses the data it collects in the compilation of the RPI to construct two measures of the underlying rates of inflation: RPIX and RPIY. These seek to provide a picture of the inflationary pressures building up in the economy.

- RPIX is RPI minus mortgage interest payments. RPIX was also known as the target rate, as until November 2003 this was the rate on which the government's target for inflation was based.
- RPIY is RPI minus not only mortgage interest payments but also indirect taxes. RPIY is also known as the core inflation rate.

The government now places more emphasis on the CPI. This has a wider coverage than the RPI but it excludes housing. It has the advantage that it can be compared directly with other EU countries and is now the measure on which the government's inflation target is based.

Definition

RPIX: the RPI (retail price index – see page 179) minus mortgage interest payments.

CPI: the consumers price index: a weighted price index with a wide coverage

Cost-push inflation

Cost-push inflation occurs when higher costs of production shift the aggregate supply curve to the left and trigger off a series of rises in the price level. The causes of cost-push inflation can be broken down as:
- a rise in wages
- higher raw material costs
- an increase in profit margins.

If workers in key industries get a pay rise, it is likely to encourage workers in other industries to press for pay rises. Higher wages, not matched by equal increases in productivity, will reduce profits and encourage firms to pass on at least some of the cost in the form of higher prices. In turn, the higher prices will be likely to stimulate workers to press for higher money wages in order to maintain their real wages. A **wage-price spiral** may be set in motion with prices continuing to rise. In the UK, changes in wages are a significant factor since they account for approximately two-thirds of total costs.

Higher import prices could result from a fall in the exchange rate. The higher prices of finished imported goods and services will directly increase the CPI and other measures of inflation. In addition, the higher cost of imported raw materials will raise costs of production that may be passed on to consumers in the form of higher prices. Domestic producers, facing less fierce price competition from overseas, may be more inclined to raise prices.

If workers respond to the rise in the price level by demanding and receiving higher wages, prices will rise still higher. These higher prices will reduce the country's international price competitiveness. The resulting fall in demand for exports may reduce the exchange rate further. This will once more raise the general price level and encourage workers to press for wage rises.

Higher raw material costs may also result from shortages due, for example, to a failure of a crop, a hurricane or from producers forming a **cartel** and exerting their increased market power. It is also possible that profit-push inflation may occur, with prices being forced up as a result of firms raising their profit margins.

Demand-pull inflation

Demand-pull inflation may occur for a number of reasons. One is a consumer boom. When consumers are very optimistic about the future, they are likely to spend more. If the higher aggregate demand occurs when the economy is approaching or at full employment, the price level will be pulled up.

Another possible cause is demand for exports increasing when the economy is at or near full capacity. If more exports are not offset by more imports, there will be more income coming into the country with fewer goods and services on which to spend the income.

Demand-pull inflation may also be initiated by an increase in government spending. One of the reasons governments impose taxation is to try to ensure that spending does not cause inflation. For example, a government may believe that its economy is capable of producing £120 billion worth of products. It estimates that, in the absence of taxation, private sector spending will be £110 billion. If it wants to spend £40 billion, it will reduce private sector spending via taxation by £30 billion to ensure that total spending does not exceed £120 billion.

Definitions

Wage-price spiral: a rise in wages which triggers off rises in the price level and in turn leads to higher wage claims.

Thinking like an economist

Why do increases in the price of oil have a significant impact on the rate of inflation?

Thinking like an economist

Explain why an increase in government spending on training is less likely to lead to inflation than an increase in government spending on pensions.

Of course, in practice, it is difficult to get these estimates right. There is also the problem of time lag. A government may decide to increase its spending when private sector spending is low. However, by the time public sector spending is increased, the economy might have picked up anyway and the extra government spending may result in an excess of aggregate demand and hence demand-pull inflation.

Monetarists argue that the key cause of excessive increases in aggregate demand is excessive increases in the money supply – too much money chasing too few goods (see section 6.12).

Quickies

1   A Family Expenditure Survey indicates that 1/10th of people's expenditure goes on food, 2/10ths on housing, 2/10ths on clothing and footwear, and 1/10th on alcoholic drink. The price of food rises by four per cent, the price of housing rises by ten per cent, the price of clothing and footwear falls by five per cent and the price of alcoholic drinks rises by thirty per cent. Calculate the rate of inflation.
2   Using aggregate demand and aggregate supply diagrams, explain why cost-push inflation may be considered more detrimental for an economy than demand-pull inflation.
3   Identify two possible causes of demand-pull inflation.
4   Explain in what circumstances an increase in aggregate demand may not result in a rise in the price level.

Puzzlers

1   Why has the weighting given to food in the construction of the RPI fallen over time?
2   Why is it often difficult to determine the initial cause of inflation?

The effects of inflation will depend on a number of key factors. These include its level, its stability or otherwise, whether it has been correctly anticipated or not, its rate in comparison to other countries' inflation rates and how the government responds to it. An accelerating inflation rate above that of rival countries and above that expected is likely to cause more harm than a low, stable and fully anticipated rate. In analysing the effects of inflation, it is possible to consider the impact on individuals and on the economy as a whole.

Effects on individuals

Some people tend to gain (for example, borrowers) and some tend to lose (for example, lenders) as a result of inflation. This is because the nominal rate of interest does not usually keep pace with inflation, which means that the real rate of interest falls. If, for example, the nominal rate of interest is six per cent and inflation is two per cent, the real rate of interest is four per cent. If, then, the inflation rate rises to five per cent but the nominal interest rate only rises to eight per cent, the real rate of interest will fall to three per cent. There have even been times when the real rate of interest has been negative. In such circumstances, lending will make people worse off.

One of the main reasons that people borrow large sums of money is to buy a house. Mortgage holders are often beneficiaries of inflation. This is because while the real interest rate they pay back is usually reduced by inflation, the real value of their houses tends to rise, since the price of houses increases by more than the rate of inflation.

Inflation also usually redistributes income from those workers with weak bargaining power towards those with strong bargaining power. Those workers who can gain wage rises above the rate of inflation will experience increases in real income, while those whose wages do not keep pace with inflation will suffer a fall in real income. People on state benefits may also experience a fall in real income because, for instance, Jobseeker's Allowance may not be raised in line with inflation.

Unanticipated inflation will create uncertainty and some confusion. People will not know, for instance, whether it is better to take out a fixed or variable rate mortgage and what wage rise to ask for. Inflation also generates inflationary noise, with distorted information being sent out about relative prices. As people will be unsure whether price rises are in line with inflation or not, they may make inefficient choices.

In addition, taxpayers will lose if the government does not adjust tax margins in line with inflation. In such circumstances, taxpayers will be dragged into higher tax brackets when their nominal incomes rise.

The consequences of inflation

Synoptic link

This section builds on AS section 2.5. Before you start this section, check your understanding of the consequences of inflation.

Thinking like an economist

What are the economic arguments for and against index-linking state pensions?

Effects on the balance of payments

As mentioned at AS level, if a country has an inflation rate above that of its main competitors, its products will become less price competitive. This fall in international price competitiveness is likely to result in a rise in imports and a fall in exports, and thus a deterioration in the current account balance.

The balance of payments may also be affected in other ways. If the country is experiencing high and accelerating inflation, portfolio and direct investment into it may also be discouraged.

Additionally, government policy measures to reduce inflation may harm the balance of payments. For instance, if the Bank of England raises the rate of interest to reduce aggregate demand, this may raise the country's exchange rate. A higher exchange rate increases the price of exports and reduces the price of imports. If demand for exports and imports is price elastic, a higher exchange rate will cause export revenue to fall and import expenditure to rise.

Effects on output

A low level of anticipated demand-pull inflation may cause a rise in output in the short run. This is because the higher aggregate demand and the higher prices are likely to encourage firms to raise their production. However, inflation can have a detrimental effect on national output.

Hyperinflation is particularly harmful to economic activity. When the price level is rising rapidly it can be difficult for an economy to operate. In Germany in the 1920s, inflation reached phenomenal levels. Money became worthless and people asked to be paid in a range of items, including cigarettes, which they believed would prove to be more acceptable when it came to paying for goods and services. Barter also made a comeback with people directly exchanging goods and services. The disruption caused to the economy and people's lives led to political unrest and contributed to the rise of Hitler.

A rate of inflation well below hyperinflation levels but still considered high and unstable may also have a detrimental effect on output. This is because:
- it will increase firms' costs
- it will create uncertainty
- it may decrease aggregate demand.

Inflation raises firms' costs in a number of ways – for example, by imposing **menu costs** and **shoe leather costs**. If money is losing its value at a high rate, it cannot be left idle. So firms receiving payments are likely to try to gain interest on the money, even if they are going to pay it out in a few days' time. Staff time has to be used in assessing where the highest interest is being paid and moving the money around.

There are also other financial costs imposed on firms as a result of inflation.

- Extra time and effort has to be taken in searching round for the lowest prices of raw materials, adjusting accounts, estimating appropriate prices and negotiating with unions about wage rises.
- Unanticipated and accelerating inflation makes it particularly difficult for firms to plan ahead and this may discourage them from investing.
- As with the balance of payments position, output may also be harmed by short-term government measures to reduce inflation. This is particularly the case if the measures are of a deflationary nature.
- Even without such policies, inflation may reduce aggregate demand. This is because the uncertainty it generates may reduce consumption and investment and because the effect it may have on international competitiveness may reduce net exports.
- As well as reducing aggregate demand, a fall in investment will have an adverse effect on economic growth.

Thinking like an economist

Explain why government measures to reduce unemployment may increase inflation.

Effects on employment

If a low and stable rate of inflation is accompanied by an increase in output, unemployment may fall. However, there are a number of reasons for thinking that inflation may have an adverse effect on employment. These reasons have been touched on earlier. If inflation makes the country's products less price competitive, raises firms' costs and creates uncertainty, output is likely to fall and may therefore cause unemployment.

Again, some government measures implemented to reduce inflation may have a harmful effect on employment. Deflationary fiscal and monetary policy measures may reduce output and thus increase unemployment. However, some longer-term measures, designed to reduce inflation by increasing aggregate supply, may have a beneficial effect on employment. For instance, increasing and improving education and training is likely to improve the skills, occupational mobility and therefore employability of labour.

Thinking like an economist

Discuss how a fall in the rate of inflation may improve a country's economic performance.

Quickies

1 In what circumstances will the real rate of interest be negative?
2 Identify three groups who are likely to suffer as a result of unanticipated inflation.
3 In what sense may inflation be self-sustaining?
4 Why may an increase in inflation reduce unemployment?

Puzzler

Is unemployment or inflation currently imposing greater costs on the UK economy?

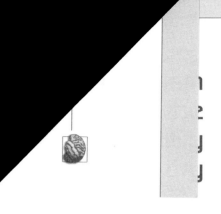

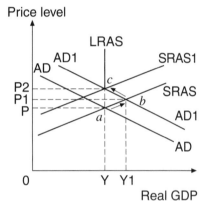

Figure 1: The effect of an increase in the money supply

M onetarists believe that inflation is caused by excessive increases in the money supply. Such increases, they believe, will spark off a series of increases in aggregate demand and decreases in short run aggregate supply – both of which push up the price level. In this section, you will examine the monetarist model of the inflationary process, the theory they use to support their view and the contrasting view of Keynesians.

Monetarist model of the inflationary process

Monetarists argue that the cause of inflation is the money supply growing faster than output. They argue that if the supply of money increases faster than the demand for money, the value of money will fall and inflation will occur.

Monetarists think that an excessive growth of the money supply will cause people to use some of the extra money to buy goods and services. This higher consumption will increase aggregate demand, shifting the AD curve to the right. In the short run, the higher demand will lead to an increase in output and the economy will move to point *b* on the short run aggregate supply curve, as shown on Figure 1.

The increased demand for resources will, however, bid up their prices and so increase costs of production. So the **SRAS** curve shifts to the left. The economy moves to point *c* as workers and firms adjust to the rise in costs and prices. Output and employment return to their previous levels and aggregate demand again equals aggregate supply. The price level, however, has risen. Firms and workers will now expect the price level to continue to rise and so will act in a way that continues to push up the price level.

'Inflation is always and everywhere a monetary phenomenon.'
Milton Friedman

Transmission mechanism

The monetary **transmission mechanism** is the process by which changes in the money supply work through the economy. Changes in the money supply may affect output, employment, the price level and even the balance of payments. Monetarists and Keynesians have different views on the impact of changes in the money supply, as discussed below.

The Fisher equation

In discussing the effects of a change in the money supply, monetarists refer to the **Fisher equation**, also sometimes called the equation of exchange. This is MV = PY (or MV = PT), where:

- M is the money supply

- V is the **velocity of circulation**
- P is the price level
- Y is the level of output
- T stands for transactions and is equivalent to output.

As it stands, the equation is a truism. One side represents total expenditure and the other is the value of goods sold so, by definition, they must be equal.

Quantity theory

To provide an explanation of their view of the monetary transmission mechanism, monetarists developed the Fisher equation into a theory. This theory is called the Quantity theory of money (so-called because of the emphasis it places on the quantity of money in the economy).

To convert the equation into the **Quantity theory**, monetarists assume that V and Y are constant. They argue that, in the long run, output will be at the productive capacity level (full employment) and that V is largely stable. So they think a change in M will have a direct and proportional effect on P. For instance, initially M may be £50 billion, V 6, P £10 and Y £30 billion. Then, if M increases by 50 per cent to £75 billion and V and Y are unchanged, P will also increase by 50 per cent to £15. Now £75 billion × 6 = £15 × £30 billion.

The Keynesian view on the Quantity theory

Keynesians do not believe that the equation MV = PY can be converted into a theory. This is because they think V and T can be influenced by changes in M and so cannot be assumed to be constant. An increase in M may be accompanied by a fall in V and/or a rise in Y and have little effect on P. For example, M may be £80 billion, V 5, P £4 and Y £100 billion. If M increases to £100 billion and this increase in the money supply is accompanied by an increase in output to £125 billion, P will remain at £4.

The Keynesian transmission mechanism

The Keynesian transmission mechanism explains how an increase in M may result in a change in either P or Y, or a combination of the two.

According to Keynesians, an increase in the money supply will initially affect mainly those dealing in financial markets. These people will buy more financial assets, including government bonds. The increase in demand for bonds will raise the price of bonds and lower the rate of interest. A fall in the rate of interest is likely to generate increases in consumption and investment. It may also result in a rise in net exports if it leads to a fall in the exchange rate.

Definitions

Velocity of circulation: also sometimes called the income velocity of circulation, it is the number of times money changes hands in a given time period.

Quantity theory: the view that a change in the quantity of money causes a direct and proportionate change in the price level.

Thinking like an economist

Calculating the velocity of circulation: if £1,000 billion worth of products have been traded using a money supply of £200 billion, it means that, on average, each pound must have changed hands five times. V = PY/M.

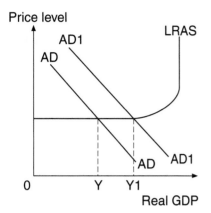

Price level

AD1
AD
LRAS

AD
AD1

0　　　Y　Y1

Real GDP

Figure 2: An increase in aggregate demand having no effect on the price level

The effect of higher aggregate demand will depend on whether the economy is initially operating with spare capacity and the extent to which productive capacity rises with higher investment. It is possible that output may increase but the price level may remain unchanged, as shown in Figure 2.

Line of causality

Monetarists argue that it is increases in the money supply that cause inflation. Keynesians accept that inflation is a monetary phenomenon in the sense that it will be accompanied by a rise in the money supply. However, they argue that it is a rise in the price level that leads to a rise in the money supply, and not the other way round. If the price level is rising, firms and households will demand more money in order to cover higher costs and prices. The rise in bank lending will increase the money supply.

Exam hint

It is important to remember that the price of government bonds and the rate of interest are inversely related. For example, a government bond issued for £1,000 may pay £100 interest (that is, ten per cent). If the price of the bond rose to £2,000, the £100 interest would now be five per cent.

Quickies

1　If M is £20 billion, V is 5 and Y is £40 billion, what is P?
2　What does monetarist theory suggest about V and T?
3　Why might an increase in M have no effect on P?
4　Assume M is £30 billion, V is 4, P is £2 and Y is £60 billion. If M increases to £45 billion, what will happen to P according to the monetarists?

Puzzler

Why do you think that the velocity of circulation increases during the Christmas period? What effect do you think an increase in the velocity of circulation will have on the economy?

I n recent years there has been a shift away from relying on fiscal policy to influence aggregate demand in the short run to greater reliance on interest rate changes. This is one of the monetary policy tools. The other two are changes in the money supply and changes in the exchange rate. The prime aim of monetary policy has been to try to achieve price stability. However, it is also used to achieve the other main government objectives – that is, full employment, economic growth and balance of payments equilibrium.

Changes in the money supply

Measures of the money supply became prominent when the Conservative government of 1979 started to target the growth of the money supply. Measures are still produced today and, while they are not given the prominence they once were, they are still taken into account by the Monetary Policy Committee (MPC). The two main measures of the money supply are:

- M0, which includes notes, coins and high street banks' accounts at the Bank of England, sometimes referred to as the monetary base or narrow money
- M4, which covers the items in M0, plus bank and building society deposits (accounts), sometimes known as broad money.

The amount of money in existence is heavily influenced by the lending policies of the high street banks. When banks lend, they open up deposits for the borrowers. As these deposits can be spent, they are money and are included in the M4 measure of the money supply. Banks lend when they are able to back-up their loans with liquid assets (assets that can be turned into cash quickly and without loss) and when demand for loans is high.

Measures to reduce the growth of the money supply

The Bank of England, acting on behalf of the government, can seek to reduce the growth of the money supply by reducing the ability of the banks to lend and/or by reducing demand for loans. There are a number of policy measures they can implement to achieve this, including the following.

- Open market operations. This involves buying and selling government bonds. If the Bank of England is seeking to restrict bank lending, it will sell government bonds. The intention is to use up some of the banks' liquid assets and thereby reduce their ability to lend.
- Funding. This involves converting government debt from short term to long term with the intention of reducing the value of liquid assets that banks can get hold of.
- Moral persuasion. This involves the Bank of England asking banks to lend less.
- Interest rates. Raising interest rates works on the demand for loans by increasing the price of the loans. This is thought to be the most effective

Synoptic link

This section is based on the understanding of monetary policy you gained from AS sections 2.13 and 2.16.

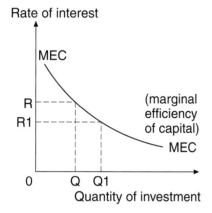

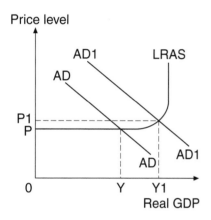

Figure 1: The monetary transmission mechanism

way to control bank lending and is the main way in which the
authorities seek to control the growth of bank deposits.

Monetary transmission mechanism

As noted on pages 186–9, the monetary transmission mechanism is the
process by which changes in the money supply come to affect output,
employment, inflation and the balance of payments. For example, an
increase in the money supply will mean that people will have more money
to spend on financial assets. This will raise the price of financial assets and
reduce the rate of interest.

A rise in the price of financial assets results in a fall in the rate of interest.
Lower interest rates stimulate consumption and investment. They also tend
to reduce demand for the currency, thereby lowering its value, and
increasing demand for exports, and lowering demand for imports.

So three components of aggregate demand are likely to rise. The effect of
the shift to the right of the **AD** curve will depend on the level of output at
which the economy was initially operating. If, for example, the economy
was operating close to full employment, the effect is likely to be to raise
both output and the price level. The monetary transmission mechanism is
illustrated in Figure 1.

Role of the Monetary Policy Committee

The MPC sets the rate of interest with the prime objective of achieving the
government's target rate. Subject to meeting that objective, it has been
instructed to support the economic policy of the government, including its
objectives for employment and economic growth.

The MPC consists of five members drawn from employees of the Bank of
England, including the Governor of the Bank of England, and four
economists nominated by the Chancellor of the Exchequer. It meets monthly
to review evidence on the performance of the economy and indicators of
changes in inflationary pressure. This information includes figures on:

- the current and predicted growth of the money supply
- the exchange rate
- wage rates
- employment
- productivity
- retail sales
- surveys of business
- consumer confidence.

Research task

By assessing relative data,
decide whether the MPC should lower,
raise or leave interest rates unchanged
this month.

If the MPC believes that the information points to the risk that inflation will
rise above the target, it will raise interest rates.

Independence of the Bank of England

The government gave the Bank of England operational independence to set interest rates in May 1997. In January 2000, the newly appointed shadow chancellor, Michael Portillo, stated that the Conservative Party accepted that the Bank of England should remain independent, so now there is agreement between the two main political parties on the issue.

The arguments for permitting the Bank of England to decide on the appropriate level of interest rates are that:

- it has considerable experience in financial markets
- it is more likely to take a longer-term perspective
- it will not be tempted to lower interest rates just prior to an election to win popularity, which permits the government to concentrate on other policy measures.

However, some argue that the Bank of England is too concerned with price stability and is sometimes prepared to sacrifice jobs to pay for it. The independence of the members has also been questioned, as the Governor of the Bank of England and the four economists are appointed by the Chancellor of the Exchequer.

Exam hint

In discussing monetary policy, concentrate on the rate of interest as it is currently the main monetary policy measure used.

Monetary policy stance

A tight (restrictionist or contractionary) monetary policy approach is one that aims to reduce aggregate demand, or at least the growth of aggregate demand, usually in a bid to lower inflation or improve the balance of payments position. In contrast, an expansionary monetary policy approach (loosening monetary policy) is one that encourages a growth in aggregate demand. So reducing the rate of interest would be regarded as an expansionary approach.

Quickies

1 Distinguish between narrow and broad money.
2 Explain two ways in which the Bank of England could seek to reduce the money supply.
3 Why may profitability and liquidity conflict for a bank?
4 Explain three factors that could cause the MPC to consider raising interest rates.

6.14 exchange rate

Countries can operate fixed or floating exchange rates. In the first case, the exchange rate is largely a policy target. In both cases, the exchange rates are influenced by changes in government policy. Changes in the exchange rate can also have a significant impact on the country's inflation rate, unemployment and the balance of payments.

Synoptic link

This section builds on AS sections 2.13 and 2.18. Before you start this section, check your understanding of the exchange rate and exchange rate adjustment.

Definitions

Fixed exchange rate: an exchange rate fixed against other currencies that is maintained by the government.

Floating exchange rate: an exchange rate determined by market forces.

Devaluation: a deliberate reduction in the value of a fixed exchange rate by the government.

Depreciation: a fall in the value of a floating exchange.

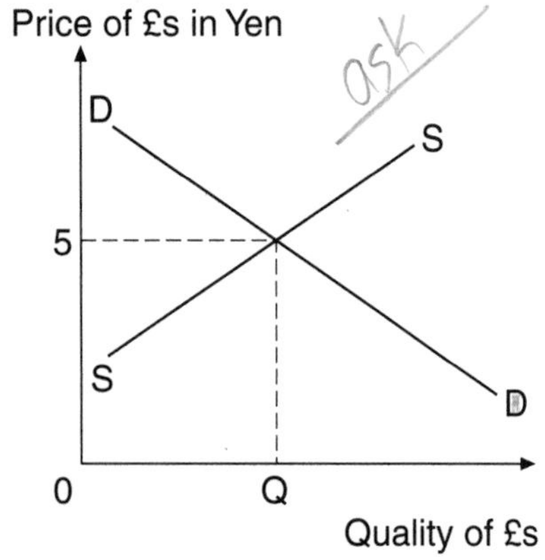

Figure 1: The exchange rate

Thinking like an economist

What action would a central bank take to reduce the exchange rate?

Target

If a government operates a **fixed exchange rate**, the exchange rate is likely to become a policy target or objective. A fixed exchange rate is one where the price of the currency is pegged against other currencies (for example £1 = US$1.5). If the price comes under threat by market forces, the central bank, acting on behalf of the government, will step in to maintain the value by either buying or selling the currency and/or changing its interest rate. For example, Figure 1 shows an exchange rate set at £1 = ¥5. If, perhaps, due to a fall in demand for the country's currency the exchange rate comes under downwards pressure, the government would intervene by buying its currency and/or increasing its interest rate.

A government may also, on occasions, try to influence the value of a **floating exchange rate** if it thinks it is rising too high (to a level that is not sustainable and that is harmful for the economy), falling too low or is too unstable. In this case, it is effectively changing the exchange rate from a floating to a managed exchange rate.

If a government aims to maintain an exchange rate at a certain value, it may have to sacrifice other policy objectives to achieve this. As noted earlier, a government may have to raise the interest rate, and such a measure may reduce output growth and raise unemployment.

Instrument

A government may change the value of a fixed exchange rate from one price to another or it may seek to influence the value of a floating exchange rate. In this case, the exchange rate becomes a policy instrument (tool or measure). For example, a government may undertake a **devaluation** of its fixed exchange rate or encourage a **depreciation** in a floating exchange rate in order to improve the current account of the balance of payments, raise output and/or increase employment.

Effects of exchange rate movements

The first effect of a change in the exchange rate is a change in the price of exports and imports. A rise in the exchange rate will:

- raise the price of the country's exports in terms of foreign currencies
- reduce the price of imports in terms of the domestic currency.

This will put downward pressure on inflation, because the price of imported raw materials will fall, thereby reducing the cost of production and the price of imported finished products that count in the calculation of the country's inflation rate. In addition, domestic firms, facing cheaper imported rival products at home and the prospect of their products becoming more expensive abroad, will be under pressure to cut their costs in order to keep their prices low.

A rise in the exchange rate will improve the **terms of trade**. The sale of each export would enable more imports to be purchased. However, the change in prices will affect demand. If demand for exports is elastic, the revenue earned from selling exports will fall, thereby reducing the overall purchasing power of the country. Elastic demand for exports and imports will also mean that a fall in the value of currency will result in a deterioration of the balance of payments.

Higher priced exports and cheaper imports caused by reducing net exports will lower aggregate demand. A fall in aggregate demand is likely to reduce the rate of economic growth and increase unemployment. A higher exchange rate may, indeed, reduce aggregate demand so much that it results in a reduction in the industrial base of the country. Some firms may not be able to compete at home and/or abroad as a result of the higher exchange rate and some may go out of business.

Frequent changes in the exchange rate can have harmful effects on the economy. Firms will be uncertain how much they will have to pay for imported raw materials and how much they will earn from exporting. This uncertainty is likely to reduce investment and therefore economic growth.

A fall in the exchange rate and balance of payments

A lower exchange rate will make export prices cheaper in terms of foreign currencies, while making import prices higher in terms of the domestic currency. Initially, a lower exchange rate may worsen the country's trade position. This is because it takes time for people to realise that relative prices have changed and to alter their spending plans. In the longer run, when people have had time to recognise that prices have changed and previous orders have expired, demand usually becomes more elastic.

This tendency for the trade position to get worse before it gets better is known as the **J curve effect** and is illustrated in Figure 2. The Marshall-Lerner condition states that for a fall in the exchange rate to be successful in improving the trade position, the combined elasticities of demand for exports and imports must be greater than one.

Definitions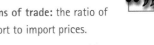

Terms of trade: the ratio of export to import prices.

[handwritten notes:]
Strong Xchange
- low inflation
- BoP deterioration
- loss international competitiveness
- Economic growth falls
- Unemployment falls

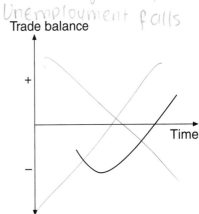
Figure 2: The J curve effect

Definitions

J curve effect: the tendency for a fall in the exchange rate to make the trade position worse before it gets better.

[handwritten notes:]
Weak Xchange
- Improvement in BoP
- Increase employment
- Rise in inflation
- Increase EG

Relationship between the interest and exchange rates

A country's interest rate and its exchange rate are closely linked. If the rate of interest is increased, it is likely that the exchange rate will also rise. This is because a higher exchange rate usually results in an increase in demand and a fall in the supply of the country's currency.

More foreigners will want to buy pounds to place into UK financial institutions to take advantage of the higher returns. Fewer UK citizens will sell pounds to buy foreign currencies to place into foreign financial institutions; they will switch their financial investment to the UK.

A country's exchange rate can be affected indirectly by changes in other countries' and areas' interest rates. For instance, if the European Central Bank and the Federal Reserve Bank of the USA raise their interest rates, the Bank of England is likely to follow suit. This is because the UK government and the Bank of England try to avoid destabilising changes in financial flows into and out of the country.

Again, a higher interest rate is likely to result in a rise in the exchange rate. However, the effect is actually influenced by changes in relative interest rates. If the UK's interest rate rises in line with that of the EU and the USA, the relative interest rate has not changed and the exchange rate may not be affected.

Changes in the exchange rate can also influence the rate of interest. A central bank, for instance, may cut its interest rate if it thinks that the country's exchange rate is rising too much. It may be concerned that the higher exchange rate is putting too much pressure on exporting firms and those firms that compete with imported products.

Research task

Using recent newspaper articles, decide whether the value of the pound sterling is currently thought to be too high, too low or about right.

Only effective if one country on its own increases exchange rates.

Quickies ✔

1 Explain why the government may seek to reduce the exchange rate.
2 Why is an increase in the rate of interest likely to raise the exchange rate?
3 What effect is an unstable exchange rate likely to have on employment?
4 Explain the likely effect on the government's four main macroeconomic objectives of a rise in the exchange rate.

Puzzler

Why might the value of exports still rise despite a high exchange rate?

Taxes have a significant impact on households, firms and the economy as a whole. In assessing this impact it is important to consider the types of taxes imposed, the qualities of a good tax, and the relative merits of direct and indirect taxes.

Types of taxes

Most tax revenue in the UK comes from income tax, followed by value added tax (VAT).

→ As income rises so does tax

- Income tax is a direct and progressive tax; as income rises, both the amount and the percentage that a person pays in tax rises.
- VAT is an indirect and largely regressive tax. It is imposed on the sale of goods and services at different rates. *→ Inequitable - Takes more out of a poor persons income than a rich person*

The standard rate of VAT is 17.5 per cent, but a few items, including sanitary protection, are taxed at 5 per cent. Some products – for example, most foods, children's clothing, prescription medicines, books and newspapers – are zero-rated. This means that the firms selling the products cannot charge VAT but can reclaim any VAT paid on their inputs. Others, including education, finance and health services, are VAT exempt. In this case, the firms do not charge VAT but cannot claim back any VAT they have paid.

Other taxes include excise duty, capital gains tax and inheritance tax.

- Excise duty is an indirect tax imposed on specific products – for example, alcohol, petrol and tobacco. The rate varies depending on the product.
- Capital gains tax is a tax on the increase in the value (difference between purchase and selling price) on items such as shares, property and paintings. A large number of assets are exempt, including agricultural property, private motor cars and winnings from gambling.
- Inheritance tax is a tax on transfers of wealth above a certain amount.

Qualities of a good tax

Four qualities of a good tax were identified by the eighteenth-century economist Adam Smith. He argued that a good tax should be equitable, certain, convenient and economical.

- Equitable. This means that the amount of tax a person or firm pays should be fair. Economists now discuss horizontal and vertical equity. Horizontal equity occurs when people or firms with the same income and financial circumstances pay the same amount of tax. Vertical equity occurs when the amount that people and firms pay is based on their ability to pay, so that people with high incomes pay more than those with low incomes.

Some economists argue that taxes should be based not on the **ability to pay principle** but on the **benefit principle**. The latter suggests that people should pay taxes related to the benefit they receive from public expenditure. It would be relatively easy to apply this principle in connection with services that can be provided privately and that do not have significant externalities.

Synoptic link

This section draws on the knowledge and understanding you gained on AS section 2.12.

Prescription medicines are among the zero-rated VAT products

Research task

Check details on the most recent budget to discover which tax rates have changed and why.

Definitions

Ability to pay principle: the rule that people with higher incomes should pay more in tax.

→ However

Benefit principle: the rule that the amount people pay in tax should be related to the benefit they derive from public expenditure.

It is more difficult to apply when it is hard to estimate who benefits and to what extent they benefit.

- Certain. This means that it should be clear to people and firms how much tax they will have to pay.
- Convenient. The tax should be easy for taxpayers to pay and for the government to collect.
- Economical. An economical tax is one that, relative to the revenue raised, is cheap for people or firms to pay and for the government to collect.

Since Adam Smith's time, economists have added two additional criteria – flexible and efficient.

- Flexible. It must be possible for the tax to be changed relatively quickly in the light of changing market conditions.
- Efficient. An efficient tax is one that increases efficiency in markets. An example of an efficient tax is a Pigouvian tax (see section 6.17).

Exam hint

When considering the impact of taxation on fairness (equity), make sure you discuss both the ability to pay and the benefit principles.

Direct and indirect taxes

In the last two decades there has been a shift in the UK and other EU countries from reliance on direct to indirect taxes. In the UK, income tax rates have been cut while excise duty rates have increased.

Direct taxes are progressive and, depending on their rates, contain a degree of equity. They also help to make the distribution of income more equal. In addition, they help to stabilise economic activity – revenue from direct taxes rises automatically during an economic boom since incomes and profits increase. Tax revenue falls automatically during a recession when incomes and profits decline.

However, governments have reduced their reliance on direct taxes mainly because they believe they can act as a disincentive to work and effort. The argument is that high marginal rates of income tax may discourage some workers from working overtime, some from taking promotion and some workers from entering the labour force altogether. It is also thought that high marginal rates of corporation tax discourage entrepreneurs from expanding their firms and high marginal tax rates on savings reduce the incentive to save. There can also be the problem of savings effectively being taxed twice – once when the income is earned and again when it is saved.

Additionally, direct taxes can take some time to change. For example, changes in income tax rates can take some time to implement, since PAYE (pay as you earn) codes have to be adjusted. Changes in indirect tax can usually be implemented more quickly. It is also claimed that indirect taxes have less of a disincentive effect, since they are based on spending rather than earning and, in part, because they are thought to be less obvious to the payers. They are also difficult to evade.

Taxes can also be used to influence the consumption of particular products. For example, demerit goods can be taxed highly. Indirect taxes, as well as direct taxes, have a stabilising effect, since spending rises in line with the trade cycle. Indirect taxes, however, tend to be regressive.

The zero rating of VAT on some products reduces the regressive effect, but some claim that, overall, VAT takes a higher proportion of the income of the poor. It is also argued that the coverage of excise duty results in horizontal inequity. For example, two families of the same size and with the same income will pay different amounts of tax if one family enjoys walking and reading (which are not taxed) and the other enjoys driving and drinking alcohol (which are taxed).

Indirect taxes can be inflationary if a rise in indirect tax stimulates a further rise in prices. This is thought to be a particular risk with taxes on petrol that feed through to increased costs of production.

Indirect taxes also reduce consumer surplus and distort the pattern of consumption. They may be introduced to eliminate negative externalities. However, unless negative externalities can be measured accurately, there is a danger that indirect taxes will result in a less efficient allocation of resources.

substitution

Thinking like an economist

Analyse the arguments for and against cutting tax on wine.

Depends on what people do.

Taxing the right goods

Hypothecated taxes

A **hypothecated tax** is one that is raised, or raised in part, for a specific purpose. So the revenue, or some of the revenue, is 'ring fenced'. In November 1999, the Chancellor of the Exchequer, Gordon Brown, announced that some of the revenue raised from tobacco duty would be earmarked for the National Health Service to spend directly on fighting smoking-related diseases. It was the first time he had specifically earmarked revenue for public spending, although later that month he also said that any further increases in petrol and diesel duties would be spent on improving public transport.

Hypothecation gives consumers some choice, can give some idea of how much people are prepared to pay for a particular service, and can be used to take money from those creating negative externalities and using it to compensate those who suffer from the negative externalities. However, hypothecation reduces the Chancellor's flexibility in changing tax revenue and government spending to influence economic activity. The revenue earned is itself also subject to changes in economic activity. It is debatable whether many people would want spending on the NHS to fall during a recession, for example. Additionally, there is the question of financing categories of government spending that are less popular than education and health and, if adopted on a large scale, the technical problems of aggregating individual preferences.

Quickies

1. What effect would a shift from direct to indirect taxes be likely to have on the distribution of income?
2. What are the advantages and disadvantages of hypothecated taxes?
3. What are the qualities of a good tax?
4. Is income tax based on the ability to pay principle or the benefit principle?

Public expenditure and the Budget

Synoptic link

This section draws on the knowledge and understanding you gained in AS section 2.12. Before you start this section, check your understanding of public expenditure (government spending).

Definition

Transfer payments: money transferred from one person or group to another not in return for any good or service.

Changes in the level and distribution of public expenditure can have a significant impact on households, firms and the economy as a whole. Public expenditure compared to tax revenue gives the government's budget balance.

Forms of public expenditure

Public expenditure can also be referred to as government spending. It includes spending by both central and local government and public corporations, and can be divided into:

- capital expenditure – on hospitals, schools and roads and so on
- current spending – on the running of public services (including teachers' pay and the purchase of medicines to be used in the NHS)
- **transfer payments** – money transferred from tax payers to recipients of benefits (for example, pensioners and the unemployed)
- debt interest payments – payments made to the holders of government debt (for example, holders of National Savings Certificates).

Capital and current expenditure are sometimes referred to as real or exhaustive expenditure, as they make use of resources directly. When the government builds a new school, it is paying for the use of the land, materials and other resources.

On the other hand, transfer payments and debt interest are non-exhaustive forms of expenditure. In their case, the government is not buying the use of resources, but enabling others to do so, and it is the recipients of the benefits and interest that will determine the use of resources.

Forms of government spending

The four most important areas of government spending are:

- social security payments
- education
- health
- debt interest.

The amount and proportion spent on different items is influenced by a number of factors. For example, spending on social security, while influenced by benefit rates, is much more significantly affected by economic activity. It rises during periods of increasing unemployment and falls during periods of falling unemployment. Expenditure on health and education is affected by government priorities, government policies (for example, the replacement of student grants with loans) and changes in the age composition of the population among other factors.

Debt interest payments are affected by the level of government debt and the rate of interest. Spending on other categories is influenced by a number of factors. For instance, spending on defence rose in 2003 due to Gulf War 2.

The Labour government of 2003 has introduced a comprehensive spending review that decides on the amount that departments can spend over the next three years.

Effects of higher public expenditure financed by borrowing

It is generally thought that higher government spending will lead to a multiple increase in aggregate demand. However, new classical economists argue that an increase in government spending financed by borrowing will not always cause aggregate demand and economic activity to increase. This is because they believe it can lead to 'crowding out', which means that the extra government spending does not add to total expenditure, it merely replaces some private sector spending.

The thinking is that the higher borrowing used to finance the increased spending pushes up demand for scarce funds and thereby raises the rate of interest. The higher rate of interest discourages private sector consumption and investment. It may also cause a rise in the rate of exchange rate, which will further reduce demand for the country's output.

However, Keynesians argue that increased government spending can cause a rise in private sector spending – 'crowding in'. They believe that higher government spending will encourage firms to increase their output, either because the government is buying directly from them or because the recipients of benefits will buy more from them. The higher incomes that arise will result in increased savings, which can finance the borrowing.

Effects of higher public expenditure financed by higher taxation

It might be expected that higher government spending financed by taxation would have a neutral effect on aggregate demand. In practice, this is rarely the case. This is because the recipients of government spending often spend a relatively high proportion of their disposable income, while tax payers, especially high tax payers, tend to spend a lower proportion of their income. So higher public expenditure will tend to increase aggregate demand. If the economy is initially operating below its full capacity output, higher aggregate demand should raise output and employment. It may also have an inflationary impact if output rises close to full capacity.

Changes in the distribution of public expenditure

Even if the level of public expenditure does not change, the government can use its spending to influence economic activity and affect the distribution of income. Increased government spending on unemployment benefits and assistance to areas of high unemployment and decreased compensatory spending on higher education and government offices based in prosperous areas is likely to make income more evenly distributed. It is also likely to increase aggregate demand, as the poor spend more of their income than the rich.

Reduced government spending on higher education may have an adverse effect on aggregate supply and the economy's long-term economic prospects.

Some government benefits are what are known as universal benefits, while others are means tested.

■ Universal benefits are paid to everyone in a certain category – for example, the basic state pension is paid to all those of retirement age. These benefits have the advantage of being cheap to administer. They also avoid the problem of poor take-up, as there is no stigma attached to receiving them and there are no complicated forms to complete by recipients. However, they can be expensive and some who receive them do not really need them.

■ In contrast, means-tested benefits are targeted to particular individuals. They are income related and only paid to those who are considered to be in need of assistance – for example, working families' tax credit. These can be relatively cheap in total. However, they are expensive to administer, often have a low take-up and are frequently disliked by the recipients.

The effect of a switch from universal to means-tested benefits will depend crucially on the rate of take-up and the extent to which the means-tested benefits are changed in value. If there is a high take-up and the level of means-tested benefits is raised, the distribution of income will become more even. However, new classical economists would be concerned about disincentive effects unless relatively stringent conditions were to be attached to the recipient of the benefits.

The Budget

The Budget is presented annually by the Chancellor of the Exchequer, usually in March. To calculate the country's budget position, tax revenue and government spending are compared. A budget surplus arises when tax revenue exceeds government spending. A budget deficit occurs when government expenditure exceeds tax revenue. A budget deficit will increase demand in the economy, as the government is injecting more spending into the economy than it is withdrawing from it.

Quickies

1 Distinguish between exhaustive and non-exhaustive government spending.
2 Identify three possible reasons why the government may increase its spending on health.
3 Why might higher government spending not increase aggregate demand?
4 Is housing benefit a universal or a means-tested benefit?

Puzzler

What effect would a reduction in child benefit and an increase in child tax credit have on the distribution of income?

changes in public expenditure and taxation have effects on particular markets and the economy as the whole. Some of these effects are intentional, but others are not.

Microeconomic effects

A government may raise fuel and vehicle excise duty in an attempt to reduce the growth of road use and thus negative externalities – including pollution, damage to wildlife habitats and congestion. Such a move, however, is also likely to raise firms' costs of production. Indeed, an indirect tax is equivalent to a rise in costs of production and shifts the supply curve to the left. Transport is a significant cost for many firms and firms may find it difficult to switch from using road to rail to move their products and raw materials.

A government may make cuts in income tax to increase incentives in the labour market. However, it is difficult to predict what effect a cut in income tax will have on the number of hours worked. This is because:
- some workers will not be able to change the number of hours they work
- some may chose to work more hours
- some may work less because they can effectively stay on the same wage and therefore enjoy more leisure time.

Imposing different taxes and different rates of tax on products influences the pattern of consumer expenditure. Again, sometimes this is intentional (see below) and sometimes not. For example, while shaving equipment does not have VAT imposed on it because shaving is regarded as an essential activity, sanitary protection carries a five per cent rate of VAT.

Public expenditure also has microeconomic effects. For instance, the government may give a subsidy to encourage the production of a particular industry. A subsidy shifts the supply curve to the right and lowers price, as shown in Figure 1. Throughout the world, one of the most heavily subsidised industries is agriculture.

Pigouvian tax

The **Pigouvian tax** is named after Arthur Pigou (1877–1959), who wrote extensively about economic welfare. It has the prime aim of not raising tax revenue but correcting a negative externality. The tax is imposed to turn the external cost into a private cost and thereby achieve allocative efficiency. However, for the tax to be efficient, it must be possible to measure the external costs accurately. Figure 2 shows that the tax does improve the allocation of resources.

Sin taxes are a form of Pigouvian tax. They are designed to discourage unhealthy living. As well as possibly harming those who partake of them, smoking and drinking alcohol generate negative externalities.

Synoptic link

This section draws on the knowledge and understanding of fiscal policy, the budget and aggregate demand you gained in AS section 2.12.

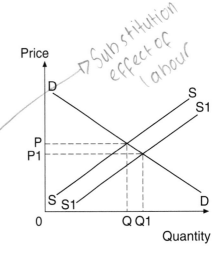

Figure 1: The result of a subsidy shift

Definitions

Pigouvian tax: a tax designed to correct a negative externality.

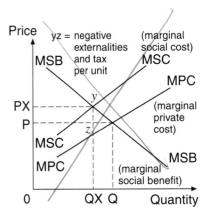

Figure 2: A Pigouvian tax

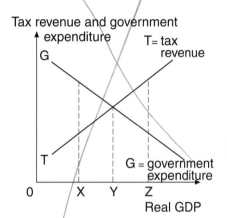

Figure 3: The effect of changes in economic activity on tax revenue and government spending

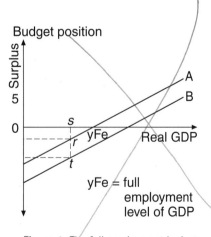

Figure 4: The full employment budget

Fiscal stance

Fiscal policy can have a significant impact on aggregate demand. Fiscal stance refers to whether the government is seeking to raise or lower aggregate demand through its fiscal policy measures. A **reflationary, or expansionary, fiscal policy** is one that is increasing demand. A **deflationary, or contractionary, fiscal policy** aims to reduce aggregate demand.

However, it is harder to assess a government's fiscal stance than might initially appear to be the case. A government may be trying to raise aggregate demand, but may end up with a budget surplus. This is because the budget position is influenced not only by government policy, but also by changes in the level of economic activity.

Figure 3 shows how tax revenue rises and government expenditure falls as real GDP rises. At income level X, there is a cyclical deficit, government expenditure is exeeding tax revenue due to the low level of real GDP. At income level Y, there is a balanced budget. At income level Z, there is a cyclical surplus.

A number of forms of government expenditure and taxation adjust automatically with economic activity to dampen down the fluctuations. These are referred to as automatic stabilisers. For example, spending on Jobseeker's Allowance falls when economic activity picks up. Of course, some forms of government expenditure and taxation are not automatic stabilisers. For example, spending on child benefit is not linked to the economic cycle.

1) helps achieve growth trend

Full employment budget position

To try to assess how a budget's position is influenced by cyclical fluctuations, economists sometimes make use of the full employment budget concept. This plots the budget position that would occur taking into account only cyclical factors achieving a balanced position at full employment – shown in Figure 4 by line A. Then the government's actual budget position is plotted on line B.

If GDP is at *s*, there is budget deficit of *st*. Of this, *sr* is the cyclical deficit component and *rt* is the structural deficit. A structural deficit arises from government policy on taxation and spending. It is the result of government spending being too high relative to tax revenue over the whole economic cycle.

Reflationary and deflationary fiscal policy

A government may implement a reflationary fiscal policy by increasing public expenditure and cutting taxation during a recession.

If the economy is overheating, the government may implement a deflationary fiscal policy by reducing its level of spending and/or raising taxes. However, this may not be that easy, as households and firms get used to higher levels of government spending and do not like tax rises.

Seeking to influence the level of aggregate demand in the economy is sometimes referred to as demand management. Governments do this to create greater stability. They try to act counter-cyclically, injecting extra demand when private sector demand is thought to be too low and reducing its own demand when private sector demand is thought to be too high.

In the past, governments frequently engaged in fine-tuning. This involved short-term changes in government spending and/or taxation with the aim of achieving a precise level of aggregate demand. However, they now accept that fiscal policy cannot be used so precisely, so they may be said to engage in coarse-tuning, which is less frequent changes in policy designed to move the economy in the right direction.

Public Sector Net Borrowing

The **Public Sector Net Borrowing (PSNB)** is the excess of public expenditure over tax revenue. It arises when the government has a budget deficit. To finance such a gap between expenditure and revenue, the government will borrow either from the banking sector (high street banks or the Bank of England) or the non-bank, private sector (households, insurance companies and so on). The government borrows by selling – for example, government bonds and National Savings certificates on which it pays interest. A negative PSNB means that revenue exceeds expenditure. This would enable a government to repay past debt.

Thinking like an economist

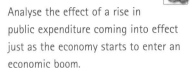

Analyse the effect of a rise in public expenditure coming into effect just as the economy starts to enter an economic boom.

Exam hint

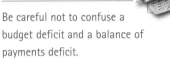

Be careful not to confuse a budget deficit and a balance of payments deficit.

Definitions

Public Sector Net Borrowing (PSNB): excess of public expenditure over revenue.

Quickies

1 Explain two reasons why a government's budget position may move from a deficit into a surplus.
2 What is meant by crowding out?
3 Distinguish between a structural and a cyclical deficit.
4 Explain the relationship between the PSNB and the economic cycle.

Puzzlers

1 Should a tax be imposed on high-fat foods?
2 What might be the consequence of a government confusing a cyclical surplus with a structural surplus?

Changes in fiscal and monetary policy

Synoptic link

This section builds on AS sections 2.12 and 2.13 on fiscal and monetary policy.

In recent years, there have been a number of changes in the operation of UK fiscal and monetary policy caused in part by experience and in part by the government's desire to achieve greater stability.

Current government's fiscal policy

The Labour government of 2003 has stated that its aims for fiscal policy are to:
- raise sufficient revenue to pay for the services that its policies require
- pay necessary interest on national debt while keeping the burden of taxation as low as possible
- promote fairness
- encourage work, saving and investment.

It has also sought to increase stability in fiscal policy by introducing the comprehensive spending review and fiscal policy rules.
- The first is called the 'golden rule'. This is a commitment that, over the economic cycle, the government will only borrow to finance capital spending.
- The second is the 'public debt rule'. This is the requirement to keep public sector debt at 40 per cent of GDP during the period of the economic cycle.

The motives behind promoting stability of government policy is to make it easier for government departments, firms and consumers to plan.

Fiscal policy and the EU

If the government decides to enter the single currency, it would have to accept a limit on any budget deficit to three per cent of its GDP. This could be difficult, especially during a downturn in the economy. UK fiscal policy is already being influenced by its membership of the EU. Under the Conservative government in 1992, the UK entered into an agreement which linked its VAT rates to those in the EU.

There are calls for greater tax harmonisation (that is, the standardisation of tax rates) within the EU. The main argument behind such a move is that for an area to operate as a single market, similar, if not identical, rates of taxes must operate in the different member countries. Without such standardisation, countries can gain a comparative advantage in product, labour and capital markets by operating lower rates of taxation. For example:

- workers may be tempted to work in countries with low income tax rates
- consumers may be tempted to buy in countries with low excise duty
- firms may be tempted to relocate to countries with low corporation tax.

Probably the best-known evidence of the effects of differences in tax rates are the 'booze cruises' – UK citizens travelling to France, where tax rates are lower, to stock up on alcohol and cigarettes.

Thinking like an economist

Explain why tax harmonisation may increase economic efficiency.

Changes in monetary policy

When the Conservative party came to power in 1979, its main priority was to reduce inflation. As the Conservatives believed that inflation was caused by excessive growth of the money supply, they sought to reduce the growth of the money supply. They found this very difficult to achieve, and statistical evidence for the period suggests there was no clear link between the growth of the money supply and inflation. So, in 1990, the emphasis of monetary policy switched to the exchange rate.

In that year, the UK joined the Exchange Rate Mechanism (ERM). This was a pegged exchange rate system in which currencies could vary only by a small amount relative to the other member currencies. The UK went in at a high exchange rate in the belief that this would put downward pressure on domestic inflation. However, the rate was not sustainable and the UK left the ERM in 1992.

It then decided to target inflation and to use the rate of interest to influence its level. (It is thought that setting an inflation target may itself reduce inflationary pressure by persuading firms and consumers that the government is taking a determined approach to keeping inflation low.) This is still the approach of the government, although the responsibility for determining the rate of interest has been given to the Bank of England.

Monetary policy and the EU

Entry into the European single currency means that a country loses autonomy over its monetary policy, since euroland operates one exchange rate and one interest rate. The European Central Bank (ECB) sets the interest rate and can influence the exchange rate. Some commentators have expressed concern that the interest rate policy pursued by the ECB and the value of the euro may not benefit the UK. However, it could be argued that is one of the reasons why it is important for a country's economy to converge with that of euroland before it considers membership.

Even outside euroland, the UK's monetary policy is influenced by the ECB's actions. If, for example, the euro falls in value relative to the pound sterling, the UK's price competitiveness against its main trading partners declines. In addition, if the UK's interest rate falls below that of the ECB's, money may flow out of UK financial institutions into those of the euro area, which would put downward pressure on the value of the pound.

Fiscal and monetary policy

In recent years the main use of macroeconomic policy has been to control the rate of inflation. The main policy instrument used has been the monetary policy instrument of the rate of interest. What are often perceived as fiscal policy measures have actually been used as supply-side measures to increase the trend rate of economic growth. For instance, the bottom rates of income tax have been cut to increase the gap between paid employment and unemployment, and thus increase the incentive to work.

Policy instruments

In considering how to use their policy instruments (also known as measures or tools), governments often take into account **Tinbergen's rule**. Jan Tinbergen, a Dutch economist, argued that a government should use a separate policy instrument for each objective it wishes to achieve. For example, a government wishing to improve the balance of payments position may raise the rate of interest, and to increase employment it may reduce employers' National Insurance contributions.

Quickies

1 What are the advantages of a stable fiscal policy?
2 Explain the government's rules for fiscal policy.
3 Why might an exchange rate be unsustainable?
4 Why did targets for the money supply prove ineffective in reducing inflation?

Puzzler

Why has the government chosen to use the rate of interest as the main measure to influence aggregate demand in the short run?

I n practice, there are a number of reasons why government policy measures may not be as effective as expected. There is also the possibility, particularly in the short run, that there may be conflicts between policy objectives.

Views on government policy

Keynesians believe that markets do not work efficiently. They think that market failure is a real problem. They also think that governments have the appropriate knowledge, skills and tools to intervene and improve the performance of the economy. In contrast, new classical economists argue that markets work efficiently and that there is a real risk that government intervention will make the situation worse. They believe that governments should:

- remove some past policies, laws and regulations that are hampering the smooth working of free market forces
- keep tax low
- concentrate on creating a low inflationary climate, which will provide the basis for achieving the other three macroeconomic objectives of economic growth, low unemployment and a satisfactory balance of payments position.

Government failure

Government failure occurs when government intervention makes the performance of markets worse rather than improving them. As noted earlier, new classical economists, more than Keynesians, believe that government failure is a significant problem. There are a number of possible causes of government failure, including:

- poor quality of information
- the effects of economic theory
- time lags
- unexpected responses
- complexity
- conflicts of objectives
- government self-interest
- rigidities
- policy constraints.

Poor quality of information

If a government lacks information or has inaccurate, information it may make the wrong policy decisions. For example, if the Bank of England wrongly believes that aggregate demand will rise too rapidly in the future, it may raise interest rates now. If the economy is actually on the brink of a recession, this will reinforce the downturn in demand.

The government employs a high number of economists who supply it with analysis and advice. The government also receives advice from other economists working in academia, the media and industry. Some of these

Synoptic link

This section builds on the knowledge and understanding you gained in AS sections 2.12–2.18 on fiscal policy, monetary policy, supply-side policies, policies to reduce unemployment, inflation, promote economic growth and improve the balance of payments.
It is also linked to A2 section 5.18 on government intervention in markets.

Conflicts can occur between supply side and demand side

One sets out to achieve something and a consequence conflicts with the aim of another policy.

economists now use very sophisticated models, but the accuracy of these models is influenced by the information and theories fed into them and how the predictions are interpreted.

In assessing the expected effect of changes in government policies on the economy, economists make use of the concept of the multiplier. This is the relationship between an initial change in aggregate demand and the final change in income. For example, the government may increase its spending by raising the state pension. Pensioners receiving more money will spend some of the extra. The shopkeepers who benefit from the rise in spending will, in turn, spend some of the extra revenue they receive and so on. The size of the multiplier can be measured as either:

$$\frac{\text{Final change in GDP}}{\text{Initial change in AD}} \quad \text{or} \quad \frac{1}{1 - \text{proportion of extra income which is spent}}$$

For example, if people spend 80 per cent (or 0.8) of their extra income, the multiplier would be:

$$\frac{1}{1 - 0.8} = \frac{1}{0.2} = 5$$

Keynesians believe that it is possible to calculate the multiplier reasonably accurately, while new classical economists do not think it is. New classical economists believe it is difficult for a government to assess, in advance, the effect that changes in government spending and taxation will have. They also argue that markets provide higher quality information and provide it more quickly.

Economic theory

The policies adopted are influenced by the economic theories followed by politicians and their economic advisers. However, there are disagreements as to which are the appropriate theories to follow.

Time lags

By the time some government policies take effect, the situation that caused them to be implemented has changed. For example, a government may cut income tax to increase consumer spending but by the time the tax rates are changed, the economy may be entering a boom period. The three main time lags involved with government policy are:

- recognition lag – this refers to the time it takes for a government to recognise there is a problem
- implementation lag – it can take time for a government to decide on the appropriate policy measure and implement
- behavioural lag – this is the time it takes for people and firms to change their behaviour in the light of government policies. For example, a government may cut income tax but people may take time to adjust their spending.

Unexpected responses

Economics is a social science. It deals with people, and people and the firms they run do not always react in the way the government expects or wants. For example, in 1998 the Japanese government cut interest rates and income tax, hoping to stimulate a rise in aggregate demand. However, this failed to materialise because consumers and firms were pessimistic about the future and so actually saved more.

Economists have also noted that targeting can itself alter the behaviour of what is being targeted. This phenomenon was identified in Goodhart's law, which states that any measure of the money supply behaves differently when it is targeted.

Complexity

The world is a complex, increasingly integrated and constantly changing place. Economic growth of a country can be knocked off trend by sudden and unexpected events abroad. For example, a recession in the USA, one of the UK's main trading partners, will reduce UK aggregate demand and so may reduce the UK's economic growth rate and increase its unemployment rate. The UK economy is also significantly affected by the economic performance of the rest of the EU. This is because the EU is the main destination of UK exports and the main source of UK imports. In addition, changes in EU policy, such as reform of the CAP, impact on the UK economy.

Conflicts of objectives

Policy instruments simultaneously affect a number of objectives. So, a rise in income tax designed to reduce inflation may also raise unemployment. However, it is interesting to note here that new classical economists argue that policy objectives do not need to conflict. They think that if the government keeps inflation low, largely by avoiding the temptation for itself to increase aggregate demand, the other three objectives will be achieved.

There is increasing agreement that supply-side policies can, in the long run, help a government to achieve all of its major objectives. The new economic paradigm (see page 158) also holds out the promise of increasing the ease with which all four major objectives can be achieved simultaneously.

Government self-interest

The recommendations and decisions made by politicians and civil servants may be influenced by their own self-interest. For example, a government may receive advice from economists that now would not be an appropriate time to cut income tax. However, if it is approaching a general election, it may go ahead with such a change. Ministers and civil servants might resist cuts in the spending of their department for fear that a smaller department will reduce their status and, in the case of civil servants, their pay.

Rigidities

Thinking like an economist

Analyse the effect on the UK economy of a cut in the rate of interest by the European Central Bank.

As noted earlier, while market conditions are constantly changing it is difficult to change some aspects of government policy. For example, laws take time to change. Some forms of public expenditure are difficult to change. Once a government has started to build a hospital, it is difficult and costly to stop. If governments are reluctant to admit their mistakes, they may continue to spend money on a project that does not have long-term viability.

However, where consumers and firms need to make long-term plans, frequent and large changes in government policies can cause problems. For example, a decision to remove grants to firms that have located in a depressed region three years after they were first announced may put the viability of those firms in question. A doubling of the rate of interest would also cause major problems for those with mortgages.

Policy constraints

Membership of international organisations and increasing globalisation limit the autonomy of national government policy. The UK government cannot impose tariffs on EU members, and its rate of interest cannot be significantly out of line with that of the EU and the USA.

Quickies

1   Why may the objectives of low inflation and low unemployment conflict?
2   Explain three constraints on government policy.
3   Explain how supply-side policies can strengthen the long-term performance of the economy.
4   Why are income tax rates unlikely to be increased just before a general election?

Puzzler

What effect would a decision by the MPC to lower interest rates have at a time when the economy is just beginning to enter a downturn?

The UK economy is operating in a global economy. Advances in technology and reductions in transport costs are enabling UK consumers to access markets throughout the world. UK firms are selling their products throughout the world and locating separate parts of their production processes in a range of countries. However, some people are concerned about the effects of **globalisation**.

The meaning of globalisation

Globalisation means that national barriers are being broken down in terms of:

- where firms make their products
- where people buy their goods and services.

Countries have always traded with each other, but now the scale of the movement of goods and services, ideas and capital investment between countries is increasing rapidly. The production processes and patterns of consumption are becoming more and more integrated. Consumers in, for example, China, France and Nigeria can buy the same products – say, a Manchester United football strip and Coca-Cola. Parts of products, including cars and toys, are being assembled in a number of industrialised and developing countries.

Features of globalisation

Globalisation is manifesting itself through:

- the rapid increase in international trade, which is growing faster than world output
- an increase in FDI – that is, the movement of physical capital between countries.

Other periods – for example, the end of the nineteenth and start of the twentieth centuries – have witnessed rapid increases in international trade and international capital movements, but this time these have also been accompanied by the following.

- The growth of **multinational companies** (MNCs). These are increasingly thinking and operating globally, not only owning plants in different countries but also engaging in the fragmentation of production. This involves MNCs spreading different stages of production around the world, sometimes using their own plants and sometimes a combination of their own plants and other firms' plants. So when the managers of MNCs plan their production processes, they do not simply consider producing a product in one location. Instead, they think transnationally – they consider assembling parts in a range of countries and they use a decentralised management structure.
- An increase in the number of countries producing manufactured goods for export.

The pattern of international trade

6.20

Synoptic link

This section builds on the knowledge and understanding you gained in AS section 2.7 on international trade.

Definitions

"

Globalisation: the development of the world into one marketplace.

Research task

Using the *ONS Monthly Digest of Statistics*, analyse the extent to which China has become a more important trading partner for the UK.

Definitions

"

Multinational companies: a company that produces products in several countries.

Causes of globalisation

Globalisation is occurring as a result of the following.

- Improved communication. Advances in information and computer technology are increasing the ease with which consumers can find out about and buy products from other countries and the ease with which producers can co-ordinate production throughout the world. For example, consumers in the UK now regularly use the Internet to order CDs, books and so on from the USA and other countries. Managers of UK MNCs keep in touch with their staff in other countries using a range of information and computer technology, including e-mail and teleconferencing.
- Reduced transport costs. Over time, with the development of containerisation and increasing use of larger ships and planes, transport costs have been falling.
- Trade liberalisation. Since the Second World War, the barriers to the free movement of goods, services and capital have been reducing.
- Increased competition in manufactured goods. This is coming from developing countries, particularly from the **newly industrialised economies** or countries (NIEs) of South-East Asia such as South Korea and Singapore.
- The rise in skill levels throughout the world. This is enabling MNCs to assemble products and parts of products not only in industrialised countries but also developing countries.

Definition

Newly industrialised economies (NIEs): economies that have experienced a rapid rate of growth of their manufacturing sector – most noticeably, the Asian tigers.

Web link

Find out more about the World Trade Organisation by visiting www.heinemann.co.uk/hotlinks and entering express code 0810P.

Consequences of globalisation

Globalisation is having a number of significant effects, including those that follow.

- It is changing the nature of international trade. An increasingly higher percentage of international trade consists of the exchange of similar products from the same industries (for example, different makes of computers from China to the USA and from the USA to China). A smaller percentage consists of different products from different industries (for example, textiles from India to France and cars from France to India). At the start of the twentieth century, manufactured goods were being exported from Europe and the USA to developing countries in return for raw materials. Now, at the start of the twenty-first century, Europe and the USA are still exporting manufactured goods to developing countries – but in return for manufactured goods.
- It is causing more and more firms to think globally. As already noted, advances in technology and transport are enabling firms to target consumers throughout the world and to operate in a range of countries.
- It is increasing FDI. This is linked to the point above. MNCs are seeking out the lowest cost countries in which to locate production and parts of the production process. Indeed, some are now being referred to as

transnational companies, as they have substantial operations in a large number of countries and have a decentralised management structure.

■ It is increasing the susceptibility of countries to external crises. The increased integration of economies means that the problems in one part of the world quickly spread to other countries. This was seen in the aftermath of 11 September 2001, when the slowdown in the USA economy and the resulting uncertainty contributed to a downturn in economic activity in Europe and East Asia.

■ It is increasing the role of international organisations in overseeing world trade, including the World Trade Organization (WTO) and the International Monetary Fund (IMF). The WTO was formed in 1995, replacing the General Agreement on Tariffs and Trade (GATT). It seeks to reduce tariffs and other restrictions on international trade, and provides a means by which countries can settle their trade disputes. The IMF was established in 1947 with the main aim of encouraging world trade. It acts as an international bank offering assistance to countries in financial difficulties.

■ It is changing countries' comparative advantage (see section 6.21). The rise in the level of competition coming particularly from the newly industrialised economies is causing a shift in resources in Europe and the USA.

■ It is reducing price differences between countries. A market is said to be completely integrated when identical products sell at the same price in different countries.

Thinking like an economist

Analyse the effects that globalisation is likely to bring about in demand for labour in industrialised countries and in developing countries.

Encourages efficiency
Fall in unemployment
low inflation
Increase in consumer surplus
Affect BoP → but is
dependant
Comparative advantage
• Exploit labour intensive
  countries →Inequity
• Negative externalities,
  Pollution
• Too dependant of good
  relations between countries
• Susceptability of countries
  to external crisis.
[• Harsh on infant industries]
Oligopoly type
  situation

Quickies ✓

1 What is causing globalisation to occur?
2 Explain two possible advantages and two possible disadvantages of globalisation for UK consumers.
3 Why do countries trade with each other?
4 What factors could slow down globalisation?

Puzzler

Will globalisation lead to greater international prosperity or greater international inequality?

Comparative advantage

As section 6.20 noted, international trade continues to grow. The principle of **comparative advantage** illustrates the benefits of international trade. It has to be remembered, though, that international trade may generate costs as well as benefits.

Absolute advantage

In the past, some international trade could have been explained in terms of **absolute advantage**. A country is said to have an absolute advantage in producing a product when it is better at producing it than other countries. More technically, it means that it can produce more of the product from each unit of resource than other countries – that is, it has a greater productivity.

Table 1 is based on the assumption that there are ten workers in the USA and ten in Malaysia. Initially, each country divides its workers equally between car and rubber production. It is further assumed that each worker in the USA can make either six cars or ten units of rubber, and each worker in Malaysia can make either two cars or sixty units of rubber.

The table shows that the USA has the absolute advantage in the production of cars, as it can make three times as many cars per worker as Malaysia; alternatively, Malaysia has the absolute advantage in rubber production, as it can make six times as much rubber per worker as the USA.

	Output	
	Cars	Rubber
USA	30	50
Malaysia	10	300
Total	40	350

Table 1: Position before specialisation and trade

In this case, it is clear that the USA should specialise in the production of cars and Malaysia in the production of rubber. Both countries would gain as a result of specialisation and trade. In our simplified example, if the USA now specialised in cars and Malaysia in rubber, output would rise to the levels shown in Table 2.

	Output	
	Cars	Rubber
USA	60	–
Malaysia	–	600
Total	60	600

Table 2: Position after specialisation

Synoptic link

This section explains the basis of international trade. AS section 2.7 described the main features of UK international trade.

Definitions

Comparative advantage: relative efficiency – the ability to produce a product at a lower opportunity cost than other regions or countries.

Absolute advantage: the ability to produce output using fewer resources than other regions or countries.

Rubber tapping in Malaysia – Malaysia has an absolute advantage in rubber production

The USA could then export twenty cars to Malaysia in return for two hundred rubber units, and both countries would be better off in comparison to the situation before specialisation and trade – see Table 3.

	Consumption	
	Cars	Rubber
USA	40	200
Malaysia	20	400
Total	60	600

Table 3: Position after specialisation and trade

Comparative advantage

Although absolute advantage explains a small amount of current international trade, most is now based on comparative advantage. A large proportion of the UK's trade, for example, is with countries producing products that the UK is either making or could make in fairly similar quantities per worker. As implied in section 6.20, globalisation is also increasing the imports of manufactured goods from NIEs.

As its name suggests, comparative advantage is concerned with relative efficiency. A country may have an absolute advantage or an absolute disadvantage in more than one product. It is said to have a comparative advantage in a product when it is even better at making that product or not so bad at making the product. This can also be expressed in terms of opportunity cost. A country has a comparative advantage if it can produce it at a lower opportunity cost than another country.

The principle or theory of comparative advantage states that both countries will benefit from specialisation and trade, even if one country is more efficient at making both products, as long as there is a difference in its relative efficiencies.

Table 4 assumes there are ten workers in the USA and ten in Malaysia, and that the workers are divided equally between the two products. In the USA, each worker can make either six cars or 120 toys. In Malaysia, each worker can make either two cars or eighty toys.

	Output	
	Cars	Toys
USA	30	600
Malaysia	10	400
Total	40	1,000

Table 4: Position before specialisation and trade

Exam hint

Including a simple numerical example helps to explain comparative advantage.

The USA has the absolute advantage in the production of both goods. However, its comparative advantage lies in the production of cars. It can produce three times as many cars as Malaysia, but only 1.5 times as many toys. The opportunity cost of one car in the USA is lower than in Malaysia, twenty toys as opposed to forty toys.

Malaysia's comparative advantage is in toys. It can produce two-thirds as many toys as the USA, but only one-third as many cars, and it has a lower opportunity cost in the production of toys.

Table 5 shows the situation if the USA concentrates mainly on car production, devoting eight workers to car production and two to toy production, with Malaysia specialising completely in toy production. This specialisation has caused total output to rise.

	Output	
	Cars	Toys
USA	48	240
Malaysia	–	800
Total	48	1,040

Table 5: Position after specialisation

Countries will benefit from trade if the exchange rate lies between their respective opportunity cost ratios. If it does not, the countries would gain more of a particular product by switching its own resources. For example, if the USA wanted more toys and it could only exchange one car for ten toys through international trade, it would be better moving workers from car production to toy production. However, if the exchange rate does lie between the opportunity cost ratios, both countries can gain. Table 6 shows the position if the exchange rate is one car for thirty toys and the USA exports thirteen cars.

	Consumption	
	Cars	Toys
USA	35	630
Malaysia	13	410
Total	48	1,040

Table 6: The position after specialisation and trade

Limitations of the principle of comparative advantage

While the principle of comparative advantage highlights the importance of differences in relative productivity, it does have its limitations in explaining the pattern of international trade that actually occurs.

It is often expressed, as here, in terms of a few countries and a few products. Of course, in the real world, as there are many countries, many products and as situations are always changing, it is more difficult to work out where comparative advantages lie.

The principle ignores transport costs that may outweigh any comparative advantage, particularly in terms of heavy products. However, as noted earlier, one feature of globalisation is reduced transport costs.

The principle also assumes constant opportunity cost ratios and productivity as resources are shifted. Therefore, in our example shown in Table 5, when Malaysia doubled the number of workers producing toys, the output of toys doubled. However, in practice the workers most suited to toy production are likely to be employed first, so that when more are employed, these are likely to be less productive. This would mean that the opportunity cost of increasing toys would rise and so the returns from specialisation would be reduced.

The benefits of specialisation and trade are also reduced in the real world by the existence of import restrictions and, for some countries, by differences in bargaining power. A country may have a comparative advantage in a particular product, but may have difficulties exporting it because other countries impose tariffs, quotas or other trade restrictions on it. Developing countries may also find that exchange rates are set in a way that disadvantages them.

In addition, a country may not specialise to the extent that the principle suggests because it may wish to keep a more diversified industrial structure in order to reduce the risks arising from sudden shifts in demand and supply. There are a number of other reasons why a country may seek to maintain industries in which it does not currently have a comparative advantage, including strategic industries and new industries. These are examined in more detail in section 6.22.

Quickies

1. Distinguish between absolute and comparative advantage.
2. Why might a country have a low cost of employing labour per unit hour but still have high unit wage costs?
3. What causes comparative advantage to change?
4. What are the advantages of having a comparative advantage in knowledge-based industries?

Handwritten margin notes:

Ignores transport costs
Does not take into account other countries and goods.
↳ Only assumes two goods and two countries.

• Does not take into account the process of fragmentation

• Marginal physical product for each worker is different

• Does not take into account restrictions.

need different Δ skills to produce different goods.

Δ • Some countries may wish to stay diversified, in order to not be too dependant

Benefits and costs of international trade

Synoptic link

This section develops the knowledge and understanding you gained in the previous two A2 sections.

Globalisation is interlinked with comparative advantage

In section 6.21, the nature of comparative advantage was examined. In this section, the effects of globalisation on comparative advantage are discussed. The benefits and costs of international trade are also considered.

Globalisation and comparative advantage

As noted in section 6.20, globalisation is changing countries' comparative advantage. Developing countries are becoming more efficient at producing manufactured goods. Their comparative advantage at the moment is mainly in manufacturing industries that make use of low skilled labour. They have a large supply of low-skilled workers, which means their wage rates are lower.

In the past this did not result in a comparative advantage because although wages were low, so was productivity and as a result, unit wage costs were high. However, now with rises in productivity, particularly in NIEs, unit wage costs have been falling. Some commentators have expressed the concern that this will result in a rise in unemployment and a fall in wages in industrialised countries. Their fear is that multinational companies will locate more of their processes in developing countries, and that developing countries' firms will gain a larger share of the market for manufactured goods.

However, this is only part of the picture. It is not so much that industrialised countries are facing a fall in demand for their output, but that a shift in demand from some products towards other products results from changes in relative efficiencies. Resources will have to shift to reflect these changes and this process is already underway.

Average wages are not falling in most industrialised countries, but the wages of unskilled workers are falling relative to those of skilled workers. Industries producing goods and services requiring high skilled labour are experiencing rises in demand, while some relying on low skilled labour are facing lower demand. In the case of the UK, some processes are being relocated to lower production cost countries, but at the same time FDI is being attracted by the high skilled labour force of the country.

Therefore, while jobs requiring low skill levels are declining, jobs requiring high skill levels are increasing. To ease the shift in resources, educational and vocational qualifications need to rise.

Of course, the situation is always changing, and economies and their citizens have to be adaptable. Currently, the UK has a comparative advantage in, for example, oil, financial services, business services and scientific instruments. However, in a few years' time, with skill levels rising throughout the world and patterns of demand and supply changing, this may alter.

Benefits and costs of international trade

If countries specialise and trade, total output should be greater than otherwise. The resulting rise in living standards is the main benefit claimed for free international trade.

Consumers can benefit from the lower prices and higher quality that result from the higher level of competition that arises from countries trading internationally. They also enjoy a greater variety of products – including a few not made in their own countries.

Although firms will face greater competition in their domestic markets, they will also have access to larger markets in which to sell their products (enabling them to take greater advantage of economies of scale) and from which to buy raw materials.

However, despite all these advantages and increasing trade liberalisation, restrictions on exports and more particularly imports still exist. This is explained, for example, by governments being concerned that certain undesirable products may be imported, that the continued existence of new and strategic industries may be threatened and other countries may not engage in fair competition. These points are examined in more detail in section 6.23.

International trade provides countries with challenges. Competition from other countries and access to their markets results in some industries contracting and some expanding. This requires the shifting of resources, which can be unsettling and may be difficult to achieve due to, for example, occupational immobility of labour.

Thinking like an economist

Explain three benefits a UK insurance company could gain from engaging in international trade.

Quickies

1 Why is productivity rising in NIEs?
2 Why does the UK no longer have a comparative advantage in textiles?
3 What is the main benefit of international trade?
4 Which firms benefit from international trade?

Puzzler

Why did James Dyson relocate his vacuum manufacturing firm from Swindon to Malaysia?

Synoptic link

Before starting this section it would be useful to look over AS section 2.18 on import restrictions.

Definition

Protectionism: the restriction on the free movement of products between countries.

Tariff: a tax on imports.

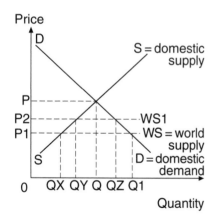

Figure 1: The effect of a tariff

Free trade occurs when there are no restrictions imposed on the movement of goods and services into and out of countries. In contrast, **protectionism** refers to the deliberate restriction of the free movement of goods and services between countries and trade blocs. A government engages in protectionism when it introduces measures to protect its own industries from competition from the industries of other countries. The methods of protection can be divided into **tariffs** and non-tariff measures.

Tariffs

Tariffs (which can also be called customs duties or import duties) are taxes on imported products. They can be imposed with the intention of raising revenue and/or discouraging domestic consumers from buying imported products. For example, the EU's common external tariff, which is a tax on imports coming into the EU from countries outside, does raise revenue but its main purpose is to encourage EU member countries to trade with each other.

Tariffs can be *ad valorem* (percentage taxes) or specific (fixed sum taxes). The effect of imposing a tariff is to raise the price to consumers and, in the absence of any retaliation, shift demand from imports to domestically produced products.

Figure 1 shows the effect of a specific tariff. Before the country engages in international trade, price is P and the quantity purchased is Q, all of which comes from domestic suppliers. When the country engages in international trade, the number of producers in the market increases significantly. The increase in competition drives price down to P1.

The quantity demanded extends to Q1. Of this amount, QX is now bought from domestic suppliers and QX–Q1 from foreign firms. So domestic supply falls from Q to QX.

The imposition of a tariff causes the world supply to decrease to WS1. It raises the price to P2 and causes the quantity to be purchased on the domestic market to fall to QZ. Domestic supply rises to QY and imports fall to QY–QZ. Domestic producers gain but this is at the expense of domestic consumers.

Non-tariff measures

These include:

- quotas
- voluntary export restraint or restriction (VER)
- exchange control
- embargoes
- import deposit schemes
- time-delaying customs procedures
- quality standards
- government purchasing policies
- subsidies.

Quotas

A **quota** is a limit on the supply of a good or service. It can be imposed on exports. For example, a developing country may seek to limit the export of food during a period of food shortages. However, quotas on imports are more common. For example, a quota may place a restriction on the imports of cars to, say, 40,000 a year or alternatively to, say, £400,000 worth of cars.

The effect of a quota is to reduce supply. This is likely to push up price. Foreign firms will experience a reduction in the quantity they can sell, but they may benefit from the higher price if demand for their products is inelastic and if the quotas are not operated via the selling of import licences.

Voluntary export restraint or restriction (VER)

This measure is similar to a quota, but this time the limit on imports arises from a voluntary agreement between the exporting and importing countries. A country may agree to restrict its exports in return for a similar limit being put on the exports of the importing country or to avoid more damaging import restrictions being imposed on its products. VERs have been used frequently by the EU and the USA. For example, the EU entered into several VERs with Japan, which restricted the sale of Japanese cars.

Exchange control

A government or an area may seek to reduce imports by limiting the amount of foreign exchange made available to those wishing to import goods and services or to invest or to travel abroad. This measure was used by a number of European countries, including the UK, in the 1960s and 1970s and is still found in some developing countries.

Embargoes

An embargo is a ban on the export or import of a product and/or a ban on trade with a particular country. For example, a country:
- may ban the export of arms to a country with a poor human rights record
- may prohibit the importation of hard core pornography
- is likely to break off trading relations with a country during a military conflict.

Import deposit schemes

The UK made use of import deposit schemes in the 1960s. These schemes involve requiring importers to deposit a given sum of money with a government before they can import products. The intention is to increase the cost, in terms of time and money, of importing.

Problems

- Retaliation.

- Encourages inefficiency
- Loss of consumer surplus/ choice/soveirgnty

- Protects domestic jobs, unemployment low
- Generate equitable world
  ↳ Extortion

- Enable infant industries to develop.
- Raise government revenue

Time delaying customs procedures

These are designed to have a similar effect as import deposit schemes. If it takes time to complete long and complex customs forms, it will be more expensive to import products.

Quality standards

A government may use quality standards as a means to limit imports. They may set high and complex requirements with the intention of raising the costs of foreign firms seeking to export to the country.

Government purchasing policies

A government may try to reduce imports by favouring domestic firms when it places orders, even when the domestic firms are producing at a higher cost or lower quality.

Subsidies

Subsidies given to domestic firms may be used as an indirect way of protecting them. The subsidies may enable relatively high cost domestic firms to undercut more efficient foreign firms in the domestic market.

Arguments for protection

Several arguments can be put forward for imposing restrictions on free trade. These include:

- raising revenue
- protecting the whole industrial base of the country
- protecting particular industries
- recently, protecting domestic standards of, for example, food safety, environment and labour market conditions.

Revenue raising

The imposition of tariffs enables governments to raise revenue. This is no longer a major motive behind industrial countries imposing import duties, but the revenue received by some developing countries is a significant proportion of their tax revenue.

Protecting the whole industrial base

Arguments for protecting the whole industrial base include the following.

- Protecting domestic employment. It was thought that if a country imposed import restrictions, it would mean that its citizens would purchase more domestic products and thereby raise domestic employment. This concentration on domestic employment at the expense of other countries led to such measures being referred to as 'beggar my neighbour' policies. However, imposing import restrictions is likely to result in a reduction in other countries' abilities to buy the country's exports and may provoke retaliation. So the country's exports may decline and any jobs created by imports may be offset by jobs lost due to the fall in exports. The level of unemployment may rise if the imposition of tariffs results in a trade war, with countries raising their tariffs higher and higher – building 'tariff walls' round their countries. There will also be a welfare loss resulting from countries not being able to specialise to any great extent in those products that give them a comparative advantage.

- Improving the country's balance of payments position. One reaction to a situation where expenditure on imports exceeds revenue from exports is to place restrictions on imports. The intention is to switch domestic expenditure from imports to expenditure on domestic products. However, the same risks and disadvantages apply as above – it may provoke a price war and it reduces the degree of specialisation. In addition, imposing import restrictions in the absence of any other policy measures does not solve the cause of the balance of payments deficit. If domestic consumers are purchasing imports because their quality is higher, for example, they may still continue to buy imports.

- Protecting the country's industries from 'unfair low wage competition' from abroad. This would involve restricting imports from certain countries. Some argue that if the wages paid to workers in developing countries are very low, then firms in industrial countries will not be able to compete unless they reduce wages to unacceptably low levels. Competition from low wage countries may also reflect the fact that those countries have a comparative advantage in low-skilled, labour intensive industries. Unemployment in certain industries may rise, but the rise in unemployment may be a temporary situation if that labour can move into the industries in which the country does have a comparative advantage.

  The case for imposing restrictions has more justification where wages are being held below the equilibrium rates, the working conditions are poor and child or slave labour is employed.

- Improving the terms of trade. If a country is a dominant buyer of a product or products, then placing restrictions on imports may force the sellers to lower their prices in order to remain competitive on the domestic market. If this occurs, the country will be able to purchase its imports more cheaply.

Key concepts

The argument to protect domestic employment was used by a number of countries in the 1930s, when countries in the West were going through a depression.

Key concepts

Low wages do not always mean low unit wage costs. Due to a lack of capital equipment and education, labour productivity in a number of countries is low.
Being able to sell products without restrictions to industrial countries may enable income levels to rise in developing countries. This may result in their levels of investment, education, wages and purchases of products from industrial countries rising.

Key concepts

The terms of trade refers to the relationship between a country's export and import prices and is measured by:

$$\frac{\text{Index of export prices} \times 100}{\text{Index of import prices}}$$

Protecting particular industries

Arguments for protecting particular industries include the following.

■ To prevent **dumping**. Dumping occurs when firms sell their products at less than cost price. Foreign firms may engage in dumping because government subsidies permit them to sell at very low prices or because they are seeking to raise profits by price discriminating. In the latter case, the initial reason for exporting products at a low price may be to dispose of stocks of the good. In this case, consumers in the importing country will benefit. However, their longer-term objective may be to drive out domestic producers and gain a strong market position. In this case, consumers are likely to lose out as a result of the reduction in choice and the higher prices the exporters feel able to charge.

■ To enable **infant industries** to grow. Infant industries (which are also called sunrise industries) are newly established industries. The firms in such industries may find it difficult to develop because their average costs may be higher than their well-established foreign competitors. However, if they are given protection in their early years, they may be able to grow and thereby take greater advantage of economies of scale, lower their average costs and become competitive. At this stage the protection could be removed. The infant industry argument is thought to be particularly strong in the case of high technology industries, which have high fixed costs and a potential comparative advantage. However, there is a risk that the industries may become dependent on protection.

■ To permit declining industries to go out of business gradually. Declining industries (also called sunset industries) are likely to be industries that no longer have a comparative advantage. However, if they go out of business quickly there may be a sudden and large increase in unemployment. Protection may enable an industry to contract gradually, thereby allowing time for resources, including labour, to move to other industries.

■ To enable industries to regain their comparative advantage. Industries may have lost their comparative advantage due to a lack of investment. A case may be made to protect them temporarily while additional investment is made.

■ To protect strategic industries. This is more of a political than an economic argument. Many countries believe it is important to have a degree of self-sufficiency in certain industries, including arms and agriculture, in case disputes or military conflicts cut off supplies.

Protecting domestic standards

Countries have traditionally placed restrictions, including embargoes, on demerit goods – for example, drugs and pornography. However, in recent years domestic regulations on food safety, labour conditions and environmental standards have increasingly been acting as trade restrictions.

Although countries may be keen on free trade in theory, in practice many are reluctant to compromise domestic policy in sensitive areas such as genetically modified foods.

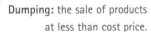

Definition

Dumping: the sale of products at less than cost price.

Definition

Infant industry: a newly established industry that has not yet grown large enough to take full advantage of the available economies of scale.

Making connections

Identify three internal economies of scale that a newly established car company is likely to be able to take advantage of.

Trade blocs

The breakdown of trade barriers has actually occurred mainly within groups of countries operating as trade blocs. There are four main types of trade blocs, with increasing degrees of integration:

- free trade areas
- customs unions
- common markets
- economic and monetary union.

Free trade areas

Countries within a free trade area remove restrictions between each other but are free to operate whatever trade restrictions they wish on non-members. The members have to make some provision, usually via maintaining customs points, to prevent imports to the area coming in via the country with the lowest tariffs.

Examples of free trade areas include the North American Free Trade Agreement (NAFTA) consisting of Canada, the USA and Mexico. There is also ASEAN (Association of South East Asian Nations), which consists of Brunei, Indonesia, Malaysia, the Philippines, Singapore and Thailand.

Customs unions

The members of a customs union not only remove trade restrictions between each other but also agree to operate the same import restrictions on non-member countries. An example is MERCOSUR, which consists of Brazil, Argentina, Paraguay and Uruguay, and operates a common external tariff.

Common markets

These not only have no import restrictions between member countries and a common external tariff, but also permit the free movement of labour and capital between its members. In 1986, the Single Market Act was signed which moved what was then the EC, but has since become the EU, towards a single market.

Economic and monetary union (EMU)

This takes integration several stages further by introducing a single currency, similar labour market policies and some degree of tax harmonisation. The Maastricht Treaty of 1992 started the move of the EU towards EMU.

Trade blocs and conflicts

As the EU has become more integrated and a more powerful economic force, it has come into conflict with the USA and NAFTA. The USA complains particularly about the EU's protection of its farming and film industries.

Exam hint

In answering essay questions on the arguments for and against protectionism, make sure you focus on the arguments. Do not devote too much time to only describing the methods of protection.

In 1997 and 1998, the US protested to the WTO about the privileged market access given to the export of bananas from former British and French colonies in Africa, the Caribbean and Pacific under the Lome convention at the expense of cheaper Latin American bananas.

In 1999, it imposed retaliatory tariffs of more than US$190 million on a range of European goods after the EU failed to comply with a WTO ruling requiring it to restructure its banana import regime to prevent the discrimination against Latin American exporters.

The EU, in turn, is concerned about noise levels caused by US aeroplanes, hormone-treated beef and genetically modified food. The start of the 2000s saw a trade dispute over the EU's ban on US hormone-treated beef.

Countries outside trade blocs, particularly developing countries, feel discriminated against. They do not enjoy any of the benefits of belonging to a trade bloc, but have restrictions imposed on their products by the EU, USA and other countries.

The role of the WTO

The WTO, which currently has 136 member countries, seeks to promote trade liberalisation through a series of negotiations (which are often referred to as rounds). For example, the Uruguay Round achieved agreement to reduce trade barriers in textiles. The WTO also operates a trade dispute-settlement mechanism, which is binding on member countries.

The role of the WTO has been criticised by developing countries, who argue that the rounds have benefited mainly industrial countries by devoting more attention to reducing the tariffs imposed mostly by developing countries. For example, tariffs on tobacco have been reduced to four per cent while tariffs on tobacco products remain at forty per cent.

Thinking like an economist

Why do you think tariffs are higher on cigarettes and coffee than on tobacco and coffee beans?

Developing countries argue that the differential has nothing to do with health concerns, but is concerned with keeping industrial processing, where higher profits are made, in the West. They also claim that the WTO, by allowing industrial countries to impose restrictions on dumping in certain circumstances, is often enabling those countries to protect jobs in sensitive industries, which would prove politically unpopular if allowed to decline.

Quickies

1   What factors influence the effect of a tariff on domestic output?
2   Assess four arguments that could be advanced for protecting a UK industry.
3   Distinguish between a free trade area and a customs union.

T he two main components of the balance of payments are the current account and the financial account (which is still often referred to by its old name of the capital account). Both of these sections are affected significantly by both short-term and long-term capital flows.

The section of the balance of payments

As noted in AS section 2.7, the balance of payments account consists of a number of sub-groups. These are:

- the current account   *— Invisible*
- the capital account
- the financial account.

The current account is influenced by:

- the international competitiveness of the goods and services produced
- the amount of income earned and paid on overseas investments and financial assets and liabilities.

The capital account is a term now applied to a relatively small account that includes, for example, debt forgiveness and the purchase and sale of copyrights.

The much more important financial account covers the flow of investment into and out of the UK – including direct investment, a significant amount of which is carried out by multinational companies.

Short-term international capital flows

Short-term international capital flows involve money going into and out of an economy to take advantage of changes in interest rates and exchange rates. For example, if UK banks are paying out relatively high interest rates, some foreign individuals and firms are likely to buy pounds to open up accounts in UK banks.

Similarly, the expectation that the value of the pound will rise in the near future will increase demand for the pound. When money flows into the UK, the value of the pound rises. UK financial institutions will also benefit.

However, short-term capital flows can be destabilising. This is because the money can be pulled out quickly if interest rates or exchange rates change, or if expectations about future interest rates and exchange rates change.

Long-term international capital flows

Much of the money invested in a country for the long term is accounted for by foreign direct investment (FDI). UK multinational companies invest abroad and foreign multinational companies invest in the UK. This investment includes:

Synoptic link

This section is based on AS section 2.7.

How exchange rates and interest rates affect the BoP

Thinking like an economist

Analyse the effect that a fall in the US rate of interest may have on the value of the pound.

- the establishment of new plants
- the expansion of existing plants
- the purchase of existing plants and firms.

Multinational companies seek the highest return on their capital. So the amount of foreign direct investment attracted by a country is influenced by the productivity and flexibility of its workers, its tax rates, the stability of its economic policies, its rate of economic growth, the size of its market and the perception of its future economic prospects.

The UK is currently an attractive location for FDI because of:

- government grants – especially for multinationals setting up in the poorer regions of the UK
- its flexible labour force
- its time zone advantage in financial services
- its membership of the EU; setting up in the UK gives, for example, a Japanese or US multinational company access to the EU market without having to pay the common external tariff, but, as noted in section 6.26 of the AS book, some economists believe that if the UK continues to stay out of the single currency, FDI may be reduced
- the use of the English language; this is the main language of the Internet and is frequently used in international business. In addition, it is spoken by Americans and is the most popular foreign language learnt by the Japanese and South Koreans.

Handwritten margin note: Output/worker employed

Handwritten margin note: Adaptability of workers to adopt to changes in A.D.& A.S

Making connections

Explain why advances in technology are increasing FDI throughout the world.

Handwritten margin notes:
How to reduce trade balance deficit

- Protectionism
- Weaken currency
- Subsidies / Govt Spending
- Interest rates both up & dwn

Effects of foreign direct investment

The effects of FDI include the following.

- An initial inflow of investment, which will appear as a credit item in the financial account. However, in the longer run, money will flow out of the country in the form of investment income (profit, interest and dividends), which will appear in the current account. The goods and services that the multinational company sells abroad will count in the country's exports. The net effect on imports is rather more uncertain. Some goods and services that had previously been bought abroad from the MNCs may now be purchased from their plants in the home country. However, the MNC may purchase some of their raw materials and services from their home countries.
- MNCs may cause a rise in employment. This is one of the key reasons that governments give grants to MNCs to set up in their countries. They hope that the MNCs will increase employment directly by taking on workers and indirectly by increasing economic activity and demand in the area in which they are based. However, some of those employed by the MNCs, particularly in top management posts, may be bought over from the home country. Even more significantly, if the competition from MNCs leads to domestic firms going out of business, they will not be creating employment, merely replacing jobs.

- MNCs, especially in developing countries, can help to spread knowledge and understanding of recent technological advances. A high proportion of MNCs are high tech, capital intensive firms.
- MNCs can bring in new ideas of management techniques. The establishment of Japanese and South Korean MNCs in a range of countries has resulted in their host countries reviewing their management styles (see page 63).
- MNCs' output counts in the home country's GDP and, in many cases, their contribution to output and growth is significant.
- MNCs tend to have high labour productivity. This is mainly because of high capital/labour ratios. This may encourage domestically owned firms to raise their productivity levels and may reduce inflationary tendencies.
- A rise in tax revenue may occur, but some MNCs try to reduce their tax payments by moving revenue around their plants in different countries in order to minimise their payments.
- Pollution levels may rise. This is particularly the case in developing countries where MNCs may locate in order to get round tighter environmental regulations at home. MNCs may also be attracted by less strict labour market policies in terms of working hours, health and safety, minimum wages and lowest working age.

Research task

In a group, research the impact that MNCs are having in your area.

International competitiveness

MNCs that do introduce new technology will help to raise the international competitiveness of a country. International competitiveness can be defined as the ability of a country's firms to compete successfully in international markets and thereby permit the country to continue to grow.

Sometimes, referring to a country being internationally competitive is taken to mean that it can produce products more cheaply than most other countries. However, it is more commonly taken by economists in a wider context to include competitiveness in terms of quality and marketing.

Indicators of international competitiveness

In assessing how internationally competitive an economy is, economists examine a range of indicators – including the following.
- Growth rates. Competitive economies tend to grow faster than non-competitive ones because their products are in high world demand.
- Productivity levels. Higher productivity levels increase the country's productive capacity and allow long-term growth to occur.
- Unit labour costs. This is obviously linked to productivity levels. If output per worker rises more rapidly than wages and other labour costs, unit labour costs will fall.

- Share of exports in world trade. It is becoming increasingly difficult for an industrial country to maintain its share of world trade in the face of increasing competition from a number of developing countries, particularly the NIEs.
- Balance of trade in goods and services. This is linked to the point above. A competitive country is not likely to have a large deficit on its trade in goods and services balance.
- Investment as a proportion of GDP. Investment is seen as an important cause of economic growth.
- Education and training. As with investment, these are thought to be very important indicators. A country with high quality education and training is likely to have a flexible, high skilled and highly productive labour force.
- Investment in research and development. High levels of expenditure on research and development are likely to develop and encourage the implementation of new technology.
- Communications and infrastructure. Good communications and infrastructure will increase the efficiency of firms by lowering their costs and increasing their speed of response to changes in market conditions.
- Industrial relations. Good industrial relations increase the quantity and quality of output.
- Composite indicators. Each year, the Swiss-based International Institute for Management Development (IMD) publishes a global league table for international competitiveness. This ranks 46 countries on 259 criteria designed to measure factors providing a good business environment. These include economic performance, infrastructure, the role of government, management, the financial system and technological competence. Two-thirds of the criteria are based on statistical data and one-third comes from an opinion survey of more than 4,000 business executives worldwide. So far, the USA has always come top of the league table.

Thinking like an economist

Explain two policy measures the UK government could take to increase UK international competitiveness.

Quickies

1. What is the difference between the current account and the financial account?
2. Explain the connection between the financial account and the investment income section of the current account.
3. What attracts foreign direct investment to a country?
4. Identify three benefits a country may gain from attracting foreign direct investment.

A country or area may operate a freely floating exchange rate system or its government may intervene to influence or fix the exchange rate. These different exchange rate systems have both advantages and disadvantages.

Determination of exchange rates

As noted in section 6.14, a fixed rate is one that is determined by the government. If market forces threaten to move from its set rate, the government will intervene. For example, if demand for the currency is falling, the government will either demand some of the currency itself (paying in foreign currencies) and/or will seek to generate private sector demand by raising the domestic rate of interest.

A floating exchange rate is one that is determined by the market forces of demand and supply. If demand for the currency rises, this will raise the exchange rate; if the supply of the currency increases, the exchange rate will fall in value.

A managed exchange rate is effectively a combination of a floating and fixed exchange rate. The exchange rate is largely allowed to be determined by market forces, but the government will intervene to affect its value if it thinks the rate is in danger of falling too low, rising too high or fluctuating too much.

Factors affecting exchange rates

A number of factors influence the value of a floating exchange rate and put upward or downward pressure on a fixed and managed exchange rate:

- relative inflation rates
- income levels
- relative quality
- relative interest rates
- levels of foreign direct investment
- speculative capital flows.

Relative inflation rates

A country that is experiencing an inflation rate above that of its competitors is also likely to experience a decrease in demand for its exports and a rise in demand for imports. This would cause demand for the currency to fall and supply of the currency to rise. These changes would put downward pressure on a fixed exchange rate. Figure 1 shows the effect on a floating exchange rate.

Income levels

Rises in income levels abroad will tend to increase a country's exchange rate. This is because foreigners will have more income to spend on the country's exports. In contrast, rises in income at home may reduce a country's exchange

Synoptic link

This section draws on the knowledge you gained in the AS sections 2.13 and 2.18. Before you start this section, check your understanding of interest rate and exchange rate changes.

- Income abroad
- Interest
- Imports
- Exports

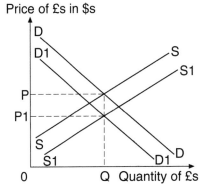

Price of £s in $s

Figure 1: The effect of inflation on a floating exchange rate

rate. This is because a buoyant home market may suck in more imports and encourage some firms to switch sales from export markets to the home market.

Relative quality

If a country's products rise in quality relative to its competitors, demand for its products both at home and abroad will increase. This will cause a rise in the floating exchange rate and put upward pressure on a fixed exchange rate. Improvements in marketing and after-sales service will have a similar effect.

Relative interest rates

If a country's interest rate rises relative to other countries' interest rates, it is likely to attract an inflow of funds from abroad into its financial institutions. This will increase demand for the currency and raise the exchange rate or put upward pressure on it. As noted earlier, a government seeking to influence its currency may use changes in its interest rate to achieve its objective.

Levels of foreign direct investment

A country that attracts more investment from foreign MNCs than its MNCs invest abroad will experience an increase in demand for its currency and upward pressure on its exchange rate.

Speculative capital flows

A high percentage of the dealing in foreign exchange markets is now accounted for by speculation. Speculators buy and sell currency, hoping to make a profit from movements in interest rates and exchange rates. Speculation can have a stabilising or a destabilising effect on exchange rates. The rate will be driven down even further if speculators respond to a falling exchange rate by selling some of their holdings of the currency. However, if they think the rate will soon start to rise, they will purchase the currency, thereby preventing a large fall. Speculation is something of a self-fulfilling principle; by their action, speculators bring about what they expect to happen.

Advantages and disadvantages of a fixed exchange rate

The main advantage claimed for a fixed exchange rate is the certainty it provides to traders, investors and consumers. A firm buying raw materials from abroad will know how much it will have to pay in terms of foreign currency. A firm selling products abroad will know how much it will receive in terms of its own currency. Investors will know the cost of, and expected return from, their investment, and consumers going on holiday abroad will know how much they will have to pay.

Thinking like an economist

What effect is a favourable report on the future prospects of the UK economy by an international organisation likely to have on the value of the pound?

Another advantage claimed is that a fixed exchange rate imposes discipline on government policy. For example, if the country is experiencing inflation, a government could not rely on the exchange rate falling to restore its international competitiveness; it would have to tackle the causes of inflation.

To maintain the **parity**, however, other policy objectives may have to be sacrificed. For instance, if the exchange rate is under downward pressure, the government may raise its interest rate, which could slow down economic growth and cause a rise in unemployment. There is also no guarantee that the parity set will be at the long run equilibrium level. If it is set too high, this will put its firms at a competitive disadvantage, since exports will be relatively high in price while its imports will be relatively low in price. In this case, the rate would not be sustainable and the value of the currency would have to be reduced.

In addition, reserves of foreign currency have to be kept in case the central bank has to intervene to increase demand for the currency. This involves an opportunity cost – the foreign currency could be put to alternative uses.

Advantages and disadvantages of a floating exchange rate

Operating a floating exchange rate means that the exchange rate no longer becomes a policy objective. The government does not have to sacrifice other objectives and does not have to keep foreign currency to maintain it.

Also, in theory, a floating exchange rate should move automatically to ensure a balance of payments equilibrium. For example, if demand for the country's exports fall, demand for the currency will fall and supply will rise. This will cause the exchange rate to fall, making exports cheaper and imports more expensive.

In practice, however, the exchange rate is influenced not just by demand for exports and imports. A country may have a deficit on the current account of its balance of payments, but speculation may actually lead to a rise in the exchange rate.

A floating exchange rate can create uncertainty, with traders and investors being unsure how much the currency will be worth in the future. Some may seek to offset this uncertainty by agreeing a price in advance, but this involves a cost. The degree of uncertainty will be influenced by the extent of fluctuations in the currency.

Definitions

Parity: the price of one currency in terms of another currency or group of currencies.

Making connections

Explain why a fall in the exchange rate may create inflation.

Quickies

1   Identify three factors that could cause a fall in a country's exchange rate.
2   Distinguish between a fixed and a floating exchange rate.
3   Explain why operating a fixed exchange rate involves an opportunity cost.
4   Why might a floating exchange rate create uncertainty?

6.27 Economic and Monetary Union (EMU)

Synoptic link

This section builds on A2 section 4.5, Monetary policy and the euro.

Research task

Investigate whether the UK currently meets the conditions necessary for entry into the single currency.

The timetable for Economic and Monetary Union (EMU), which is also sometimes known as European Monetary Union, was set out in the Maastricht Treaty signed in 1992. Stage 1 was already in progress with the creation of the single market. The main features of stage 2 were to be increased co-ordination of national monetary policies and governments seeking to achieve greater similarity of economic performance (convergence). The third stage was to be the introduction of the single currency and the establishment of the European Central Bank (ECB). The ECB is based in Frankfurt. Its prime objective is to maintain price stability within euroland. It implements monetary policy, and foreign exchange and reserve policies.

The European single currency

The European single currency, the euro, is currently operated under a floating exchange rate system. However, the European Central Bank (ECB) reserves the right to intervene if it considers it to be necessary. In addition, the changes to its interest rate, which it makes mainly to control inflation, have an impact on the value of the euro.

The single currency came into existence on 1 January 1999. So far in 2003, twelve of the fifteen members of the EU have joined. This group is referred to as euroland, the euro area or the euro zone. The three countries that have not joined are Denmark, Sweden and the UK.

Convergence criteria

To join the single currency (sometimes referred to as joining EMU), a country has to show that its economy is operating at a similar stage of the economic cycle as the rest of the members. The specific criteria are as follows.
- The government budget must not exceed three per cent of GDP.
- Government debt should not be above 60 per cent of GDP.
- The inflation rate should not exceed the average of the three members with the lowest inflation rates by more than 1.5 percentage points.
- Long-term interest rates should not be more than two percentage points above the average of the three members with the lowest inflation rate.
- A stable exchange rate.

Those members in the single currency have to continue to meet the limits on the fiscal deficits.

UK government's criteria

Chancellor of the Exchequer Gordon Brown has set down five conditions that must be met before the 2003 UK government will consider entry to the single currency.
- There must be sustainable convergence between the UK economy and the economies of the euroland countries.

The ECB in Frankfurt

- There must be flexibility within the euro area for coping with economic change.
- Entry will be beneficial for promoting foreign direct investment in the UK.
- Entry will benefit UK financial services.
- Entry will be good for jobs and growth.

Effects of belonging to the single currency

Joining the single currency would have a number of effects for the UK.

Benefits

The possible benefits of joining the single currency include the following.
- There would be a reduction in transaction costs. UK firms and consumers would not have to spend money and time converting pounds into euros.
- The exchange rate risk with euroland countries would be eliminated. For example, UK firms would no longer be caught out by unexpected changes in the value of the pound against the euro.
- There would be increased transparency. This is thought to be an important advantage. Having one currency makes it easier for firms and consumers to compare prices throughout the EU. Consumers and firms will not have to spend time and effort converting prices into pounds before they decide which are the best offers. Competition should increase and price discrimination should decrease.
- There would be increased influence within the EU. Being part of the single currency would give the UK more say in the future direction of the EU. It would also make the EU a stronger economic power.
- There would be lower interest rates. Since its inception, the EU has had a lower rate of interest than the UK. A lower interest rate may stimulate investment and growth in the UK.
- There would be increased FDI. Some claim that membership of the euro would attract more MNCs to set up in the UK. It is argued that the UK would become a more attractive location because of the reduced transaction costs and reduced exchange rate uncertainty.

Handwritten margin notes:
- Price transparency
- lower Transactional costs
- lower exchange rate risk
- lower interest rates
  ↳ Uniform rate

Costs

There would be transitional costs, which are the costs of changing over from using the pound to using the euro. For example, firms would have to convert their IT systems, show for a period of time prices in both pounds and euros, and train staff. However, transitional costs are one-off costs and are not a major consideration in deciding whether to join the single currency. More significant are the disadvantages that may be longer lasting – including the following.
- Reduction in independence of macroeconomic policy. The ECB sets the rate of interest in the euro area. In addition to no longer being able to operate

Handwritten margin notes:
Reduction in independance of macroeconomic policy
↗
• no control over interest rates

its own interest rate, the UK government would lose the exchange rate as a policy tool and would have constraints imposed on its use of fiscal policy.

- An asymmetric policy sensitivity. The UK economy differs from the rest of the EU in three main ways, which may mean that it would be affected more significantly than other members by changes in policy.

  1 More UK borrowing is undertaken on variable interest rate terms than in most EU countries. So if the euro area's interest rate were to rise, this would affect UK home buyers and firms more than those in other EU countries. However, there is an increasing tendency for loans to be taken out on fixed interest rate terms.

  2 The UK trades more with the USA than other EU countries and is therefore affected more by changes in the level of economic activity in the USA and changes in the value of the dollar.

  3 The UK is also still a major exporter of oil, so its economy is influenced more (and in a different way) by changes in the world price of oil than other EU countries that import oil.

Thinking like an economist

A country joins the single currency. Analyse the possible effect this may have on the efficiency of the country's firms.

The effects of staying out

The UK government has not yet decided on entry. Staying out of an arrangement that most of the EU members have joined may have a number of effects on the UK economy, including the following.

- A tendency for its exchange rate to be high because of its higher interest rate.

- A risk of loss of FDI. Euroland has formed a large market that may prove more attractive to FDI than the UK. This may particularly be the case if companies decide to locate close to each other to benefit from external economies of scale. Currently FDI is very important for the UK. Indeed, the UK is the third largest recipient of FDI, after the USA and China.

- A risk that some of the UK's financial institutions may move to euroland to be closer to the main financial dealings.

Quickies

1 What is the main role of the ECB?
2 Why is it thought necessary for members of the single currency to limit any budget deficit?
3 Explain how membership of the single currency reduces a country's economic sovereignty.

Puzzler

Does membership of the single currency increase a country's economic performance?

Government policy

1. Distinguish between:
   a) monetary and budgetary (fiscal) policy
   b) supply-side and demand management policy.

2 Explain the importance of each of the following in government economic policy:
   a) output gaps
   b) interest rates
   c) the inflation target
   d) the 'natural rate' of unemployment
   e) the Monetary Policy Committee of the Bank of England
   f) trend growth
   g) actual growth and potential growth.

3 Distinguish between different types of unemployment, for example, cyclical, structural, seasonal. Why is it important for a government to be able to identify the type of unemployment?

4 'The government should take responsibility for the total level of demand in the economy.' (J. K. Galbraith)
'Supply creates its own demand.' (J. B. Say)
Discuss these apparently contradictory views.

The national economy

5 These figures show index numbers for the price of a loaf of bread in Germany, with base year 1913.

Year	Price index
1913	100
1921	1,440
1922	10,100
January 1923	278,500
November 1923	75,000,000,000,000

   a) What name is given to a period of inflation of this sort?
   b) What are the economic consequences of this type of problem?
   c) Why might the social and political consequences be even more serious than the economic ones?

6 The measured national income of Country A is twice that of Country B. Does this mean that the average citizen of A has twice the standard of living of the average citizen of B? Justify your answer.

7 Discuss, with examples, the usefulness of each of the following economic principles as tools for analysing the national economy:
   a) the production possibility curve
   b) the Phillips curve
   c) aggregate supply and aggregate demand analysis.

8 Explain and discuss the problems of (i) defining and (ii) measuring:
   a) unemployment
   b) inflation.

The international economy

9 Read this newspaper extract then answer the questions that follow.

INDUSTRY IS NOT MOTORING

The strength of the Rubomark (Rm) against other leading currencies is having an adverse effect on the Rubovian motor industry, which last year accounted for Rm six billion of Rubovia's Rm twenty billion deficit in the balance of trade. With an over-supply of cars on world markets, and higher prices for most of the items which Rubovia imports, the terms of trade have moved against Rubovia's manufacturing sector. If it were not for Rubovia's strong financial sector, the balance of payments of Rubovia would be heavily in deficit. Instead, it is only mildly in deficit, and at the same time the government is running a small budget deficit.

Professor Michelle Potter of Havard Business School recently conducted an investigation into the Rubovian economy, and concluded that it needed to liberalise its markets and invest in human capital if it wished to gain competitive advantage in today's globalised markets.

Source: *The Rubovia Financial News*, 1 November, 2003.

   a) Carefully explain why the 'strength' of a currency can cause problems for exporters.
   b) Distinguish between:
      (i) the balance of trade and the terms of trade
      (ii) the balance of trade and the balance of payments
      (iii) a balance of payments deficit and a budget deficit.
   c) Discuss critically the idea that countries need to 'liberalise' their markets and invest in 'human capital' in order to 'gain competitive advantage in today's globalised markets'.

10 'Governments can achieve national policy aims such as low inflation or full employment, or they can achieve international policy aims such as a stable currency or equilibrium in the balance of payments. They cannot, however, achieve all these things at once.' Critically discuss this statement.

In Section A, answer all parts of the question.
In Section B, answer one question.

Section A

Study the extracts and answer all parts of the question.

Extract A: What is globalisation? Is it important?

Internationalisation of trade has been taking place for centuries. Many economists argue that globalisation is not quite the same thing, and has only been taking place for decades, coinciding with new communication technologies and the liberalisation of money and capital markets.

Global free trade is clearly beneficial to the managers and shareholders of the multinationals, who would like nothing better than to receive profits generated from the economies of scale that would be created if everyone in the world were to drive the same motor car, eat the same hamburger, or wear the same baseball cap. Some observers believe that globalisation has automatic benefits for the majority of the world's population. Such observers tend to believe in a 'trickle-down' theory of economic distribution. They believe that although globalisation might lead to a more unequal share-out of the world production cake, it will result in a bigger overall cake and thus benefit poorer sections of world society as well as the better off. Other observers believe that growth of the cake will be insufficient to benefit everyone, and that the 'haves' will take progressively bigger slices than the 'have nots'.

If global free trade is such a good thing, why are so many countries grouping themselves into regional trading blocs like the EU? A substantial minority of economists argues that protectionism is not always a bad thing, and that protective barriers might surround some things that actually are worth protecting, such as a distinctive culture, or a region that depends on a particular industry for its way of life.

UK policy-makers appear to have wholeheartedly accepted the idea of globalisation and, like other countries operating in the global economy, the UK is constrained by what has been called the 'golden straitjacket'. If a country wants to have access to global communications, information technology, world markets and inward investment, then it has to accept the rules of 'club' membership: low taxes, privatisation, deregulation, and free movement of capital.

Extract B: Inward investment – the high point of globalisation?

Country	FDI, 2001	FDI, 1997	% change
All EU	2,648,651	1,225,507	+116.0
UK	496,776	252,945	+96.3
Germany	480,899	192,151	+150.0
France	310,430	195,910	+58.4
Spain	158,405	100,021	+58.3
Ireland	74,831	14,975	+400.0
Greece	14,059	15,234	-7.7

Table 1: Foreign direct investment, selected countries, $m

Sources: text adapted from C. Smith, *Understanding International Trade*, Anforme, 1999; figures: United Nations, 2003.

1 a) Explain what economists mean by the term 'globalisation'. (4 marks)
  b) Using Extract B describe the main changes in the pattern of Foreign Direct Investment between 1997 and 2001. (6 marks)
  c) Discuss the extent to which globalisation has increased prosperity in the world. (10 marks)
  d) Identify and evaluate arguments for and against protection from international competition. (30 marks)

Section B

2 a) Discuss the likely causes of inflation. (20 marks)
  b) Assess the success or otherwise of the UK Treasury's policy of setting an inflation target then delegating the control of interest rates to the Bank of England. (30 marks)
3 a) Explain the role of the government budget in influencing both the level of aggregate demand, and the pattern of demand for various goods and services. (20 marks)
  b) Is a government budget deficit necessarily a bad thing? Justify your answer. (30 marks)
4 a) Discuss the various factors that might lead to a current account balance of payments 'problem' for the UK. (20 marks)
  b) Evaluate the likely impact on the UK economy of a balance of payments deficit on the current account. (30 marks)

Specific hints

1   a) A good working definition, based on a description of the
       phenomenon by Milton Friedman, and used by Peter Jay, economic
       editor of the BBC, is: 'The ability to make a product anywhere, use
       resources from anywhere, sell it anywhere, and place the profits
       anywhere.'
       It is well worth considering this definition and thinking about its
       implications. However, you should note that globalisation is a
       contested concept. Politicians appear to have accepted globalisation
       wholesale, and believe that it affects their ability to raise taxes and
       provide public services such as health and pensions. While many
       economists support this point of view, others along with political
       scientists regard globalisation as a myth, as another word for
       Americanisation or as 'hype'. See, for example, B. Milward,
       'Internationalisation and the impact on labour markets'
       (*Developments in Economics*, edited by G. Atkinson, Vol. 19,
       Causeway Press, 2003).

    b) You should be able to define Foreign Direct Investment (capital
       investment from companies in other countries). Among the points
       you could note are that:
       ■ FDI appears to be increasing throughout the EU
       ■ the UK has a large share in absolute terms
       ■ however, smaller countries like Ireland are making gains in
         percentage terms. Ireland has achieved this through focusing on
         'sunrise' industries like electronics, telecommunications,
         information technology and pharmaceuticals. Other countries, like
         Greece, have not replicated this strategy.

    c) The principle of comparative advantage predicts that trade is
       potentially beneficial to all countries, rich or poor. However, there is
       a view of globalisation that sees it as a type of 'victory', a 'win' for
       rich countries over poor ones, the west over the east, the north over
       the south, capitalism over socialism, markets over governments, large
       companies over small ones. Many candidates write about
       globalisation uncritically. It is worth looking for faults in the 'rose-
       tinted' view of globalisation. For example, globalisation is leading to
       the free movement of resources, capital and jobs (production can be
       based in countries with weak environment laws, profits can be placed
       in low tax countries, jobs can be exported to low wage countries).
       However, it is clearly not leading to the free movement of labour.
       Workers are probably less free to move around the world today than
       they were 100 years ago, as you will have noticed from tabloid press
       publicity about 'economic migrants'.

    d) Among the issues you could discuss here are the various methods of
       protection (tariffs, quotas), and arguments about 'infant' industries,
       'sunset' industries, and the 'dumping' of goods internationally at

prices below production costs. The ideas of 'trade creation' and 'trade diversion' are relevant, and you should read up on these. As in part (c), the idea of comparative advantage is relevant. For added value in your evaluation, you could introduce some recent examples of politics becoming intertwined with economics: for example, the United States' argument that the EU's insistence on the labelling of GM products is a 'restriction' on free trade.

Section B

2 a) Among the issues you could cover here are:
- definition of inflation in terms of persistently rising prices and a fall in the spending power of money
- measures of inflation (CPI, RPI, RPIX)
- the distinction between demand-pull and cost-push.

Modern output gap theory is particularly relevant.

b) You should have some knowledge of the 'symmetrical' inflation target set by the Treasury and the Chancellor of the Exchequer. This is currently 2.0 per cent in the CPI. Note that inflation can be too low as well as too high. Deflation can cause a number of problems, as Japan has recently experienced.

Generally speaking, the MPC is widely regarded as having been a success story, and has succeeded in bringing the UK's inflation rate in line with that of its competitors (in modern parlance it has achieved 'convergence'). This is important in a trading world: if our inflation rate is 2.5 per cent and everyone else's is also around 2.5 per cent then in trading terms there is no inflation problem in Britain. However, some observers claim that the MPC has been lucky, and that world conditions are counter-inflationary. World problems, such as the reduction in tourism following 11 September 2001, have been deflationary. The MPC has yet to be tested in a situation of unexpected inflationary shocks in the world economy.

3 a) You should note that budgetary policy includes both taxation and government expenditure. An important economic principle to use here is the idea of upward and downward multiplier effects. Aggregate demand and aggregate supply analysis would also be very useful.

The pattern of demand refers to the composition of demand, that is, how demand is allocated between different goods and services. You could answer this with the use of plenty of examples of instances where the government tries to discourage us from buying certain products (for example, tobacco) and tries to encourage us to consume others (for example, private pensions). The role of subsidies should be discussed as these can be regarded as 'negative taxes', instances where the government actually gives us something in money or in kind.

b) Explain what is meant by a deficit budget. Modern governments do not like deficit financing, but occasionally have to rely on borrowing. This is usually regarded as potentially inflationary, because the danger is that governments will repay their debts by, in effect, printing money. The International Monetary Fund (IMF) has 'Structural Adjustment Policies', the EU's euro members have a 'Stability and Growth Pact' and the UK Treasury has its 'Golden Fiscal Rules'. All have virtually the same effect: they restrict government borrowing. However, there are circumstances when borrowing can be justified. Sometimes it is more costly not to borrow than to borrow, for example, where it is necessary to invest in infrastructure, such as new roads or modern railways, in order to improve a country's efficiency for the future.

4 a) Although a budget deficit should definitely not be confused with a 'balance of payments' deficit, this question is rather similar to the previous one. Balance of payments deficits and budget deficits often appear as 'twin' deficits. A country that is not paying its way internationally is likely to be failing to earn enough income domestically to finance government expenditure. For extra marks, you could consider whether a balance of payments surplus is a problem. Remember that one country's surplus is another country's deficit, and so a surplus is not necessarily 'good'. If it impoverishes your main trading partner it is definitely 'bad' and will rebound on you in the long run.

   b) No country can afford to run a balance of payments deficit forever. It means that one generation is importing goods and services and enjoying a higher standard of living than it is paying for through exports. At some time in the future another generation will have to pay the debts that build up. However, as the USA has discovered, living with a balance of payments deficit is a very tempting idea. In America's case it has flooded the rest of the world with dollars and made businesses, individuals and governments around the world dependent on the dollar as a currency in which to place their savings, profits and pension funds. However, the USA is now trying to reduce its budget deficit and this involves cutting back on demand at home, with clear economic and political consequences.

   As is often the case in economics, it is worth considering short run factors versus long run factors. A short run current account deficit might be worthwhile, if a trading nation, for example, is importing machinery or raw materials which are essential for creating exports which it can sell in the future.

Further exam guidance

General hints

This guidance applies to both units ECN5 and ECN6. You should also read the note on synopticity in the general guidance in section 5.26 of this book.

Your examination papers for units 5 and 6 each consist of one compulsory data-response question and one essay question from a choice of three. Both questions are worth 50 marks.

The data-response question is in four parts, worth (a) 4, (b) 6, (c) 10 and (d) 30 marks respectively. You should note that these part-questions are organised along an incline of difficulty, with the higher-scoring parts demanding higher-order skills. You should allocate your time accordingly. You have 90 minutes for a paper worth 100 marks, so as a rough rule of thumb that is just under one minute per mark. Therefore, you should devote about 45 minutes to each question, and on the data response question about 3 minutes to part (a) and 30 minutes to part (d) and not the other way round. Note that part (d) is marked using a levels of response mark scheme (you can see full details of this in the AQA specifications and specimen papers). To reach the highest levels (4 and 5) you will need to show evaluation skills. Level 4 starts at 18 marks, and so if you offer no evaluation you are limited to just over half marks. Examiners will often also impose a cap on candidates who fail to display analysis and/or application skills.

The essay question is in two parts, and again there is an incline of difficulty. Part (a) is marked out of 20, using a 'points' mark scheme, which allocates specific marks for points made. It follows that you should make as many points as you can. However, do not write your essay in point form, as this is an exercise in extended writing, not in the presentation of 'notes'. Do not make 'lists': instead of bullet points or (i), (ii) etc. Write 'Firstly..., secondly...,' and so on. Part (b) is marked using the same levels of response scheme for 30 marks as the data-response part (d), and the same considerations about evaluation apply.

6.2

C. Bamford & S. Grant. *The UK Economy in a Global Context*. Heinemann, 2000. Chapter 7.

D. Smith. *UK Current Economic Policy*, 3rd edition. Heinemann, 2003. Chapter 6.

6.3

C. Bamford & S. Grant. *The UK Economy in a Global Context*. Heinemann, 2000. Chapter 7.

D. Smith. *UK Current Economic Policy*, 3rd edition. Heinemann, 2003. Chapter 6.

6.4

D. Burningham & J. Davies. *Environmental Economics*, 3rd edition. Heinemann, 2003. Chapter 4.

S. Grant. *Economic Growth and Business Cycles*. Heinemann, 1999. Chapter 5.

6.5

C. Bamford & S. Grant. *The UK Economy in a Global Context*. Heinemann, 2000. Chapter 7.

6.6

C. Bamford & S. Grant. *The UK Economy in a Global Context*. Heinemann, 2000. Chapters 2 & 7.

G. Hale. *Labour Markets*. Heinemann, 2001. Chapter 5.

D. Smith. *UK Current Economic Policy*, 3rd edition. Heinemann, 2003. Chapter 5.

6.7

C. Bamford & S. Grant. *The UK Economy in a Global Context*. Heinemann, 2000. Chapter 6.

G. Hale. *Labour Markets*. Heinemann, 2001. Chapter 5.

6.8

C. Bamford & S. Grant. *The UK Economy in a Global Context*. Heinemann, 2000. Chapter 6.

G. Hale. *Labour Markets*. Heinemann, 2001. Chapter 5.

6.10

C. Bamford & S. Grant. *The UK Economy in a Global Context*. Heinemann, 2000. Chapters 2 & 6.

M. Russell & D. Heathfield. *Inflation and UK Monetary Policy*, 3rd edition. Heinemann, 1999. Chapters 2 & 4.

6.11

C. Bamford & S. Grant. *The UK Economy in a Global Context*. Heinemann, 2000. Chapter 6.

M. Russell & D. Heathfield. *Inflation and UK Monetary Policy*, 3rd edition. Heinemann, 1999. Chapter 3.

6.12

M. Russell & D. Heathfield. *Inflation and UK Monetary Policy*, 3rd edition. Heinemann, 1999. Chapters 4 & 5.
D. Smith. *UK Current Economic Policy*, 3rd edition. Heinemann, 2003. Chapter 4.

6.13

C. Bamford & S. Grant. *The UK Economy in a Global Context*. Heinemann, 2000. Chapter 3.
M. Russell & D. Heathfield. *Inflation and UK Monetary Policy*, 3rd edition. Heinemann, 1999. Chapters 2–4.
D. Smith. *UK Current Economic Policy*, 3rd edition. Heinemann, 2003. Chapter 4.

6.14

M. Russell & D. Heathfield. *Inflation and UK Monetary Policy*, 3rd edition. Heinemann, 1999. Chapter 7.

6.15, 6.16

C. Bamford & S. Grant. *The UK Economy in a Global Context*. Heinemann, 2000. Chapter 3.

6.17

D. Smith. *UK Current Economic Policy*, 3rd edition. Heinemann, 2003. Chapter 3.

6.18

D. Smith. *UK Current Economic Policy*, 3rd edition. Heinemann, 2003. Chapter 1.

6.19

C. Bamford & S. Grant. *The UK Economy in a Global Context*. Heinemann, 2000. Chapters 5 & 8.

6.20–6.24

C. Bamford & S. Grant. *The UK Economy in a Global Context*. Heinemann, 2000. Chapters 4 & 5.

6.25

C. Bamford & S. Munday. *Markets*, Heinemann, 2002. Chapter 6 .

6.26

B. Hill. *The European Union*, 4th edition. Heinemann, 2001. Chapter 6.
M. Russell & D. Heathfield. *Inflation and UK Monetary Policy*, 3rd edition. Heinemann, 1999. Chapter 10.
D. Smith. *UK Current Economic Policy*, 3rd edition. Heinemann, 2003. Chapter 9.

Glossary

Ability to pay principle	the rule that people with higher incomes should pay more in tax
Absolute advantage	the ability to produce output using fewer resources than other regions or countries
Benefit principle	the rule that the amount people pay in tax should be related to the benefit they derive from public expenditure
Bottom line	the ultimate profitability of providing a product or service
Common Agricultural Policy (CAP)	the agricultural policy measures of the EU
Common market	a group of countries with free movement of products, labour and capital
Comparative advantage	relative efficiency – the ability to produce a product at a lower opportunity cost than other regions or countries
Counter cyclical policies	government policies designed to offset fluctuations in economic activity by stabilising aggregate demand
Customs union	a group of countries with free trade between them and a common external tariff on imports from outside the area
Cyclical unemployment	unemployment arising from a lack of aggregate demand
Deflationary fiscal policy	decreases in public expenditure and/or increases in taxation designed to decrease aggregate demand
Depreciation	a fall in the value of a floating exchange
Devaluation	a deliberate reduction in the value of a fixed exchange rate by the government
Discouraged workers	people who have given up looking for work
Discrimination	when a group of workers and potential workers is treated differently than other workers in the same job in terms of pay, employment, promotion, training opportunities and work conditions
Dumping	the sale of products at less than cost price

Economic and Monetary Union (EMU)	a group of countries that operate a single currency and co-ordinate economics policies
Economic cycles	fluctuations in economic activity
Exchange control	restrictions on the purchase of foreign currency and on the export of capital
Fisher equation	an equation that shows the relationship between the money supply, the velocity of circulation, the price level and output: $MV = PY$. (Irvin Fisher, 1867-1947, was an American economist who developed the equation of exchange.)
Fixed exchange rate	an exchange rate fixed against other currencies that is maintained by the government
Floating exchange rate	an exchange rate determined by market forces
Foreign direct investment (FDI)	investment by companies in one country in other countries in the form of setting up production facilities or purchasing existing businesses
Free trade area	a group of countries with free trade between them
Frictional unemployment	unemployment arising because workers are in between jobs
Globalisation	the development of the world into one marketplace
Hypothecated tax	a tax raised for a specific purpose
Hysteresis	the view that unemployment generates unemployment
Infant industry	a newly established industry that has not yet grown large enough to take full advantage of the available economies of scale
J curve effect	the tendency for a fall in the exchange rate to make the trade position worse before it gets better
Keynesians	a group of economists whose ideas are based on the work of the economist John Maynard Keynes. They believe that

government intervention is necessary to correct market failure and ensure full employment

Law of diminishing returns   if a firm seeks to increase production in the short run, its average costs of production will first fall, then bottom out, then rise. This means that the short run average cost curve is always drawn as being 'U' shaped

Long run Phillips curve   a curve that indicates there is no long run trade off between unemployment and inflation

Marginal cost   the change in cost brought about by selling one more unit

Marginal revenue   the change in revenue brought about by changing production by one unit

Marshall-Lerner condition   the view that for a fall in the exchange rate to be successful in improving the balance of payments, the combined elasticities of demand for exports and imports must be greater than one

Menu costs   costs involved in changing prices in, for example, catalogues and advertisements due to inflation

Monetarists   a group of economists who believe that increases in the money supply in excess of increases in output will cause inflation

Monopsony   a single buyer; a factor market in which there is theoretically only one employer of a given factor of production, for example ((to come))

Multinational company   a company that produces products in several countries

NAIRU (the non-accelerating inflation rate of unemployment)   the level of unemployment that exists when the labour market is in equilibrium

Natural monopoly   a market in which full economies of scale can be achieved only if there is ine firm

New economy paradigm   the view that economies are entering a new era of high, sustained economic growth, low unemployment and low inflation

Newly industrialised economies	economies that have experienced a rapid rate of growth of they manufacturing sector – most noticeably, the Asian tigers
Oligopoly	a market dominated by a few large firms
Parity	the price of one currency in terms of another currency or group of currencies
Phillips curve	a graph showing the relationship between unemployment and inflation
Pigouvian tax	a tax designed to correct a negative externality
Poverty trap	a situation in which an individual is better off not working and claiming welfare benefits than he or she would be in work and not eligible for benefits
Protectionism	the restriction on the free movement of products between countries
Public Sector Net Borrowing (PSNB)	excess of public expenditure over revenue
Quantity theory	the view that a change in the quantity of money causes a direct and proportionate change in the price level
Quota	a limit on the quantity of a product that can be imported
Reflationary fiscal policy	increases in public expenditure and/or cuts in taxation designed to increase aggregate demand
Relative poverty	being poor in comparison to others
Replacement ratio	the relationship between unemployment benefit and income from employment
Restrictive public procurement policies	policies that favour domestic procedures
Retail price index (RPI)	a weighted measure of changes in the prices of consumer goods and services
Shoe leather costs	costs involved in reducing holdings of cash and seeking the highest rate of interest.
Social benefits	the private benefits and positive externalities attributable to a particular use of economic resources

Social cost	both the private cost and negative externality attributed to a particular use of economic resources
Strategic industry	an industry regarded as important to the operation of the economy
Structural unemployment	unemployment arising from changes in demand and supply affecting particular industries
Tariff	a tax on imports
Tax burden	the total amount of tax paid as a percentage of GDP
Terms of trade	a ratio of the export to import prices
Tinbergen's rule	the view that a separate policy instrument needs to be used to achieve each government objective
Trading bloc	a group of countries with preferential trading arrangements
Transfer payments	money transferred from one person or group to another not in return for any good or service
Transmission mechanism	the process by which changes in the money supply influence the economy
Velocity of circulation	also sometimes called the income velocity of circulation, it is the number of times money changes hands in a given time period
Wage-price spiral	a rise in wages which triggers off rises in the price level and in turn leads to higher wage claims

Index